T5-AFR-194

Interviewing & Investigation

SECOND EDITION

Kerry Watkins, John Turtle, and James Euale

2011
Emond Montgomery Publications
Toronto, Canada

Copyright © 2011 Emond Montgomery Publications Limited. All rights reserved. No part of this publication may be reproduced, stored in a retrieval system, or transmitted, in any form or by any means, photocopying, electronic, mechanical, recording, or otherwise, without the prior written permission of the copyright holder.

Emond Montgomery Publications Limited
60 Shaftesbury Avenue
Toronto ON M4T 1A3
http://www.emp.ca/college

Printed in Canada.
17 16 15 14 13 12 11   1 2 3 4 5

We acknowledge the financial support of the Government of Canada through the Canada Book Fund for our publishing activities.

Acquisitions editor: Bernard Sandler
Developmental editor: Sarah Gleadow
Marketing manager: Christine Davidson
Director, sales and marketing, higher education: Kevin Smulan
Supervising editor: Jim Lyons
Copy editor & typesetter: Nancy Ennis
Proofreader: Debbie Gervais
Text designer: Tara Wells
Indexer: Paula Pike
Cover image: Janaka Dharmasena

Library and Archives Canada Cataloguing in Publication

Watkins, Kerry (Kerry G.)
   Interviewing & investigation / Kerry Watkins, John Turtle, James Euale. —
2nd ed.

Includes index.
Previous ed. published under title: Interviewing and investigation / James Euale
   and John Turtle.
ISBN 978-1-55239-379-6

   1. Police questioning—Canada—Textbooks.   2. Interviewing in law
enforcement—Canada—Textbooks.   3. Criminal investigation—Canada—
Textbooks.   I. Turtle, John W. (John Warren), 1961-   II. Euale, James,
1947-   III. Euale, James, 1947- . Interviewing and investigation.
IV. Title.   V. Title: Interviewing and investigation.

HV8073.3.W38 2011   363.25´40971   C2011-901056-9

Contents

Chapter 4: Interviewing Suspects II: Approaches and Techniques

Chapter 5: Detecting Deception

Chapter 6: Eyewitness Identifications

Chapter 7: Portals of Discovery: Investigative Failures and the Lessons Learned

Appendix A: Selected Case Law

Appendix B: Review Scenario

Glossary of Terms

References

Index

Preface

There is perhaps no skill more important to an investigator than the ability to gather information from victims, witnesses, and suspects through the process known as the investigative interview. This text is intended to serve both as a practical guide for novice investigators who are seeking to acquire basic interviewing skills and as a professional reference for experienced investigators who wish to continue their professional development in this important area of investigative practice. To this end, the text provides an overview of current interviewing techniques and information and research findings about investigative interviewing that have emerged over the past several decades in closely related fields such as law, criminology, and psychology.

In the past, many believed that common sense and the ability to ask questions was all that was required to be a good interviewer. However, years of attention from the law enforcement and legal communities, and a considerable body of scientific research, have shown that the interview process is considerably more complex than was first thought. A skilled interviewer must not only possess knowledge of practical interviewing techniques, but must also have an understanding of the greater legal and psychological context in which such interviews take place. This text is designed to aid investigators in gaining that understanding, and in so doing to help them build a solid foundation for sound professional practice.

In their discussion of interviewing techniques and related legal and psychological issues, the authors of this text draw on their more than seven decades of combined practical experience and academic study in the fields of criminal investigation, criminology, psychology, and educational instruction. The discussion is augmented by reference to realistic investigative scenarios designed to assist the reader in understanding key concepts and techniques, and the ways in which these are applied in the field. Review questions at the end of each chapter enable the reader to reflect on the application of particular techniques and assess their suitability for use in specific situations. Finally, a carefully selected list of suggested readings in each chapter provides readers with an opportunity to further their knowledge with respect to the various topics covered.

The discussion of interviewing techniques—such as the enhanced cognitive interview, the Reid technique, and the PEACE model—examines how the techniques were developed, explains how they work and are applied in practice, and evaluates their relative strengths and weaknesses. In addition, efforts to detect deception by observing interviewees' behaviour, analyzing their language, and measuring changes in their physiological state using the polygraph are discussed at length, as are the many myths and misconceptions that abound in this area. This critical thinking approach equips the reader with an understanding of the limitations inherent in all techniques, and with the knowledge required to make informed choices about which techniques are the most appropriate in specific situations.

The legal context in which investigative interviews take place is discussed with reference to the *Criminal Code*; the *Charter of Rights and Freedoms*; the *Youth Criminal Justice Act*; and case law decisions, especially as they relate to the issue of admissibility. Through a comprehensive examination of the Supreme Court of Canada case of *R v. Oickle* (2000), the reader will gain a clear understanding of the key issues that a court considers when determining the admissibility of a suspect's statement and the steps that investigators can take to help ensure the admissibility of the statements they take from suspects and accused persons.

The text concludes with a detailed review of what can be learned from past investigative failures. The review includes a discussion of the most common errors an investigator is likely to encounter when conducting a criminal investigation and suggests a number of strategies to assist investigators in managing the risk of error—a danger inherent in all investigative work.

Kerry Watkins, John Turtle, and James Euale
February 2011

Acknowledgments

The authors would like to acknowledge the support of the following individuals whose experience, expertise, and comments were of great assistance in the preparation of this book: Ms. Joan Barrett, Crown Counsel, Ministry of the Attorney General, Ontario, for her careful scrutiny of select chapter drafts and her valuable suggestions as to how they might be improved; Mr. Bernard Power (Durham College) and Mr. James Pardy (Sault College), for their detailed feedback regarding ways in which the first edition might be enhanced to serve as a more valuable resource; Breana Vandebeek, for her legal research with respect to the case law in select chapters and Appendix A; and Douglas Grace, a lawyer, federal Crown attorney, and good friend, for the role he played as devil's advocate and sounding board in the development of scenarios and questions for this new edition.

We would also like to express our gratitude to Sarah Gleadow, developmental editor, for her sound editorial judgment, which proved to be of great assistance in our attempt to achieve balance, clarity, and utility in the text; Nancy Ennis, who copy-edited the manuscript; and the editorial staff at Emond Montgomery Publications.

Introduction to Interviewing and Investigation

1

"A man should look for what is, and not for what he thinks should be."

Albert Einstein

INTRODUCTION

An investigation is a search for the truth. The word "investigate" comes from the Latin verb meaning "to search after" or "to follow a track," and that's exactly what an investigator does. He or she searches after the truth by following a trail and making detailed, systematic observations and inquiries along the way. Although this may sound simple, it is difficult to do well because there are typically many obstacles along the path, each with the potential to knock the investigator off course.

Of all the potential obstacles that stand between an investigator and the truth, perhaps the most difficult to overcome are the investigator's own limitations as a human information processor and decision-maker. It's a point that led the late, Nobel prize-winning physicist Richard Feynman, famous for his research into the truths of how the universe works, to identify the first principle of investigative work as "not fooling yourself," because you are the easiest person to fool (Feynman, 1999, p. 212). Similarly, Albert Einstein is often quoted as saying that "[c]ommon sense is just the accumulation of inaccurate information by age 18," conveying the point that we often have to be skeptical about what seems obviously true to us. Over the past several decades, a major theme from research on human judgment and behaviour has been that otherwise "normal" people are (1) often inaccurate in their perceptions, memories, and judgments, and (2) typically unaware of those inaccuracies and thus overconfident in their abilities in even the most challenging professional domains. Criminal investigators are therefore far from being alone as imperfect human information processors charged with completing a difficult task. In addition to the positive attributes they bring to an

CHAPTER OBJECTIVES

After completing this chapter, you should be able to:

- Explain what an investigation is and what sort of mindset should guide an investigator.

- Explain what a working theory of a crime is and how theories should be affected by evidence.

- Understand the responsibilities of the first officer at a crime scene.

- Describe strategies for locating witnesses.

- Outline the nature of the communication that the first officer at a crime scene should have with witnesses and the reason for this.

- Explain the differences between a witness, a confidential informant, and an agent and the different legal protections that apply to each.

- Describe the factors that affect the competence and compellability of a witness.

- Explain the difference between opinion and expert evidence and the circumstances that permit these kinds of evidence.

investigation—things like reason, experience, and dedication—investigators also often bring their biases, preconceptions, cognitive limitations, and personal motivations. When these elements combine in a situation where the information is incomplete and subject to some degree of interpretation, and where there is pressure to "figure it all out," even the best investigators can go astray.

In the 1990s, there were a number of wrongful convictions in Ontario for various offences, including murder. In those convictions, expert evidence from the field of forensic pathology played a significant role and, as a result, a judicial inquiry was ordered into the practice of pediatric forensic pathology in Ontario (Goudge Inquiry, 2008). The purpose of the inquiry was to determine the state of forensic pathology in the province and establish how errors of the kind that gave rise to wrongful convictions could be avoided in the future. In the report that followed the inquiry, a number of observations were made regarding the tenets that should guide forensic pathology; these tenets apply equally to all investigative work. Chief among them is that investigators should "think truth" as opposed to "think dirty," because the latter mindset can hinder a person's ability to investigate an event objectively. "Dirty" in this context refers to a bias toward believing a suspect is guilty, especially when there is some evidence consistent with that belief, not "dirty" in the sense of corruption or intentional misconduct—an important distinction throughout this book.

This point was well stated by one of the witnesses called during the inquiry, Ontario's then newly appointed chief forensic pathologist, Dr. Michael Pollanen. In discussing the need for a "search for the truth" framework in death investigations, Dr. Pollanen called for investigators to adopt "an evidence-based approach that keeps one's mind open to a broad menu of possibilities, and that collects objective evidence whether it supports or negates any possible theories" (Goudge Inquiry, 2008, p. 376). An investigator could receive no better advice.

Conducting a Criminal Investigation

Criminal investigation is demanding, often frustrating, and occasionally exhilarating work. There is an undeniable sense of satisfaction that comes with "figuring it out" and seeing your investigative work withstand vigorous scrutiny as it proceeds through the justice system. Although not all criminal investigations are of the mysterious "who done it" variety (many are simple and straightforward, and depend more for their success on the investigator following proper procedures for gathering evidence than on any highly developed problem-solving ability), in many cases an investigator will have to formulate a working theory (also known as a hypothesis or, simply, a theory) of the crime to guide his or her investigation. Technically, in scientific research a hypothesis is a specific prediction based on a more general theory. For example, even before humans landed on the moon, based on the more general gravitational *theory* that takes into account the moon's smaller mass, scientists *hypothesized* that an object would fall to the moon's surface more slowly than it would fall to the Earth's surface. In a criminal investigation context, however, the terms "**hypothesis**" and "theory" are often used interchangeably to refer to any tentative explanation for some as yet unexplained (or not fully explained) set of

hypothesis a tentative idea or explanation about how something happened or about how something works that an investigator uses to help guide his or her inquiries; also called a "working theory" or "theory"

circumstances, such as those typically faced by investigators in the early stages of a criminal investigation.

A hypothesis or theory about how a crime was committed is a vital tool to help focus an investigator's energy and resources, but it must not be confused with actual *knowledge* of the crime. It is simply a tool, and when the evidence gathered during an investigation contradicts it, the theory must be reformulated. Although this may sound obvious, when an investigator becomes deeply involved in a case, it can be all too easy to forget, and instead the investigator might try to reinterpret the evidence to make it fit with the theory. Investigators must always remember that the reason they are conducting an investigation is because, in their search for the truth, they *don't* have all the answers.

The Importance of Interviewing and the Scope of This Text

Ontario Superior Court Justice O'Connor emphasized the importance of interviewing to the investigative process when he said that "questioning suspects and witnesses to a crime is an essential and often the most effective investigative tool the police possess" (*R v. L.F.*, 2006, at para. 10). This is true even with the incredible advances, such as DNA matching, that have been made in forensic science over the last few decades.

In this text we focus on two of the most important sources of information available to criminal investigators—witnesses and suspects—and on the thought processes that investigators use to make sense of the information they collect during an **investigation**. Gathering information from people through the structured conversation process known as the **interview** is one of the most important ways in which you will interact with **witnesses** and victims on the one hand, and with **suspects** and **accused** persons on the other. (For simplicity's sake, we refer to these four groups using two general terms, "witnesses" and "suspects," and use more specific terminology when it is necessary to specify in order to make a particular point.) Our perspective is that the interview process is of central importance to the investigative process because, despite popular "CSI-like" portrayals of criminal investigations and the fact that physical **evidence** can of course be extremely important, more crimes are solved as a result of information gathered from witnesses and suspects than as a result of physical evidence (Eck, 2009, p. x).

To help prepare professional investigators conduct effective interviews and investigations, and to process the evidence gathered as a result, this text examines:

- the contributions that experience and science can make to the formulation of a "best practices" approach to conducting investigative interviews;
- the practical and legal issues associated with interacting with and managing witnesses and suspects;
- a model of memory based on decades of scientific research that can guide investigators to work *with* rather than *against* the ways in which people typically remember information in an investigative interview;
- how police questioned suspects in the past, and the problems associated with traditional methods of questioning;

investigation   the methodical process of exploring or examining through inquiry and observation

interview   a structured conversation between a witness, victim, or suspect and an investigator, in which the investigator asks a series of questions in order to elicit information from the witness, victim, or suspect about something that they observed, experienced, did, or have knowledge about

witness   a person who has information about a crime or suspected crime and who voluntarily gives that information to the police with no expectation of confidentiality or compensation

suspect   a person of interest (under arrest or not) suspected by the police on the basis of evidence of having committed a crime

accused   a suspect who has been formally charged with a crime

evidence   anything (for example, testimony, document, object) presented in a legal proceeding, such as a trial, for the purpose of establishing the truth or falsity of a fact in issue

- various approaches to conducting interviews in use today in North America and elsewhere, and their advantages and disadvantages;
- some common approaches to detecting deception in witnesses and suspects, and the ways in which scientific research suggests investigators should use these approaches;
- some of the potential dangers associated with eyewitness identifications, and the recommended practices as determined by research; and
- the most common ways in which investigations tend to go wrong, and how investigators can avoid these mistakes in their own professional practice.

It is important to note that the discussion of interviewing techniques in this text assumes that interviews are being conducted with average adult subjects. Interviews with individuals who belong to special groups—such as children, elderly persons, individuals with special needs, and individuals who may have difficulty speaking or understanding English—almost always require special consideration, further training, and additional planning.

IDENTIFYING KEY WITNESSES

Arriving at the Crime Scene

The primary responsibility of the first officer who arrives at the scene of a crime is, like the responsibility of any officer, the protection of life and property. Once these issues have been adequately dealt with, the officer must take all steps necessary to help preserve the scene, because its integrity will play a critical role in any subsequent criminal investigation or prosecution. A contaminated crime scene makes it extremely difficult for an investigator to reconstruct the events surrounding the crime in a manner that will yield reliable evidence that is likely to be accepted in court by the **trier of fact**.

trier of fact   the person or persons charged with making determinations of fact in a trial—namely, the jury in a jury trial or the judge in a trial by judge alone; in contrast to legal rulings that are made exclusively by a judge

The crime scene and the surrounding area are the locations most likely to contain witnesses to the criminal event and are therefore the best locations for the police to begin their search. The police officer most likely to come in contact with witnesses at the scene is the officer who arrives first. This places a responsibility on that officer not only to secure and preserve the scene and handle any emergency or life-threatening situations that he or she may encounter, but also to secure persons at the scene who may have witnessed all or part of the criminal event. These witnesses may include persons who actually observed the offender(s) commit the crime or perhaps just saw some suspicious people in the area around the time the crime was committed. It is the duty of the first officer or officers at the scene to gather information regarding the identity and contact information of all persons found at or near the scene, in addition to a brief description of what they observed (including any descriptions of the offender(s) or of any suspicious person(s) in the area). This information is important because it enables the broadcasting of descriptions to other officers in the area and will, of course, be required by the officers subsequently assigned to investigate the event.

Extending the Search

Witnesses can be reluctant to come forward at a crime scene for a number of reasons. Police officers often hear the excuse, "I don't want to get involved," but this reluctance does not extend to every member of the public; fortunately, many people believe that it is their civic responsibility to assist the police and their fellow citizens. Experienced police officers usually find that people who remain at a crime scene to assist the injured or the police *want* to tell what they saw or heard. Their involvement at the scene often instills in them the sense that they have a bond with the scene and/or the victim.

Of course, not all witnesses to a crime will be found at or near the crime scene and other methods will often have to be employed to locate them. The neighbourhood canvass is one way of locating additional witnesses. It involves officers going door to door and speaking to people who live or work in the area of the crime scene, asking if they noticed anything unusual around the time the crime was believed to have been committed. This time-consuming process can involve a large number of officers, many of whom will have to attend and then re-attend addresses until they are able to speak to the occupants. It is important that accurate records be kept of the canvass process to ensure that all addresses have been checked and that any witnesses who have relevant information to offer are interviewed in a timely manner.

The area to be canvassed is determined by its physical proximity to the crime scene and by the resources available. For an outdoor crime scene, the area for immediate attention can be identified by standing at the centre of the scene and taking a 360° view of the surroundings. Any visible window or building may produce a witness to the crime. The area of the canvass can be extended to bus or subway stops, schools, churches, or other public venues within a given area. It's easy to see how quickly the search area could grow, and how many resources would be required to effectively canvass such an area. For this reason, a neighbourhood canvass is normally appropriate only for serious crimes (for example, sexual assaults, abductions, and homicides). The neighbourhood canvass is a proven but time-consuming way to identify witnesses.

When a neighbourhood canvass is conducted, officers should look for potential sources of electronic evidence—in particular, surveillance cameras. Police services today can also draw on a variety of community resources in their search for witnesses. An effective way to get information to the residents of a specific area, or to the members of a particular group, is through community liaison officers, who can be enlisted to communicate the police appeal for witnesses to their different geographic, business, social, and cultural partners. Social media such as Twitter, Facebook, and YouTube are timely and cost-effective ways to electronically canvass for crime scene witnesses; some Canadian police services now have dedicated social media officers with extensive lists of contacts, and their expertise in using this relatively new medium of communication can be of great assistance to investigators.

Of course, the conventional news media (radio, television, Internet, newspapers) remain excellent tools for appealing to the public. Investigators should also be proactive in their search for witnesses by reviewing the media coverage of the crime they are investigating and attempting to identify any witnesses who may have been interviewed by the media regarding the event, but who have not yet come forward to police. Finally, the Crime Stoppers program, in which people can anonymously leave information that can be followed up by police, is another valuable asset that can result in information being received that may help identify witnesses as well as suspects.

Revisiting the scene of the crime, a technique for locating witnesses that is often used by investigators of serious hit-and-run collisions, can be potentially useful in other criminal investigations as well. Revisiting a crime scene on successive dates at about the same time that the crime was committed may help identify previously unknown witnesses who routinely travel a particular route. Motorists who travel the same route to work every day can often be identified in this way, as can people who work in service jobs in the area, such as delivery people, bus drivers, and cab drivers. Crimes committed within the confines of business premises, houses, or other enclosed buildings may have few if any witnesses, while those committed on the street or in other public places may have many. The greater the number of persons who could have witnessed the crime, the more extensive will be the search for witnesses who have not been identified.

MANAGING WITNESSES

First Contact

The first contact between the police and a witness is frequently made by a uniformed officer at or near the scene of a crime. As mentioned above, the first responsibility of the police in such a situation is to ensure the person's safety and well-being, which may require moving him or her to a safe location and/or obtaining medical assistance if required. Once these issues have been dealt with, if the crime being responded to is of a less serious nature and the uniformed officer will be the one investigating the matter in its entirety, then the officer should be guided by the steps for conducting a witness interview discussed in Chapter 2, Techniques for Interviewing Witnesess. However, if the crime is of a more serious nature and will likely be investigated by an officer or officers from the criminal investigation bureau (CIB), or from a specialized unit such as homicide or sex crimes, then one of the key responsibilities of the first officer(s) is to safeguard witnesses from "contamination."

In the same way that physical evidence at a crime scene must be protected from contamination, witnesses must be protected from contamination that can occur as a result of being spoken to or of speaking with other people, whether those other people are police officers, other witnesses, or members of the public. In fact, Gary Wells and Elizabeth Loftus (2002), two of the leading authorities on the issue of eyewitness evidence, argue that law enforcement and the legal system should adopt a much more scientific perspective and view what might reside in a person's *memory* in a way that is similar to the way they view physical evidence. Their suggestion is based on the notion that, just like physical evidence, eyewitness memory for an event is prone to factors like deterioration (if not recognized, collected, and stored promptly) and contamination (for example, if one witness speaks to another witness before police are able to interview them separately, or if an interviewer inadvertently provides a witness with information about the crime as part of the interview process). The analogy to the perspectives, policies, and procedures common to the collection and evaluation of physical evidence runs throughout this text.

The uniformed officer should obtain the witness's personal information and some preliminary information about what they have witnessed or experienced, but should not discuss the events with the witness in detail. Unnecessary conversation between the responding officer(s) and the witness can make it more difficult for an investigator to subsequently obtain a reliable account of the incident from the witness. For example, while "chatting" with a witness, an officer may innocently disclose a particular detail (for example, that he or she heard that the truck that fled the scene was dark blue) that the witness may subsequently incorporate into his or her recollection of events, thus affecting the reliability of the statement (whether the information was true or false) that the witness subsequently provides to an investigator. This "post-event information effect" is discussed in detail in Chapter 2.

In the event that the responding officer encounters multiple witnesses at a crime scene or elsewhere, insofar as possible these individuals should be prevented from communicating with one another, preferably by physically separating them until the investigating officer(s) have had an opportunity to interview them.

Distinction Between Witnesses, Confidential Informants, and Agents

Officers must clearly understand the differences between the categories of people who give information to the police. These categories are governed by different legal rules; failure to understand these rules and the consequences that flow from them can have a serious impact on an investigation and any subsequent prosecution.

As discussed, a witness is someone who was present at a place where they personally observed or experienced something relevant to the commission of a crime, and who voluntarily gives information about what they witnessed to the police to assist them in their investigation. A witness gives information freely, with no expectation of confidentiality or compensation. A witness's identity is required to be disclosed to the defence in a criminal prosecution.

An **informant** is someone who gives information to the police, typically with the expectation of receiving something in return, such as monetary compensation. A **confidential informant** (often referred to as a "CI") is an informant who has disclosed information about criminal activity to a police officer (or peace officer) *and* has been given an assurance of confidentiality by the officer (*R v. Brown*, 1999). Confidential informants enjoy a near absolute legal privilege that dictates that their identity cannot be disclosed to anyone by the Crown, the police, or the court, without the confidential informant first "waiving," or giving up, their privilege. The Crown must not disclose any information that might directly or indirectly identify the confidential informant, and a witness in court cannot be asked questions that might allow someone to infer the identity of the confidential informant from the responses. The issue of informant privilege is discussed at length in the Supreme Court case *R v. Leipert* (1997).

The only exception to informant privilege is a narrow one referred to as "innocence at stake," in which the informant's identity must be disclosed in order to

informant someone who provides a statement or information to the police regarding an investigation, or someone who supplies the police with facilities to observe and gather information

confidential informant an informant who has provided information to the police and has been given a guarantee of anonymity by a police officer; once a person has confidential informant status, their identity cannot be revealed to anyone by the Crown, the court, or the police without the confidential informant first waiving their legal privilege

material witness a witness who has observed "material" facts, or facts that are relevant to proving the elements of the offence with which an accused is charged

agent provocateur a person who, acting on the direction of the police, induces another person to do something that they would not ordinarily do or provides them with an opportunity to commit a crime they would not ordinarily have committed

agent an individual who acts on the direction of police to go out and become involved in an activity under investigation by the police for the purpose of gathering information about that activity and providing it to police

prove the innocence of an accused person (*R v. Scott*, 1990). In order to activate this exception, the accused must demonstrate some evidentiary basis for believing that disclosure of the informant's identity is *necessary* to prove his or her innocence. This can be demonstrated by showing that the informant was a **material witness** or an **agent provocateur**. It can also be demonstrated where a confidential informant provides information to a police officer that the officer subsequently relies on to obtain a search warrant or wiretap, and the defence seeks to challenge the ground on which the warrant was obtained. Disclosure of the informant's identity could be ordered in such a situation if the court were convinced that it is was the only way in which an effective challenge to the warrant or wiretap could be achieved (*R v. Liepert*, 1997; *R v. Barnes*, 2010).

In contrast to an informant, an **agent** is someone who, acting on the direction of the police, goes to certain places and meets with certain people who are believed to be involved in the activity under investigation and then reports back to the police with information regarding that activity. Agents may also receive compensation in exchange for their involvement in a police investigation. One example of how a police agent might function would be meeting with persons believed to be involved in criminal activity while wearing a "body pack" or recording device with which to gather information for the police (for example, *R v. Sandham*, 2008). Unlike a confidential informant's identity, an agent's identity is *not* protected by privilege. A discussion of the issue of agents, informants, and CI privilege may be found in *R v. Broyles* (1991) and *R v. Barnes* (2010).

Exercise Caution in Guaranteeing Confidentiality

Granting a person confidential informant privilege can be a valuable law enforcement tool. It allows police to gain access to sources of information that they would not otherwise have access to—sources that can be of great value in the investigation of criminal enterprises such as drug trafficking and organized crime. "CI privilege," as it is commonly referred to, protects the state's access to these unique sources of information, first by ensuring the safety of the informants themselves, and second by encouraging others to come forward knowing that their identities will also be kept confidential (*R v. Scott*, 1990, at para. 4).

On occasion, and unaware of the legal consequences, police officers have made promises of confidentiality to anxious witnesses in order to obtain information from them and maintain their cooperation during an investigation. However, officers should *not* do so because this can have serious implications for the subsequent prosecution of a case. If an officer promises a witness anonymity, that witness is now considered a confidential informant. However, if the witness is also a material witness, the defence will be able to argue that under the "innocence at stake" exception the confidential informant's privilege should be set aside and the witness's identity disclosed. In such a situation, if the witness refuses to waive their CI privilege, the Crown might be left with no option but to withdraw the charges or stay the proceedings, and the opportunity to successfully prosecute the case will be lost.

Ensuring Witness Attendance in Court

The legal authority to compel a witness to appear in court is provided by a legal document referred to as a **subpoena**, which is issued by a justice pursuant to s. 698(1) of the *Criminal Code* of Canada. A person who applies for a subpoena must provide some evidence that the potential witness likely has evidence that is relevant to the legal issues to be decided in the court proceeding; simply alleging or hoping that the witness will have **material evidence** to give the court is not sufficient (*R v. Elliot*, 2003). While agents may be compelled to testify, CIs cannot be required to attend court.

When considering whether to issue a subpoena, a justice will generally consider a sworn statement filed in support of the application for the subpoena or listen to oral evidence given by the applicant (*R v. Coote*, 2009, at para. 14(4)). Together, ss. 698 and 700 of the *Criminal Code* require that, pursuant to the authority of a subpoena, a person (1) attend court at a time and place stated in the subpoena to give evidence and bring with them, if required, anything in their possession or control relating to the proceedings (for example, records), and (2) remain in attendance at court until excused by the judge. A subpoena gives legal effect to the presumption that "[it] is not the prerogative of witnesses to criminal events to decide whether or not they will testify. They are bound to testify if called upon to do so, for it is only in this way that those guilty of crimes can be brought to justice and the public be protected" (*R v. Neuburger*, 1995, at para. 9). Failure to attend court in response to a subpoena may result in an arrest warrant being issued by the judge hearing the case.

Witnesses do not necessarily require a subpoena in order to be able to testify at a trial or preliminary hearing; oral notice from a Crown attorney or a police officer may be sufficient. However, oral notice has at least one potentially damaging consequence—a witness who has only been given oral notice cannot be arrested for failing to attend court, and such a failure can jeopardize a case where the witness has important **testimony** to give.

Note that the subpoena authority does *not* extend to compelling a witness to attend a police station for an interview; the police do not have the statutory authority to detain or arrest a witness for the sole purpose of an interview. The interview process is a voluntary one, conducted with the cooperation and consent of the witness. Witness cooperation and consent are therefore essential, and can be revoked by the witness at any time during the interview. An uncooperative witness cannot be arrested or charged with failure to cooperate with the police. In the event that a witness is uncooperative, the sole remedy available to the police is to use a subpoena to compel him or her to appear in court.

Competence and Compellability

We have seen that anyone who may be able to provide useful evidence can be made to attend court, but whether they will be permitted or compelled to *testify* is a matter determined by the rules found in the *Evidence Act*. Two concepts in particular—competence and compellability—are relevant to the determination of whether a court will allow or compel a witness to testify in a criminal proceeding.

subpoena a formal request, enforceable by the court, for a person's attendance in court to give testimony

material evidence evidence that is relevant to proving or disproving the elements of the offence with which an accused is charged

testimony the oral evidence of a witness in court

competence   being legally permitted to testify (based on the absence of factors such as age under 14 years or mental handicap)

Competence refers to whether a person may be allowed to testify under oath or affirmation in a criminal proceeding. As a general rule, every person—including a child over age 14—is considered competent to give sworn testimony, although there are some exceptions (for example, spouses, discussed below). A person who is unable to interpret or communicate what they observe due to a mental condition would not be considered competent, although not all mental conditions automatically render a person incompetent. A person who suffers from delusions, for example, may be competent to testify if those delusions do not affect their ability to perceive, remember, and communicate about the events in relation to which their testimony is being sought. The key issue is whether or not the person's mental condition would make their testimony untrustworthy.

Historically, many factors could render a witness incompetent to testify—for example, being the accused or the accused's spouse, having a financial stake in the outcome of a trial, or having been convicted of a crime. The rationale behind these prohibitions was that the evidence of such people was "tainted," and thus unreliable. Today, such prohibitions have all but disappeared, and these issues are simply factors considered in the process of determining a witness's credibility. In the past, a witness had to demonstrate some belief in a "supreme being" (God) and swear an oath to tell the truth in order to be considered competent—that is, there had to be fear on the part of the witness that they would suffer divine retribution if they were to lie; if a witness refused to take such an oath or if they were a "non-believer" (meaning that the oath would have no effect), the witness was not considered competent. Religious beliefs are no longer a requirement for competency and witnesses may choose to testify on the basis of either an oath or an affirmation to tell the truth. What is most important is that the person about to testify understands the importance of telling the truth in court (Bryant, Lederman, & Fuerst, 2009).

compellability   being without legal excuse to avoid testifying

Canadian Charter of Rights and Freedoms   the constitutional document that sets out the rights and freedoms enjoyed by all people of Canada

Compellability refers to the ability of the state to require a person to give evidence in a criminal proceeding. As a general rule, unless there is a provision to the contrary (such as the right in the ***Canadian Charter of Rights and Freedoms*** against self-incrimination), a witness who is competent is also compellable. A witness who is compellable may be forced under the power of subpoena or other process to testify in court, and refusal to do so can result in a charge of contempt. There are a number of factors that affect the compellability of a witness:

- A person who is charged with an offence is not compellable as a witness in a proceeding against themselves pursuant to their s. 11 Charter right against self-incrimination.

- Generally speaking, subject to certain exceptions (which mainly involve sexual crimes or crimes of violence against children), legally married spouses are neither competent nor compellable witnesses for the prosecution, although they are competent to give evidence for the defence (Bryant, Lederman, & Fuerst, 2009). These protections do not apply to common-law spouses.

Admissibility of Witness Testimony

The rules that govern the **admissibility** of witness testimony, as well as other forms of evidence, are something that every investigator should become familiar with. The general rule on admissibility is found in the Supreme Court case *Morris v. The Queen* (1983), which states that nothing (including witness testimony) should be admitted into evidence in court unless it is **relevant** to the charge—that is, helps to prove, actually proves, or helps to disprove at least one of the facts in issue—and everything that meets this test should be admitted into evidence in court unless it is excluded by some other legal rule (Bryant, Lederman, & Fuerst, 2009, p. 792).

Generally speaking, witnesses may only testify to facts that are within their own "knowledge, observation and experience" (Bryant, Lederman, & Fuerst, 2009, p. 771). They may *not* testify about what someone who is not before the court saw or said. Such testimony is perhaps the most common form of what is referred to as **hearsay evidence** and is, with certain exceptions, inadmissible. The central concern is that the person who made the statement is not in court and thus not subject to cross-examination. The person who made the original statement was not under oath to tell the truth when they made it and thus did not face the prospect of the charge of perjury if they lied. These factors are believed to effectively assure the quality of witness statements. In their absence, it is difficult to assess the reliability of the statement, and there is the danger that the statement will be accorded more evidentiary value than it deserves (Bryant, Lederman, & Fuerst, 2009).

In addition, witnesses may not give their opinion. **Opinion evidence** is inadmissible because it calls for an inference or conclusion to be drawn from the facts, which is the job of the trier of fact, not of the witness (Bryant, Lederman, & Fuerst, 2009, p. 771). A properly qualified person, however, may give opinion evidence to assist the trier of fact in making a judgment on a matter about which an ordinary person would unlikely be able to make a correct judgement without help because of a lack of special knowledge, skill, or expertise (Bryant, Lederman, & Fuerst, 2009, p. 771). In this case, the witness is known as an **expert witness** and the evidence is known as **expert evidence**. Professionals whom the court may deem expert witnesses include medical doctors, accountants, and scientists and may include certain police officers such as identification officers, polygraph examiners, and breathalyzer technicians. Opinion evidence is never allowed, however, in cases where the testimony concerns the mindset or intention of an accused.

In recognition of the difficulty in drawing a clear line between fact and opinion in many cases, the Supreme Court has allowed non-expert witnesses to give opinions "with respect to matters that do not require special knowledge (such as, for example, recognizing the voice of a person with whom the witness has had frequent contact), and in circumstances where it is virtually impossible to separate facts from inferences based on those facts (e.g., a person was drunk)" (Bryant, Lederman, & Fuerst, 2009, p. 771). For more on the admissibility of opinion evidence, see *R v. Mohan* (1994).

admissibility the likelihood of a piece of evidence being allowed by the judge to be presented in court

relevant tending to prove or disprove a proposition

hearsay evidence evidence based not on a witness's own knowledge but on a statement that the witness has heard from another source

opinion evidence evidence that goes beyond a statement of fact to present an opinion or conclusion

expert witness witness who by virtue of education, training, or experience has specialized knowledge or understanding beyond that of the average person, whose opinion may be relied on to assist a trier of fact in reaching a conclusion

expert evidence opinion evidence presented in a legal proceeding by a qualified expert witness drawn from their particular area of expertise

KEY TERMS

accused

admissibility

agent

agent provocateur

Canadian Charter of Rights and Freedoms

compellability

competence

confidential informant

evidence

expert evidence

expert witness

hearsay evidence

hypothesis

informant

interview

investigation

material evidence

material witness

opinion evidence

relevant

subpoena

suspect

testimony

trier of fact

witness

FURTHER READING

Burton, R. (2008). *On being certain: Believing you are right even when you're not.* New York: St. Martin's Press.

Chabris, C., & Simons, D. (2010). *The invisible gorilla (and other ways our intuitions deceive us).* New York: Crown.

Eck, J. (2009). Investigators, information and interpretation: A summary of criminal investigation research. In D.K. Rossmo (Ed.), *Criminal investigative failures* (pp. ix-xii). Boca Raton, FL: CRC Press.

Gilovich, T. (1991). *How we know what isn't so: The fallibility of human reason in everyday life.* New York: The Free Press.

Gladwell, M. (2005). *Blink: The power of thinking without thinking.* New York: Little, Brown and Company.

Levitt, S., & Dubner, S. (2005). *Freakonomics: A rogue economist explores the hidden side of everything.* New York: William Morrow. (A good discussion of issues that reveal the kind of critical thinking challenges discussed in the chapter, some of which are directly related to law enforcement.)

Levitt, S., & Dubner, S. (2009). *Super freakonomics: Global cooling, patriotic prostitutes, and why suicide bombers should buy life insurance.* New York: William Morrow.

Snook, B., & Keating, K. (2010). A field study of adult witness interviewing practices in a Canadian police organization. *Legal and Criminological Psychology, 16*(1), 160-172.

Tavris, C., & Aronson, E. (2007). *Mistakes were made (but not by me): Why we justify foolish beliefs, bad decisions, and hurtful acts.* New York: Harcourt.

REVIEW QUESTIONS

TRUE OR FALSE

T 1. The primary factor influencing a witness's compellability is mental capacity.

T 2. The immediate priority of the first officer arriving at the scene of a violent crime is to preserve any physical evidence that may be present.   *witness contamination?*

T 3. The police do not have the authority to arrest a person for the sole purpose of conducting an interview.

F 4. A witness who genuinely does not want to get involved with an investigation will not be required to testify in court.

T 5. Failure to attend court in response to a subpoena, may result in an arrest warrant being issued by the presiding judge.

F 6. Most crimes are solved by the gathering of physical evidence rather than through the interview process.

F 7. When the first officer arrives at a crime scene and encounters several witnesses, he should have the witnesses remain together to discuss what they observed in order to secure a cohesive narrative of their observations.

F 8. Hearsay evidence is not admitted in court under any circumstance.

F 9. The confidentiality privilege extends to agents acting on behalf of the police.

T 10. As a general rule, unless there is a provision to the contrary, a witness who is competent is also compellable.

MULTIPLE CHOICE

1. An investigation is or should be:

   a. a search for the person whom the investigator knows is responsible for the crime.

   b. a search for the truth.

   c. a search for evidence with which to convict the offender.

   d. a search for evidence that confirms the investigator's theory of the crime.

2. Of all the potential obstacles that stand between an investigator and the truth, perhaps the most difficult to overcome are:

   a. witnesses who refuse to cooperate with police.

   b. a lack of investigative resources

   c. the investigator's own limitations as an information processor and decision maker.

   d. defence counsel.

3. In the same way that physical evidence at a crime scene must be protected from contamination, witnesses must be protected from contamination that can occur as a result of:

   a. environmental contaminants, such as gasoline or motor oil at a vehicle crash scene, or bodily fluids, such as blood at an assault or homicide scene.

   b. listening to media reports of crime

   c. too much conversation with other people at a crime scene, such as police officers, other witnesses, or members of the public.

   d. viewing a traumatic event, such as violent crime.

4. A number of leading authorities in the field of eyewitness evidence argue that law enforcement and the legal system should adopt a more scientific perspective and view what resides in a person's memory in the same way that they view physical evidence. Their suggestion is based on the notion that, just like physical evidence,

   a. eyewitness memory for an event is prone to factors like deterioration and contamination.

   b. eyewitness memory resides in the brain, which is a physical structure.

   c. eyewitness memory can be difficult to locate because it is typically stored in many different areas of the brain.

   d. eyewitness memory can be affected by many different factors, such as mental or physical illness.

5. A confidential informant is someone who

   a. has disclosed information about criminal activity to a police officer and has been given an assurance of confidentiality by the officer.

   b. has engaged in undercover police activity, such as the wearing of a body pack in order to gather evidence confidentially.

   c. has disclosed information about criminal activity to a police officer and has been given a quantity of money in exchange for that information.

   d. personally observed or experienced something relevant to the commission of a crime and voluntarily gave that information to police.

Short Answer

1. The legal process for issuing a subpoena is found in s. 698 of the *Criminal Code*; the legal authority is found in s. 699. After reviewing an annotated Code, list the subsections relating to the content of the subpoena and service of the document. What does the case law on these subsections say?

2. Adopting the perspective of a criminal investigator, list some reasons other than those provided in the text why a witness might be uncooperative.

3. Does the *Criminal Code* allow a police officer to request a warrant for a witness in lieu of a subpoena when, on probable grounds, the officer

believes the witness may ignore a subpoena and flee the country? If so, what are the statutory requirements the police must meet?

4. Trying to find witnesses by revisiting a crime scene on successive days can have some advantages. As an investigator, in which circumstances would you revisit a crime scene and what would you hope to gain?

5. How can the first officer attending a crime scene "contaminate" the potential testimony of a witness or witnesses found there?

6. Explain the legal distinctions between a witness, a confidential informant, and an agent for the police.

7. Why must a police officer not offer confidential informant status to an anxious witness in order to obtain information from them and/or maintain their cooperation?

CASE STUDY

On January 21, 2011, at about 2:30 a.m., the police received a call from the Never Close Convenience Store at 224 Fourth Avenue, two blocks west of Main Street. The caller stated that she was a cashier at the store and had just been robbed at knifepoint by a lone male.

Two officers, Smith and Brown, attended as soon as possible but were delayed by a heavy snowfall and poor road conditions. The officers arrived at 2:45 a.m. and found a distraught clerk (Sally Little) waiting for them at the store entrance.

Sally advised the officers that she normally worked the midnight-to-eight shift at the store. At about 2:20 a.m. she had just finished serving a regular customer, Bob Black, who had purchased a package of cigarettes on his way home from work. Sally stated that Bob had been gone about 30 seconds when she noticed a middle-aged man dressed in a heavy green parka enter the store.

On entering the store, the man, who wore a black toque and gloves, stood for a moment stamping his feet on the mat to remove the snow from his boots. After looking around the store, he approached Sally, who was behind the counter, and asked for a package of Players Light cigarettes. Sally turned to pick up the package, and when she turned back to face the man he had a hunting knife in his hand and stated that he wanted all the money in the cash register. Sally said she did not move immediately because she was in shock. The man then repeated his demand, saying that if she did not do as she was told, he would have to cut her up.

Sally advised the officers that she then moved to the cash register and opened it. She took out all the cash and handed it to the man, who then asked for a bag. Sally gave the man a plastic bag and watched as he placed the cash into the bag. The man warned Sally not to call for help and he fled the store. Sally advised the officers that she watched as the man fled west toward Main Street. She could not see him for very long because he disappeared around a corner. She then called the police.

While officer Brown took a brief statement, including a full description of the robber, officer Smith inspected the area around the store. The snow continued to fall and the streets were deserted. Smith noticed an area near the southwest corner of Fourth and Main where it was obvious that a snowplow had gone around a parked vehicle that was no longer there. Smith concluded that the vehicle had departed after the snowplow had gone by, because he noticed that its tire marks crossed the mound of snow left by the plow. When Smith looked around the area from the vantage point of the store's front door, he noticed a lighted window in an apartment building across the street from the store.

1. Where should Brown and Smith begin their search for witnesses? Explain your answer.

2. Identify potential witnesses and explain your choices.

3. Describe the evidence that each potential witness might provide.

Techniques for Interviewing Witnesses

2

INTRODUCTION

Effective interviewing in a criminal investigation requires good communication skills, which include active listening on the part of the interviewer and a substantial effort by the interviewee to recall what happened. It also requires training, planning, patience, problem solving, and lots of practice. The primary objective of the investigative interview is to elicit the maximum amount of reliable information from a person's memory of an event, while being careful to minimize both errors in the person's recall and any potential contamination that might be introduced by the interviewer.

In this chapter, we typically use the term "witness" to refer to both observers and non-traumatized victims of crime. The distinction between interviewing a witness or victim versus interviewing a potential suspect is not always clear-cut, and similar techniques are often useful and necessary in both cases. (In some situations, however, special strategies are required for victims.) Furthermore, in the early stages of an investigation, it is sometimes difficult to determine who is a victim, who is a witness, and who is a suspect until information from all involved parties and evidence from other sources is obtained.

This chapter focuses on the issues common to most investigative interviews, primarily with observer witnesses, non-traumatized victims, and people who may end up as suspects after more information is gathered. The key point to remember is that, at least initially, police interviewers should treat everyone with the same reasonable degree of politeness and respect. Despite media depictions to the contrary, veteran interviewers of even the most experienced criminals know that little is to be gained from adopting a confrontational attitude at the outset with a person from whom one needs to elicit information. Establishing rapport and treating a person with respect have been shown to reliably open the lines of communication (St-Yves, 2006). Also, by treating all witnesses equally, investigators reduce the risk of displaying bias or acquiring "tunnel vision," a phenomenon we look at in greater detail in Chapter 7, Portals of Discovery: Investigative Failures and the Lessons Learned.

CHAPTER OBJECTIVES

After completing this chapter, you should be able to:

- Explain the importance of acquiring interview skills.
- Identify the single most important skill an interviewer can acquire.
- Explain theories of memory storage and retrieval and describe how they have influenced the development of interview techniques.
- Describe the fundamentals of the cognitive model of memory.
- Describe the fundamentals of the cognitive and enhanced cognitive interview techniques.
- Conduct a basic witness interview using the enhanced cognitive interview approach.

THE ROLE OF THE INTERVIEW IN AN INVESTIGATION

statement   a witness's, suspect's, or victim's account of an event, usually "taken" from a witness or a suspect in the course of a formal recorded interview, although it can be taken anywhere at anytime and may be written out; electronic recording of statements is the preferred method of preserving a statement for disclosure and court purposes

As mentioned above, the interview is a process by which the recollections of a person who made observations regarding the commission of a crime are gathered in order to create a permanent record of those observations, called a **statement**. The interview will typically be recorded (at least the audio portion, but ideally both audio and video), and a transcript of the interview may be prepared from this recording. During and after the interview, the police officer, and perhaps others, will assess both the credibility of the evidence offered by the witness and the credibility of the witness himself or herself. It is important to remember that any formal assessment based on the interview record, such as statement analysis (discussed in Chapter 5, Detecting Deception), rises or falls primarily on the quality of the interview process.

The statement is one of the pieces of evidence that the Crown attorney analyzes prior to the court process in order to determine which, if any, of the facts in issue are proven by the witness's statement. The Crown attorney can also use the statement to assess possible problems with the admissibility of the testimony. In Canada, pursuant to s. 7 of the Charter, an accused has the right to make full answer and defence to a charge. That right can only be meaningful if there is a duty on the Crown to divulge all relevant evidence that it has against a person. This principle takes effect through a process called **disclosure**. The definitive legal opinion on the issue of disclosure is found in the Supreme Court of Canada case *R v. Stinchcombe* (1991). In *Stinchcombe*, the Court said that the Crown has an obligation to provide the defence with all evidence that could possibly be relevant to the case, regardless of whether it assists the Crown's case and whether the Crown intends to use that evidence at a trial. The Court made it clear that evidence belongs to the justice system as a whole, not to the Crown: "[T]he fruits of the investigation which are in the possession of counsel are not the property of the Crown for use in securing a conviction but the property of the public to be used to ensure that justice is done."

disclosure   process in which the Crown attorney is required to reveal to the defence all of the evidence (including physical or electronic copies of all documents, statements, and any other evidence) gathered in an investigation that could be potentially relevant to the defence of the accused, including information that the Crown does not intend to use at trial

The Crown meets its disclosure obligations in the case of a witness statement when a copy of the statement is provided to the accused either directly or through his or her counsel. The Crown is obliged to give copies of all statements, and any other relevant information (with the exception of certain "privileged" information) gathered during the course of an investigation, to the defence. This obligation also applies to the evidence of witnesses who have been interviewed by the police but whom the Crown does not intend to call to testify during the course of the trial. In 2009, the Supreme Court created an additional duty on the Crown to disclose records of the discipline or misconduct of officers involved in the investigation of an accused if they might be relevant to the case; this imposed a corresponding obligation on the police to disclose any such records to the Crown (*R v. McNeil*, 2009).

When a witness is called to testify in court, he or she cannot read from the statement given to the police. The witness's statement is not evidence and cannot be read into the record of the trial except in the most extreme and narrow circumstances. However, the witness may refresh his or her memory by referring to the document before testifying. This serves to improve the accuracy of the testimony and to build confidence in the witness who, as a result of inexperience or the amount of time that has passed since the event that he or she witnessed occurred, may be nervous about his or her performance. The witness statement also gives the Crown attorney the means to confront a witness who is either hostile to the Crown from the outset or who becomes belligerent while testifying.

THE NEED FOR INTERVIEW TRAINING

Obtaining information from apparently cooperative witnesses and victims of crime has often been regarded as a process that does not require much more than asking a series of questions and accurately recording the responses. However, as we will see in this chapter, it is wrong to assume that even the most motivated witness can accurately and completely describe an event merely by responding to a series of questions from a well-intentioned investigator. The need for specialized police interview skills training was first identified in the United States in 1975, in a seminal study of criminal investigation processes conducted by the Rand Corporation. In addition, Ron Fisher and Ed Geiselman, the originators of the cognitive interview we discuss below, along with other colleagues, carefully reviewed hundreds of actual police interviews conducted in the United States and revealed a number of common shortcomings (see, for example, Fisher, Geiselman, & Raymond, 1987).

In Canada, especially over the past decade, the investigative practices of the police have attracted considerable scrutiny as a result of a number of high-profile wrongful conviction cases (for example, Sophonow, 2001; Milgaard, 2006; Dalton, Parsons, & Druken, 2006; Marshall, 2005; Driskell, 2007; Unger, 2009). Various commissions of inquiry into cases of wrongful conviction, such as the majority of those mentioned above, have reviewed police practices in these cases and produced detailed reports that set out general guidelines for conducting investigations and make specific recommendations with respect to police interviewing practices. The most common themes to come out of the inquiries with regard to the conduct of police interviews are the following:

- police investigators require a set of written, research-based interview protocols that they can follow to enhance the reliability, effectiveness, and accuracy of their interviews;
- police investigators need more training in how to conduct proper investigative interviews; and
- all police interviews with witnesses and suspects should be video recorded.

We endorse the many recommendations for the improvement of police interview practices put forth in these reports to both increase the effectiveness of police interviews and reduce the possibility of wrongful convictions. In the next section we look at some of the methods of witness interviewing that have evolved over the years, examine what they are based on, and consider the research that has been conducted into their effectiveness.

THE EVOLUTION OF MODERN INTERVIEW TECHNIQUES

Current state-of-the-art interview procedures can, in essence, be traced back to four roots: hypnosis; the concept of encoding specificity, or how similar the conditions are in which we originally experienced something to those under which we try to recall that experience from our memory; the problem of misleading post-event information; and research specifically aimed at police interview techniques, which began in the 1980s. We outline each of these roots briefly before considering various models of memory and then turning to a step-by-step examination of the interview technique we recommend: the enhanced cognitive interview.

Hypnosis

hypnosis   a technique by which a hypnotist purports to put a subject into a trancelike state in which the subject's responses and actions are under the hypnotist's control

Franz Mesmer (from whose name we get the term "mesmerized") is typically credited with refining and mastering the process of **hypnosis** in the second half of the 18th century, although similar states had been observed in various forms throughout human history (Fancher, 1995). Part medical treatment and part theatrics, it was *de rigueur* in 1770s Paris to invite Mesmer to high-society gatherings to perform his feats of "animal magnetism" for the guests' amusement. Mesmer was convinced that, just as Isaac Newton's recently developed theory of gravity explained the magnet-like attraction between objects, *animal* magnetism explained his own ability to influence other people's behaviour at a distance. No one disputed the effects of his procedure (hypnotic effects are still fairly easy to demonstrate today, especially with a large enough group of willing people), but his explanation for *how* hypnosis occurred was not well received in his day and he lost favour as a performer and practitioner of hypnosis, or "mesmerism." In fact, a century passed before hypnosis again became a subject of public and scholarly attention when Sigmund Freud and his colleagues revived interest in it in the late 19th century with the development of psychoanalysis. (Scholars still debate whether hypnosis represents a distinct state of consciousness, just as sleep is distinct from wakefulness, or whether it merely occupies an extreme ("hyper") position along some continuum of suggestibility.)

The late Canadian psychologist Nicholas Spanos of Carleton University conducted some of the best research on how hypnosis works and primarily favoured the notion of hypersuggestibility (see, for example, Spanos et al., 1991). In any event, hypnosis is a well-established if not well-understood technique, widely used around the world in therapeutic settings; for amusement by performers with large groups of people; and, most relevant for our purposes, sometimes as a technique to enhance witness recall in police investigations, although less so today than in the past.

"Hypnotically refreshed testimony" is the optimistic term often used to describe the fact that people sometimes recall a greater number of accurate details about an event under hypnosis than they do in a normal state. The problem with obtaining additional information this way is that a greater number of inaccurate details often come with the package, making it difficult to discriminate between what really happened and what a person's brain might have concocted (called "confabulations" or "intrusions") under hypnotic influence (Newman & Thompson, 2001; Geiselman et al., 1985; Orne et al., 1984). As a result, hypnotic interviews are rare, and testimony obtained under hypnosis can also be ruled inadmissible. In *R v. Trochym* (2007), the Supreme Court dealt with the issue of "post-hypnosis evidence" in Canada, stating:

> The technique of hypnosis and its impact on human memory are not understood well enough for post-hypnosis testimony to be sufficiently reliable in a court of law. Although hypnosis has been the subject of numerous studies, these studies are either inconclusive or draw attention to the fact that hypnosis can, in certain circumstances, result in the distortion of memory. The potential rate of error in the additional information obtained through hypnosis when it is used for forensic purposes is troubling. At the present time, there is no way of knowing whether such information will be accurate or inaccurate. Such uncertainty is unacceptable in a court of law.

Is there a way to reap the benefits that hypnosis apparently provides without having to cope with the erroneous details that often accompany it? Fortunately, the answer is "yes" (Wagstaff, 2008). The non-controversial fundamentals of hypnosis—such as good rapport between hypnotist and subject, a setting conducive to concentration, and a willingness on the part of the subject to exert some mental effort—can be exploited without the negative consequences associated with the actual hypnotic state. We describe the process later in this chapter when we discuss the cognitive and enhanced cognitive interviews.

Encoding Specificity

The second root of modern interviewing recommendations is based on the work of another Canadian psychologist, Endel Tulving of the University of Toronto, whose work is recognized around the world for its impact on our understanding of how memory operates and can be optimized. Tulving's seemingly simple notion of **encoding specificity** reveals that a major factor in how much we remember is the degree to which the conditions that exist during memory retrieval match the conditions that existed during one's experience of the to-be-recalled event (see, for example, Tulving & Thompson, 1973). In an investigative interview, the encoding specificity principle means that a witness will likely recall more if the physical and psychological conditions of the witnessed event can somehow be recreated. We specify how this can be done when we describe the context reinstatement phase of the cognitive and enhanced cognitive interviews.

encoding specificity a theory of memory function based on the hypothesis that a major factor in how much will be remembered is the degree to which the conditions that exist during memory retrieval match the conditions that existed during one's experience of the to-be-recalled event

Misleading Post-Event Information

The third root of modern interviewing recommendations is based on some of the best-known work on eyewitness evidence, conducted by Elizabeth Loftus, originally at the University of Washington and now at the University of California, Irvine. Loftus's early laboratory work on **misleading post-event information** (see, for example, Loftus, Miller, & Burns, 1978) has been followed by three decades of research studies; scholarly articles (for example, Bernstein, & Loftus, 2009); popular books (for example, Loftus, Doyle, & Dysart, 2008); expert testimony; case consultations; television appearances; and passionate debate on memory distortion, including the

misleading post-event information a theory of memory function that suggests that memories are easily distorted by information acquired after the original memory is formed

repressed memories
previously inaccessible
memories that are reported
to have later been recovered,
usually as a result of some
sort of therapy or
triggering event

issue of **repressed memories**. Indeed, Loftus is considered to be one of the 100 most influential researchers in psychology in the 20th century (Haggbloom et al., 2002). According to Loftus and dozens of other researchers around the world, memories are potentially vulnerable to distortion when exposed to information about an event that is inconsistent either with what really happened or with what the witness actually saw (Loftus, 1992; Loftus, 2003; Loftus, Doyle, & Dysart, 2008). The modern view of memory as a reconstructive process that attempts to take advantage of all relevant information is consistent with the finding that people often incorporate into their recall of an event information provided by other people; stories that they have read; and, most important with respect to the interview situation, questions posed by those trying to determine what happened. The effect ranges from relatively small quantitative changes in recalled details to the implantation in memory of events that never took place (see, for example, Loftus, 1997).

Research on Police Interview Techniques

Perhaps the most convincing evidence of the need for improved investigative interviewing techniques comes from the most basic source: the interviews themselves. As mentioned, one of the best-known analysis of police interviews was conducted by psychologists Fisher, Geiselman, & Raymond (1987). They found that police interviewers varied widely in their interview styles and the techniques they used; were largely unaware of the limitations of their interviewing practices; and had little logic or reasoning underlying the ways in which they interviewed witnesses (many interviews were, quite simply, haphazard). In addition, they found that the following flaws were typical of police interviews:

- officers typically asked too many closed and potentially leading questions (such as, "Was the offender young?" and "Was the car red?");
- officers did not provide sufficient time for the witness to respond to one question before asking another; and
- officers generally did not do much to encourage the witness to recall as much information as was likely available.

The psychologists concluded that police required a method for investigative interviewing that was reliable and based on what had been learned about memory through empirical research. In the light of this conclusion, in 1992 Fisher and Geiselman published the book *Memory-Enhancing Techniques for Investigative Interviewing: The Cognitive Interview*, in which they combined their analysis of police interviews with existing knowledge about hypnosis, encoding specificity, and the effects of misleading information. Both academic research on the cognitive interview and the practical application of the technique by investigators in the field have continued since the approach was first developed (for example, Fisher & Perez, 2007; Wright & Holliday, 2007; Fisher & Schreiber, 2007; Fisher & Castano, 2007; Dando, Wilcock & Milne, 2009), resulting in the enhanced cognitive interview.

MODELS OF MEMORY AND THEIR IMPLICATIONS FOR INTERVIEWING

For investigators who must access the memories of other people to obtain information about events, understanding how memory works is important. Adhering to models of memory that are inconsistent with what science has revealed about memory in recent decades is a potential barrier to gaining that knowledge. Our concern is that a belief in an inaccurate or incomplete model of memory will adversely influence an investigator's decision to accept or dismiss particular strategies for enhancing witness recall; it will also affect how an investigator responds to witnesses' claims regarding what they do or do not remember about an event.

Before examining the model that is generally accepted as the best available description of how memory works (the cognitive model), we briefly describe three of the most common models that many people incorrectly believe are accurate accounts of memory functioning.

The Freudian Model

Sigmund Freud is famous for several controversial ideas that he put forth around the turn of the 20th century (for example, Freud, 1900/1965). Perhaps Freud's most enduring legacy involves the role of unconscious influences on people's memory, thoughts, and behaviour. Freud argued that our conscious awareness is analogous to the small visible tip of an iceberg and that larger unconscious processes deep below the surface of our awareness cause us to be neurotic, narcissistic, defensive, and so forth. It is important to keep in mind that these ideas are over 100 years old and are not the subject of much training or research in modern-day psychology.

The unconscious influences that Freud was writing about were primarily memories of traumatic childhood experiences, which Freud believed continue to influence our thoughts and behaviour in adulthood, even though we may not have any conscious awareness of them. Freud argued that the only way to rid ourselves of these unconscious influences is to access the memories of our traumatic experiences through techniques such as hypnosis, word association, and the administration of "truth serum." Because accessing memory is what the investigative interview is all about, it's important to know whether memories of experiences from long ago can in fact remain intact in the deep recesses of the mind and, if so, whether there are special techniques that can be used to access them. If an investigator believes in the Freudian model of memory, the two most likely consequences of that belief are that (1) he or she believes that memories of traumatic events, such as sexual assaults in childhood, are routinely "repressed" by the unconscious and then "recovered" in their original form years or decades later; and (2) there is some sort of method that can be used to easily access information in people's memories.

Is the Freudian model convincing? A few clinical psychologists and psychiatrists claim to have helped their clients recover memories that those therapists believe to be true, but there is no universally accepted mechanism by which such repression and subsequent revelation might occur. In fact, some evidence suggests that experiences that Freudian supporters claim are candidates for repression are actually *impossible to forget* for many people, who instead have no choice but to remember them for much of their lives. It is not widely accepted that the brain automatically protects us from remembering traumatic events by repressing our memories of them, although there is also no evidence to prove that repression can *never* happen. Two landmark publications are recommended to readers who want to know more about this potentially controversial issue: Lindsay & Read (1995) and Bowers & Farvolden (1996).

In addition to the flaws that little evidence exists to support the Freudian model of memory and that much of the existing evidence actually supports an opposite conclusion, research conducted by Loftus and others (for example, Bernstein & Loftus, 2009) reveals that memory is susceptible to distortion from information acquired after the event, thus making it highly unlikely for details to remain intact in the mind for extremely long periods of time. So while it is certainly possible for an event from one's distant past to be forgotten and then remembered, we should be just as wary about the accuracy of the details from such a memory as we are about recalled details from an event that occurred last week. Despite commonly accepted beliefs in "flashbulb memories" and "photographic memories," there is no reliable research indicating that these phenomena occur in such a way or with such frequency to warrant complete faith in the veracity of anyone's recalled details from long ago (Marsh, 2007; Christianson, 1992; McCloskey, Wible, & Cohen, 1988; Turtle & Want, 2008).

With respect to the issue of "recovered" memories, certainly no one wishes to re-victimize persons who may have suffered abuse; however, the rights of suspects cannot be ignored either. The courts in Canada have taken the position that a witness should not be believed or disbelieved only because he or she claims to have repressed and then recovered a memory of a past event or series of events. Rather, such evidence should be admitted with cautions regarding its reliability (*R v. R.E.M.*, 2004; *R v. Kliman*, 1996). Our recommendation, therefore, is that a criminal allegation based on a recovered memory should be treated no differently than an allegation based on a "normal" memory; the court will decide what weight such evidence will carry during a trial.

Finally, let's consider the Freudian proposition that there are special techniques for easily accessing repressed memories. The fact is that no reliable evidence exists to support this contention. Hypnosis, as we have seen, is not a particularly useful tool for accessing reliable information from witness memories. Some of the features of a hypnotic interview can be used to an investigator's advantage, but the dangers of a full-blown trance state outweigh its benefits in most cases. Nor is word association, in which a person is asked to say the first thing that comes to mind in response to a stimulus word, a reliable method. And so-called truth serum (sodium pentathol, sodium amytal, and other agents) is merely a nervous-system depressant that, like alcohol, can reduce a person's unwillingness or inhibitions to talk about something (for example, Borrell, 2008). It does not work any better than strategies such as putting an interviewee at ease, withholding judgment about an interviewee's actions, and not creating an air of suspicion without good cause.

The Videotape Model

The videotape model of memory is, in many respects, an updated version of the Freudian model. The idea is that memory, or at least some memories, are stored in a literal, chronological form that can be accessed at a later point; in essence, the model holds that memories are passively "recorded" and later "replayed" at will in great detail. This is not a theory supported by reliable research. In one case in which police interviewed a witness who had a poor recollection of events, they pressured her in a subsequent interview to produce additional details from memory. They told her that one way to do this was to close her eyes and pretend that she was "watching a movie"; they were subsequently criticized by the judge, who stated that this approach created the potential for the production of false memories (*R v. Post*, 2005). Although many people have the impression that events such as assaults and life-threatening accidents are remembered "like a movie," in perfect detail, research has repeatedly shown that the accuracy of such memories is no greater than that of other memories (see, for example, Turtle & Want, 2008). Investigators should therefore tolerate imperfections in witnesses' memories, concentrate on what is remembered well, and not judge a witness negatively for forgetting an important detail.

The Biological Model

An apparently logical consequence of the fact that memory is based on biological processes goes something like this: memories are stored in the brain; the brain is made up of cells; therefore, memories must be stored in individual cells. Furthermore, brain cells die by the thousands each day and are typically never replaced, so the memories stored in those cells must also decay and become inaccessible.

The weak link in all of this is the assumption that memories are stored in individual cells, such as a "grandmother cell" that retains an image of your grandmother's face. Supposedly, if you lose that cell to decay, you will forget what your grandmother looked like. But research has shown that memory is much more than a simple storehouse of cells that fills up with information as we go through life. Most brain researchers now support the connectionist model of memory (for example, McClelland, Rumelhart, & Hinton, 1986), discussed below.

The Cognitive Model

Cognitive science is the study of how the brain processes information for tasks such as problem solving; language; decision making; and, most important for our present purposes, memory. It is a multifaceted approach, picking up where the other models of memory we've been discussing leave off, with an emphasis on applied issues and useful parallels with computerized information processing. The three fundamental components of the cognitive model of memory are that (1) information is processed in a series of discrete stages, (2) there is a "cognitive economy" in the brain that maximizes the efficiency of our limited cognitive capabilities, and (3) memories are stored in overlapping networks of neural connections in the brain.

Stages of Information Processing

Scientific research has shown that the brain processes information in stages, an idea first proposed by Atkinson & Shiffrin (1968), based in part on earlier work by Sperling (1960), and subsequently supported by hundreds if not thousands of additional studies and experiments (see Crowder & Surprenant, 2000 for an overview, or Baddeley, Eysenck, & Anderson, 2008 for a complete book on the subject of memory).

When we witness an event, the process goes something like this: first, our limited attentional resources typically must be allocated to an object in our visual field if it is going to have any chance of being remembered. Light waves reflected off the surfaces of the object travel through the air and into our eyes through the pupils, where they then move through the thick, vitreous fluid that fills our eyeballs before falling onto light-sensitive receptors in the retina to form an upside down two-dimensional image about the size of a dime—only a small part of which is actually in focus. The receptors convert the electromagnetic light energy into electrochemical energy, which travels along the optic nerve to the occipital cortex at the back of the brain. There, the information is decoded back into what seems like a clear, right side up, three-dimensional image, only some of which will ever make it into our memory. A portion of what we've perceived moves on to the short-term (or "working") memory stage of the process. This information is typically lost forever unless it is further processed into long-term memory. Transfer from working to long-term memory is accomplished by some combination of simple rehearsal ("his hair is brown, his hair is brown, his hair is brown"); integration with existing memory ("he looks a lot like my brother Dave"); or meaningful interpretation ("he looks more scared than I feel"). If you later want to describe what you saw, the information must be retrieved from the vast repository of long-term memory, placed into working memory, processed by speech centres in the brain, and converted into words that are created by forcing air through your larynx and moving your tongue, lips, and mouth.

Given the above, it seems incredible that we perceive and remember anything at all. This is an important fact to keep in mind when faced with a witness who claims not to have seen something that clearly was right in front of his or her eyes or who can't remember the colour of the shirt worn last month by an attacker. The cognitive interview is based on this knowledge of how memory functions and offers strategies to at least partially compensate for these built-in limitations.

The Cognitive Economy

cognitive economy
a theory of memory function that describes the shortcuts taken by the brain in an effort to store and retrieve an enormous number of individual memories

Research has also shown that the brain seeks to pare down what needs to be stored so that it is not cluttered with unnecessary details that might slow the processing of more important information. This **cognitive economy** is evidenced by the many shortcuts the brain takes to combine in memory information from similar events (called "schemas" or "scripts" by Schank & Abelson, 1975) and make decisions relatively quickly without waiting to access all of the possibly relevant information (called "heuristics" by Tversky & Kahneman, 1974). People have these mental scripts for events they experience repeatedly, such as going to a restaurant or starting a new class. After many such experiences, the brain tends to blend the details so that we don't necessarily remember the details of each occasion on which a dinner tab was delivered or the precise way that each new teacher introduced himself or herself. Instead, the brain often relies on generalized versions of familiar events that include items common to most of the events.

An interviewer, therefore, could facilitate accurate and complete recall by helping a witness remember anything that might distinguish a particular restaurant visit from all other visits. Of course, if the incident in question ended with a violent attack or robbery, it will likely stand out in the person's memory. In that case, an interviewer might have to be aware of memory schemas in order to help a bank teller, for example, who has dealt with hundreds or thousands of customers other than the one who robbed him recently, so that he does not unintentionally incorporate into his statement some aspect of a typical customer interaction that didn't actually occur in the case of the person who robbed him. And if it is only later that an incident is determined to be important to an investigation (for example, a bank teller cashing what turns out to be a bad cheque), recovering the details with knowledge of memory schemas is also important. In all these cases, the quality of the interview is likely to be improved if the interviewer employs the enhanced cognitive interview technique.

The Connectionist Model

The third component of the cognitive model of memory incorporates the connectionist model of memory alluded to earlier (for example, McClelland, Rumelhart, & Hinton, 1986). According to the connectionist model, the brain perceives and processes incoming information, such as another person's appearance, by activating a *network* of cells. Different subsets of the network are devoted to different aspects of the incoming information, such as who the person resembles and whether he or she appears trustworthy, as well as contextual information, such as the time, place, and other circumstances. When it comes time to remember the person's appearance and other details of the event, the brain attempts to reactivate the connections among the cells that were active during the initial exposure. A good interviewer can facilitate that reactivation by getting a witness to think about the many aspects of the person's face that make up the memory, the context in which the person was viewed, what the witness was doing at the time, and so on. This is part of the logic behind the cognitive and enhanced cognitive interviews.

Before turning to what the cognitive interviewing approach offers investigators, it is worth considering whether there is anything we can salvage from the other memory models. In fact, the Freudian model helps us understand some of the complexities surrounding memory, especially regarding traumatic events that occurred long ago, and the role that unconscious processes might play in forming and retrieving memories. It helps us realize that there is no simple explanation for how memory functions and that any claim based on memory—perhaps especially for traumatic events from long ago—should be investigated objectively, case by case. The videotape model gives us a useful vocabulary for helping people access their memories. For example, an investigator might say, "Dave, I'd like you to replay in your mind the details of what took place at work last Friday. When you get to the part where you say Don attacked you, I'd like you to think of the event as if it's playing back in slow motion, and when you get to the part where he pulled the weapon, I'd like you to freeze that frame and zoom in on exactly what that weapon looked like."

These are meaningful instructions for most people and may assist them in taking the time and effort required to effectively search their memory—as long as both the investigator and the witness understand that this is not how memory actually functions and as long as the investigator does not put any pressure on the witness to "play back" more than he or she can readily recall. Finally, the biological model acknowledges the complexity of our memory system and can perhaps help us account for memory abnormalities caused by illness, drug and alcohol intoxication, and/or brain injury.

THE ENHANCED COGNITIVE INTERVIEW

As mentioned above, in the 1980s American psychologists Ed Geiselman and Ron Fisher developed the **cognitive interview (CI)** in an effort to improve the quality of police interviews with witnesses. The CI has undergone a number of improvements since it was first developed and, in both its original and enhanced forms, remains one of the most researched and significant interview procedures developed over the past two decades (for example, Milne & Bull, 1999; Dando & Milne, 2009).

Background: The Cognitive Interview

As discussed, the CI is based on three ideas that arose out of psychological research on memory, which began formally in the 1970s and 1980s (see Baddeley, Eysenck, & Anderson, 2008 for much more detail):

1. An event may be represented in memory in various ways (for example, in central versus peripheral details or in semantic versus episodic information), which means that while one retrieval technique may fail, suggesting that the person has forgotten some detail, another technique may be successful at accessing that detail.

2. The principle of encoding specificity, discussed above, in which the similarity between the context in which a memory was first "made" and the context in which one subsequently attempts to retrieve it, can affect how successful a person is at remembering.

3. The phenomenon of misleading post-event information, also discussed above, helps us understand how memories can come to incorporate incorrect details from sources encountered *after* an event has occurred.

When it was first developed, the CI wasn't really an "interview"; rather, it was a group of four *techniques* designed for use *during* an interview. The techniques, which could be used either on their own or in combination, were intended to assist cooperative witnesses in recalling events or knowledge from memory and motivate them to make the effort necessary to effectively search their memories (Milne & Bull, 1999; Schollum, 2005).

cognitive interview (CI)
refers to a group of four techniques (report everything; change perspective; change order; context reinstatement) developed as a result of psychological research conducted on police interviewing practices; designed to facilitate a witness's use of their memory during an interview; *see* enhanced cognitive interview

The four original CI techniques consisted of the following points (on which we elaborate further in this chapter when we discuss the enhanced cognitive interview):

1. *Report Everything.* The interviewer asks the witness to report everything he or she remembers about the event and the circumstances surrounding it, stressing the importance of leaving nothing out, even if the witness thinks the details are unimportant or believes that the police may already know about them. The rationale for this technique is to increase both the total amount of information given by the witness and the likelihood that additional remembered aspects of the event will be "triggered" (that is, in the course of providing potentially "insignificant" information, more connections in the network of brain pathways associated with the event will be activated).

2. *Change Order.* The interviewer asks the witness to recall the events in a variety of chronological orders (for example, beginning to end, end to beginning, or from a particular point either forward or backward). The retrieval of information from memory can be influenced by prior knowledge or "mental scripts" that affect how we make sense of what we recall (that is, we piece together our stories based on inferences from our past experiences and what seems to "makes sense" in a given situation, not necessarily on the basis of specific details we can actually recall). Attempting to recall the components of an event in a different order can "shake up" our retrieval strategy and potentially limit the effect of such "mental shortcuts," resulting in improved recall.

3. *Change Perspective.* The interviewer asks the witness to consider what the event might have looked like from different perspectives (for example, from the point of view of someone else who was present during the event or an imaginary video camera in a corner of the ceiling). Research has shown that witnesses can sometimes recall more information if they think about an event from a number of different perspectives rather than from a single perspective alone. At the same time, as we discuss below, this strategy could lead to a person making inferences about what they *might* have seen from another perspective, so investigators should be wary of that problem and potential subsequent criticism from the defence.

4. *Context Reinstatement.* The interviewer asks the witness to focus his or her attention on the context surrounding the event (for example, the physical environment, or what the witness was thinking or feeling at the time) in order to mentally recreate the context of the event the witness is trying to recall. The rationale for this technique is connected to the principle of encoding specificity, which has shown that the more similar the context in which a person attempts to recall an event is to the context in which the event was initially experienced, the more likely the person is to recall it.

A number of studies conducted after the introduction of the CI indicated that the CI significantly and consistently increased the amount of correct information produced by witnesses when compared to the standard police interview or to forensic hypnosis and that it did so without an increase in the amount of erroneous information recalled (Dando & Milne, 2009). However, it became apparent that, owing to the lack of a standard police interview structure and the tendency for officers to engage in counterproductive behaviours (for example, interrupting, using short-answer questions, jumping haphazardly from one topic to another, and using judgmental language), in order to maximize the effectiveness of the CI, the techniques would need to be placed in an appropriate structure and interviewers provided with instructions on how best to use them (Dando & Milne, 2009). Additional impetus for enhancing the CI came from research that indicated that witnesses often displayed more anxiety, poorer communication skills, and more confusion about their roles in real-life interviews than subjects did in the laboratory settings in which the CI was originally developed (Gudjonsson, 1992).

In response to these issues, Fisher and Geiselman developed what has come to be called the **enhanced cognitive interview (ECI)**. In addition to the original four techniques of the CI, the ECI includes witness-compatible questioning and focused retrieval, and stipulates that all the components of the ECI be used in a particular sequence to maximize their effect. Unlike the original CI, which covered only the four memory enhancement techniques, the ECI covers the entire interview process (Dando & Milne, 2009).

Preparing for an Interview

Conducting an investigative interview can be a complex process, with a number of steps that need to be taken in the right way at the right time. Before we explore the seven steps of the ECI, we will briefly examine the preparatory steps that investigators must take to ensure that their interviews will be as effective as possible and explain how to "package" an interview.

Gathering Information and Preparing an Outline

There is no easy way to conduct a good interview, but there is no better way to try than by being prepared. The importance of thorough preparation cannot be overstated. The investigator who will conduct the interview should prepare by learning as much as reasonably possible about the case, including becoming familiar with:

- information from previous interviews with other witnesses;
- evidence collected through other aspects of the investigation (such as physical evidence collected at the crime scene or video surveillance evidence); and
- available information on any special characteristics of the witness (such as extreme youth or age, state of mind, and relationship to the suspect(s)).

The investigator should devise a plan around which to structure the interview. Flexibility is important, but no one can conduct a good interview by "winging it," so the investigator should keep a rough outline at hand in case he or she is at a loss for words at some point or wants to remember key points to address later. The headings used to describe the steps in the ECI (explored below and summarized in Figure 2.1) can be used to structure the outline.

enhanced cognitive interview (ECI)
an interview that uses the four original CI techniques, but attempts to maximize their effectiveness by placing them in an appropriate structure and providing interviewers with instructions on how best to use them to minimize the tendency of police interviewers to engage in counterproductive behaviours such as interrupting or using short-answer questions; *see* cognitive interview

CI/ECI Significantly More Effective Than Standard Police Interview

While research on the original CI had indicated that it was about 30 percent more effective than a standard police interview (Geiselman, Fisher, MacKinnon, & Holland, 1985), research on the ECI indicated that it resulted in approximately 45 percent more correct details being produced by witnesses than the original CI (Fisher, Geiselman, Raymond, Jurkevich, & Warhaftig, 1987). It was thus concluded that the ECI elicited almost 90 percent more correct details from witnesses compared to the standard police interview.

The effectiveness of the ECI has been demonstrated in both laboratory and real world conditions. North American studies have proven its effectiveness in significantly increasing the amount of information detectives are able to elicit from witnesses (Dando & Milne, 2009), and similarly positive results have been found in developing countries (Stein & Memon, 2006). Research has consistently shown that the CI/ECI enhances the *quantity* of information witnesses are able to recall without decreasing its *quality*. These effects have been demonstrated in a number of countries (the United Kingdom, Canada, Spain, and Germany) and among a number of different witness populations (children, individuals with special needs such as learning disabilities, and the elderly) (Dando & Milne, 2009).

Choosing the Time and Place

Generally speaking, a witness's ability to recall the details of a crime decreases as time passes. Witnesses and potential witnesses are usually briefly interviewed at the crime scene (assuming they are present and have been identified by the first officer or investigating officer), but this often serves merely to identify the witness and where he or she may be located at a later time. During the on-scene interview, a witness's bare-bones observations may be recorded to assist in a future determination of the evidentiary value of the witness's testimony. In addition, a rough description of an offender provided by an on-scene witness can be useful in trying to locate the offender in the area soon after the event. Witnesses should be advised that they may be contacted soon by the interviewing officer or other officers to make a formal statement.

There are several factors to consider in selecting a location for the main interview, such as the witness's age, the type of crime that he or she witnessed, the time that has elapsed since the crime was committed, and the witness's work and/or school schedules. Only some of these will be under the control of the investigator. A number of experienced investigators suggest that the best place to take a formal witness statement is in a controlled setting, such as a police station. This may in fact be the best location in many situations, but using a police station is not always possible or desirable.

Before the interview, the necessary materials and equipment must be prepared. Recording equipment should be checked and double-checked, and related supplies, such as DVDs and fresh batteries for digital audio recorders, should be on hand. Beverages, pens, and paper should be available in the interview room in sufficient quantities.

Usually, police officers must be flexible in choosing a location and must make the best of what is available. A formal witness statement can be successfully taken at a witness's home, place of employment, or in any setting that provides privacy and comfort. The location selected or agreed on should be one that allows the witness to concentrate without interruption and to reflect on his or her observations. Although a police station may provide geographical and psychological distance from, for example, the scene of a traumatizing domestic dispute or act of workplace violence, conducting an interview at the scene of the crime can have significant advantages with respect to memory recall.

The location should also provide a physical layout that allows the police officer to conduct the interview and take notes in a professional manner. A room with a table on which interview materials can be placed and a door that can be closed to minimize distractions and maintain privacy are ideal. A police officer attempting to learn the details of an event while balancing a clipboard on one knee in his or her patrol car is not presenting a professional image to the witness and may in fact give the witness the impression that the statement is not important. Also, the witness will be unlikely to exert the necessary mental effort to recall the event as completely as possible and the officer will be unlikely to listen as effectively or observe the witness as carefully.

If the statement is to be taken at the witness's residence, the officer should consider taking it at a time when the witness will not be interrupted by family members or other persons. Distractions lead to poor concentration, which in turn may produce a less than optimal interview. Privacy must also be considered when the witness suggests that the police drop by his or her office or other place of employment.

Sometimes, if it is impractical for a witness to meet with an investigator in person (for example, if the witness had been visiting the city when he or she witnessed the event and returned home before he or she could be interviewed), it may be necessary to interview a witness over the phone. Although taking a statement from a witness over the phone is not ideal, it is a reasonable option, especially when the alternative is not obtaining a statement at all. Investigators who conduct interviews over the phone should be guided by the process outlined below for conducting in-person interviews, including arranging to have the interview audio recorded.

"Packaging" the Witness's Statement

In the past, most interviews were recorded manually by the investigator, who took handwritten notes of the statement as it progressed. On the basis of these notes, the investigator prepared a summary, usually about one or two pages in length. The summary, known as a **will say**, is a summary of what a witness "will say" in his or her testimony at trial.

will say a formal witness statement prepared for disclosure to the opposing party

Today, most if not all statements taken during the course of any significant criminal investigation are recorded in their entirety (preferably on video in addition to audio; see the discussion in Chapter 3, Interviewing Suspects I: Legal Issues and Preparation, under the heading "Planning to Create a Complete Electronic Record," beginning on page 71) and that record is commonly referred to simply as a "statement." A copy (on DVD, for example) of all witness statements, and sometimes also a summary or transcript of the statement, is included in the "Crown brief," or the package of materials that is sent to the Crown attorney to assist in reviewing the case and prosecuting it in court. The law also requires that a copy of all witness statements be disclosed to the defence, whether or not the Crown intends to call a particular witness to testify at trial.

Although there is no one single format, or template, for "packaging" a statement, all statements should include certain basic information aside from the actual account of the witness. As part of establishing rapport with a witness and reducing their level of anxiety (the first step in the ECI process), an investigator can explain that, as a normal part of the interview process, certain legal steps will be taken (for example, in the form of the "KGB caution," discussed below) and certain preliminary information will be put on the record (the preamble, chronology, and so on) before the interview begins.

Investigators should start all statements with a "preamble," which is simply an introduction to the statement. The preamble provides such basic information as:

- the investigator's name and position, and the name of the investigator's partner if more than one investigator is present;
- the name of the witness being interviewed;
- the date, time, and location of the interview; and
- the fact that the interview is being recorded (if it is), and that the witness is aware of this fact and consents to being recorded.

The introductory phase of the interview process, prior to the witness giving their account, is the appropriate time to read the "KGB caution," discussed in the box feature on page 37. It is also the appropriate time to explain for the record how the witness came to be sitting in the interview room with the investigator; this can be accomplished by simply running through the chronology of events that lead up to the interview. For example:

> Mr. Smith, you are here today because on Tuesday, after the robbery occurred at the National Bank, you told the first officer who arrived at the scene, Officer Jones, that you had seen what had happened, and you gave Officer Jones your name and phone number. I then took over the investigation of the robbery, and on Wednesday I called you to make arrangements to have you come in today for an interview. And other than that, we have had no other contact or communication regarding this case. Is that correct?

The witness will normally confirm the account, if it is indeed accurate, and then the investigator can proceed to the point where the witness begins to describe what it is he or she observed or experienced. When the witness has finished giving the account and the investigator has completed all the steps in the interview process, the investigator should remember to state the time the interview concludes, prior to turning off the recording equipment.

If an investigator or a uniformed police officer has to take a full statement (as opposed to a "bare-bones" on-scene statement, referred to above) from a witness in person in the field—for example, because the witness refuses to attend a police facility—and the officer does not have access to recording equipment, an approach similar to the one described above should be used—namely, record the person's full name, date of birth, and contact information on paper; make a note of why it was necessary to take the statement in the field instead of at a location where recording equipment was available; record the starting time of the interview and the location; record the witness's statement in writing as close to verbatim as possible; and record any of the followup questions you ask and any answers the witness gives. When the interview is complete, have the witness read through your notes and make any necessary corrections (by putting a line through the entry and writing above it). When the witness is finished reviewing the statement, ask the witness to initial each page and then place the witness's signature and the date at the end of the statement. The investigator should also place his or her signature and the date at the end of the statement following the witness's entry.

The Enhanced Cognitive Interview: Step by Step

The following sections provide an in-depth examination of the seven steps of the ECI. The steps and the techniques associated with each step are summarized in Figure 2.1.

Step One: Greet, Personalize, and Establish Rapport

Prior to commencing the formal interview, the investigator identifies himself or herself; this is done again once the formal interview begins. Just as the police officer will use the interview to evaluate the witness's sincerity, reliability, and credibility, the witness will undoubtedly be evaluating the police officer's credibility and professionalism. It is therefore important for police officers to present themselves in the best possible manner. Witnesses speak more freely when a relationship of trust exists between them and the police and when they believe that the police will value what they have to say and will give them fair opportunity to tell their story. Such trust or rapport is essential to conducting an effective interview.

Rapport can be established relatively easily, but can also be lost quite quickly if the officer begins to send the witness conflicting signals. An investigator can begin establishing rapport by simply interacting with the witness on a personal level. Because an investigator is acting in an official capacity, it is easy to become overly formal, which can intimidate some witnesses. And, of course, the use of "legal" or "police" language during the course of an interview does not help to put a witness at ease. Although a degree of professional formality is required and expected, to establish a working bond with a witness a balance must be struck between the investigator's "official" persona and his or her "human side."

On first meeting a witness, it is suggested that you discuss everyday events prior to beginning the interview (for example, "Did you have any difficulty finding the office today?" "It can be hard to find a good parking spot around here, can't it?" "There is a washroom right across the hall if you would like to visit it before we start."). Ask the witness to please turn off any electronic devices for the duration of the interview—ringing phones or audible text message alerts can be significant distractions. Try to make witnesses feel comfortable. Tell them that it is normal

FIGURE 2.1   Steps and Techniques in the Enhanced Cognitive Interview

Step	Techniques
Step 1: Greet, personalize, and establish rapport	• interact on a personal level • put witness at ease • establish working bond • explain procedures • be sincere and interested • assess special needs of witness and adapt
Step 2: Explain the aims of the interview	Focused retrieval: • tell witness to report everything • transfer control to witness • tell witness not to guess • explain need to concentrate hard
Step 3: Initiate a free narrative account	Context reinstatement: • pause • do not interrupt • use non-verbal behaviour
Step 4: Questioning	• tell witness to report everything, concentrate hard, not to guess, okay to say "I don't know" and "I don't understand" • use open-ended and closed questions • use witness compatible questions • activate and probe an image
Step 5: Varied and extensive retrieval	• change the order in which events are recalled • change perspective • focus on all senses
Step 6: Summary and review	• summarize relevant information • go slowly • incorporate witness corrections • request any other relevant information
Step 7: Closure	• exchange contact information • indicate interest in hearing from witness with new information • leave a positive impression

Source: Adapted from Milne & Bull (1999).

for some witnesses to feel anxiety about sitting down to talk with the police, but that you will fully explain how the interview process works before you start. Advise witnesses that there are certain procedures that are an important part of conducting all witness interviews and that, before they can begin to give you their account of what they witnessed, you must follow these procedures. Procedures include:

- starting the recording device to ensure that everything that is discussed is "on the record" and an accurate record of the interview is created;
- reading introductory information such as date, time, and location of the interview; and
- reading any legal cautions (such as a "KGB warning," discussed in the box feature below).

Once these procedures are complete, acknowledge that some people find it stressful to be a witness to a crime. Explain to the witnesses that, if they wish, once the interview is concluded you can put them in touch with someone who can help them through the process (for example, a Victim Witness Assistance Program, if your agency offers that service). Above all, be sincere, be interested, and value your witnesses.

The aim of the first step is to defuse any unnecessary anxiety the witness might be experiencing about being interviewed. Investigators need to remember that, although they might conduct hundreds or thousands of interviews over the course of their careers, for many witnesses, an interview—especially an interview with the police—is a rare event. The investigator should judge the point at which the witness seems comfortable enough to start the interview. There is no mandatory script or time limit for establishing rapport, and once rapport has been established, it must be maintained. Witnesses will notice if you seem to have lost interest in both them and the interview process and are just "going through the motions." The following advice comes from a veteran investigator: "It takes far less time to arrange and properly prepare for an effective interview—including the time necessary to establish and maintain rapport—than it does to have to conduct a second interview because you did a poor job on the first one." Also, in some instances—such as where a witness changes their mind about speaking to the police and/or they can no longer be located—you may only get one opportunity to interview a particular witness.

A hidden advantage of the rapport-establishment phase is that it gives the investigator an opportunity to gauge the witness's language abilities and his or her mental state, and to modify the interview process as necessary. If an interviewee has language, hearing, or other difficulties, the investigator may need to ensure that the interviewee has access to, for example, a psychological counsellor, an interpreter, medications, or medical appliances (such as a hearing aid) that may be required, and/or to a legal guardian (in the case of a child or developmentally challenged or elderly person).

The investigator should also attempt to gather additional insight into any issues that may have had an effect on the witness's ability to observe and recall events. Witnesses should be asked if they normally wear glasses or contacts and, if so, whether they were wearing them when they witnessed the event. In some cases, witnesses should also be asked whether they consumed any drugs or alcohol prior

Identifying Yourself and Reading the KGB Caution

The officer must identify himself or herself to the witness, not only as a matter of courtesy and professionalism, but also as a legal precaution. Occasionally, and for a variety of reasons, witnesses may lie to or deliberately mislead the police during an interview. Witnesses who do so are liable to be charged with a criminal offence such as public mischief or obstruction of justice, but in order for the court to find the witness guilty, it must be proven that the witness was aware, at the time of deliberately making the false statement, that he or she was talking to the police.

A related issue is the situation in which the witness claims at some later proceeding, such as at a criminal trial, that what they told the police in their original statement was false and that their story has now changed. Many investigators deal with this potential legal issue during the introductory phase of the interview by reading what is commonly referred to as a **KGB caution**—named for the Supreme Court case *R v. B. (K.G.)* (1993), commonly referred to as the "*KGB* case"—to the witness. This caution informs witnesses that their statement will be taken under oath or affirmation; that they are agreeing to tell the truth; and that they could face potential criminal consequences if they knowingly give false information to or attempt to mislead the police during the course of their investigation, which of course includes the interview.

The reading of the KGB caution and the taking of the witness's statement under oath can have an impact on the admissibility of the witness's statement at a trial if the witness later "recants" their statement or claims it to be false. In a situation where a witness changes their story at trial and their original statement was voluntary, sworn, and videotaped (the essential ingredients of a KGB statement), the Crown can apply to have the original statement admitted for the truth of its contents. For recent Supreme Court discussions regarding KGB statements and prior inconsistent statements, see: *R v. Couture*, 2007 SCC 28, [2007] 2 SCR 517; *R v. Devine*, 2008 SCC 36, [2008] 2 SCR 283.

KGB caution
prepared statement read to an interviewee by the police prior to an interview, informing the interviewee that the interview will be electronically recorded and that the interviewee will be swearing an oath to tell the truth and will face potential criminal consequences if they lie to or deliberately mislead police during the interview

to witnessing the event. Determining details such as these is important, because they can become relevant later in the criminal justice process if the witness is cross-examined on their evidence in court. Such questions should be asked in a non-judgmental, matter of fact fashion. Remember, you are trying to build rapport and you do not want to send your witness signals that you believe their account may not be accurate or reliable before the interview has even begun.

Step Two: Explain the Aims of the Interview

It may seem obvious, but, in order for a witness to perform well during an investigative interview, you must explain the purpose of the interview and what you expect from the witness. Keep in mind our earlier discussion about hypnotic interviews, no longer widely used by police, and our point that the apparent advantages of hypnosis likely arose from using many of the following strategies common to the hypnotic procedure and not so much as the result of any "altered state of consciousness."

- *Focused retrieval.*   Encourage witnesses to make focused retrieval efforts by telling them that in order to use their memory effectively they must focus and concentrate. During the interview, you must give them as much time as is reasonably necessary to allow them to make those efforts.

- *Report everything.*   Tell witnesses to report everything they can remember about the event, and not to leave things out because they don't think they are important. Mention that in the early stages it's impossible to tell what information may end up being significant later in the investigation.

- *Don't guess.*   Tell witness not to guess or "fill in the gaps" while recalling events, but to say only what they actually remember ("If there are some things you don't recall, don't worry about it, no one has a perfect memory. Just do your best, tell me what you remember, and please do not guess. If you are not sure of something, just say so").

- *Transfer control.*   Make it clear to witnesses that you are transferring control of the interview to them, that you expect them to do most of the talking, and that they can do so at their own pace ("Of course, I wasn't in the bank when the robbery occurred, so I'm relying on you to tell me as much as possible about what happened. Take as much time as you need"). Make it clear to them that you are likely to ask some followup questions later in the interview, but that you will not do so until they have given their account of the event ("I might need you to clarify some of your remarks, and I might have some questions for you, but I'll try and hold my questions until after you have told your story").

Step Three: Initiate a Free Narrative Account

When conducting witness interviews, it is important for the investigator to allow the witness to provide an uninterrupted recollection of events (also called a "free narrative" or "free recall" account). For this **free recall** to be of maximum value, instruct the witness to begin the account at a point preceding the event in question. For example, if the interview concerns a bank robbery that occurred a week ago, the interviewer might say the following:

free recall   a witness's uninterrupted narrative of an incident

> Before you start to tell me everything you remember about the robbery, I'd like you to cast your mind back to what you were doing earlier that day. For example, were you on your way to work or school, or was it a day off? What other activities did you engage in before arriving at the bank? What was on your mind while you were waiting in line? The point of all this is to get you back into the state of mind you were in at the time of the robbery. It turns out that our memory for such things can be much better if we remember as much as possible about everything that was happening in our mind at the time.

context reinstatement   the establishment of background facts or conditions precedent that help put a statement into its proper context

The above is an example of **context reinstatement**—a simple extension of the encoding specificity principle discussed earlier in the chapter. Once the witness has taken the time to cast his or her mind back to the event and the context in which it occurred, ask the witness to begin the free recall account: "Now, in your own words, take as much time as you need to tell me everything you can remember about the robbery, starting with what brought you to the bank that day and what else you had been doing earlier." If all goes as planned, the witness will begin to recount the event by saying something like, "Well, I remember it was Wednesday because I get Sundays and Wednesdays off work in the summer. I had stayed out late the night before so I slept in a little later than usual [pauses] ... maybe 10, 10:15." Once the witness has begun the free recall account of the events, *be quiet.* According to Fisher & Geiselman (1992), *the single most important skill an interviewer can learn is not to interrupt witnesses* during their free recall account. Instead, pay attention; listen carefully; and take some brief, point form notes to assist you in the questioning stage that will follow.

In the example above, it would have been tempting to jump in during the pause to ask, "About what time would that have been?" *Do not fill a pause.* Leave it alone. It is crucial not to interrupt when a witness pauses during the free recall. You want the information to flow from memory the way it is stored, and you want to encourage reinstatement of the event context. During such pauses, you should convey the impression that you are willing to wait for the witness to continue—within reason, of course, for no one can be expected to wait several minutes while the witness says nothing. You can convey such willingness to wait by nodding, saying "Mmmm," raising your eyebrows slightly, and so forth—what have been termed "non-specific encouraging expressions." You need to be non-specific so that you don't provide any clues about which information you consider correct or useful. Saying, "Yes, yes, that's what we heard from the other witnesses," can "contaminate" the current witness and is a practice to be avoided when conducting an interview. The strategic use of silence, which requires conscious effort on the investigator's part, will ensure that the witness is given the best opportunity to provide the most complete and accurate recollection of the event.

In addition to encouraging total recall from the witness, you need to take notes to provide a basis for followup questions. This involves looking for "markers" in the witness's free recall to which you'll want to return later. Which aspects of the recall appear to provide the richest sources of untapped information? An extreme lack of or abundance of detail is a good indicator of an area to probe in the next phase of the interview. Consider the following example:

> So I was standing in line in the bank ... oh, it must have been about 5:45 or 5:50 because they were locking the doors so no more customers would come in before closing at 6. I remember the guy in front of me was dressed very poorly, and he was very nervous. He kept looking back at me and at the guards at the door ... then all of a sudden he pulled a gun, grabbed some money, and ran out.

This passage includes examples of both extremes of detail. On the one hand, the investigator should note that the witness had a very good opportunity to view the offender, so there is likely much more information regarding his appearance stored in the witness's memory. On the other hand, the minimal detail devoted to the climax of the event suggests that that area needs to be explored further. The investigator also needs to record any apparent inconsistencies so that they might be reconciled in the next phase.

With respect to the taking of notes during an interview, it is important to realize that if you devote too much attention to taking notes, you take away from the attention that you should devote to your witness in order to sustain rapport; a witness is not encouraged to tell the story of what they experienced if they are forced to stare at the top of your head while you scribble away trying to write down their every word. Taking notes can also limit your ability to observe your witness while they speak. And further, taking extensive notes during particular parts of an interview risks "educating" your witness about what you feel are the most, or the least, important aspects of their account. Remember, the interview is being recorded (or certainly should be), so the purpose of taking notes is not to create a record of the interview, but to serve as a guide for the investigator during the followup, questioning phase of the interview.

One good note-taking strategy is to take a pad of lined paper and draw a line down the center of the page, dividing it into two equal halves. As the interview progresses and the witness expresses certain points or touches on certain areas of interest, note these "markers" on the left side of the page; a phrase or a single sentence is often all that is necessary. The right side of the page will be used later during the questioning phase to record the witness's comments in response to your questions. Once you have made a quick note on the left side of the page, turn your attention back to your witness. This approach allows you to balance the requirement to pay attention to your witness with the suggested practice of taking notes to assist you in asking relevant questions during the latter stages of the interview.

Always remember that the rough, point-form notes you take during an interview, and any other notes that you take during the course of an investigation, must be disclosed to the defence if criminal charges are laid as a result of the investigation.

Step Four: Questioning

In this phase, the investigator follows up on the information that was produced by the witness during the free recall phase with questions designed to elicit additional information and detail. This is where you further explore the markers recorded during the free recall phase.

Before beginning the questioning phase there are number of important things the interviewer should tell the witness. Remind witnesses once again that they should *report everything* and not edit details out of their answers because they don't think they are significant. Explain to them that recalling additional detail from memory is a task that will require them to *concentrate*. Tell witnesses that, in response to any of your questions, it is okay to say, "I don't understand," and that you will take the time to repeat and clarify the question, and remind them once again that when they answer your questions they are *not to guess*; if they can't remember something it is okay for them to say, "I don't know."

Before beginning the questioning phase, you should consider how you will phrase the questions you intend to ask, because the types of questions you ask will have a significant effect on the kind of information you receive. Interviewers should begin the questioning process with **open-ended questions**—that is, questions that invite an open, unrestricted response from the witness (for example, "What else

open-ended question
question that invites a detailed answer from the subject, often phrased as a statement rather than a question—for example, "Tell me more about ..."; open-ended questions can also be phrased as conventional questions, such as, "You said x, what did you mean by that?"

can you tell me about the weather on that day?"). **Closed questions**, on the other hand, restrict an answer to a one word or short response (for example, "Was it sunny or rainy that day?"). Closed questions will be used later in the questioning process to determine fine detail, but they are not appropriate at the beginning of the questioning phase.

When phrasing questions, interviewers should avoid

- compound questions (a large question composed of a number of smaller questions);

- grammatically complex questions (the simpler the language, the better); and

- police jargon or technical language (instead of asking witnesses to tell you what happened "pursuant to the execution of the indictable offence," simply ask them to tell you what happened "after the man ran out of the bank").

With those points in mind, a good strategy for posing questions to a witness is to use the witness's own words to draw their memory back to a specific point. For example:

> You said before that the offender appeared very nervous and that he kept looking back at you and the guards at the door. I'd like you to concentrate on that point in time for a moment [*focused retrieval*] so that we can get some more detail about what he looked like. Put yourself back into that lineup in the bank and try to imagine the offender standing in front of you in that line. Close your eyes if you think that will help. Now, is there anything else about his appearance that you can remember?

If you doubt the value of having people close their eyes and pause to remember details, just consider your behaviour when you try to recall something. Most people engage in some or all of these behaviours: closing their eyes, looking at the ceiling, pursing their lips, covering their mouth with the front tips of their fingers, or talking quietly to themselves. Letting the witness know that it's normal to behave like this will work to your advantage.

When posing questions to the witness, try to use what are referred to as **witness compatible questions**. This simply means questions that are compatible with the witness's personal strengths and their mental images of the event as they describe them to you. For example, where a witness is an automobile enthusiast, the interviewer might reasonably expect to be able to elicit more detailed information about any automobiles that may have been involved in the event that the witness experienced than might be the case with a person who has no such special interest. In terms of questions that are compatible with a witness's mental images of the event, in the scene described earlier where the witness was standing behind the man in the bank lineup, in order to elicit the maximum amount of information from the witness the interviewer should initially ask the witness questions based on the witness's perspective when they experienced the event, using the words that the witness used in the free recall phase. For example, "You told me that you were 'waiting behind the guy in the bank line up, he was sloppily dressed, looked nervous, and turned to look at you'; what else can you tell me about him?" This ques-

closed question
question that invites a one word or short answer from the subject; for example, "What colour was the car?" or "Did you get a good look at his face?"

witness compatible question a question designed to take advantage of a witness's personal strengths or knowledge, and their mental images of an event as described to an interviewer; a component of the ECI designed to help maximize the amount of information an interviewer is able to elicit from a witness

tioning approach is distinct from what often occurs in police interviews, where the witness is simply asked a series of standardized questions about the suspect (gender, complexion, age, height, weight) with no effort being made to activate or probe the mental images that the witness has of the event.

During the questioning phase, the investigator's questions will move from general followup questions (such as, "What else can you tell me about the car?") to increasingly specific questions as the investigator seeks to clarify ambiguous information given earlier or elicit specific details. At this point, it is acceptable to use closed questions that invite a one-word or short answer; closed questions should only be used by an investigator to clarify a witness's observations. Improperly used, they can place a witness in the position of adopting a statement made by the investigator, and the testimony becomes that of the investigator, not the witness.

Here is an example of an acceptable closed question:

QUESTION: You stated that the incident took place on Wednesday. Would that have been last Wednesday, the 17th of August 2010?

ANSWER: Yes/No

Here is an example of an unacceptable closed question:

QUESTION: Was the man you saw entering the bank wearing a black leather jacket?

ANSWER: Yes/No

This type of closed question is unacceptable because it is "leading"—that is, the question itself suggests the answer to the witness. Moreover, if the witness did not mention earlier in their statement that the man who entered the bank was wearing a jacket, the question can also "contaminate" a witness's account. An acceptable version of this question, assuming that the witness *did* mention earlier that the man who entered the bank was wearing a jacket, might be, "You said earlier that the man who entered the bank was wearing a jacket. Was it light or dark in colour?"

Step Five: Varied and Extensive Retrieval

If witnesses appear to be having difficulty recalling information about some particular aspect of the event they are describing, the fifth step of the ECI offers a number of strategies that can be used to assist them.

One way of assisting witnesses to use their memory effectively is to ask them to make a **varied retrieval** attempt—that is, to try and recall the details of the event in a different order or from a different perspective. Recalling details in a *different order* can be an advantage for a witness who has told the story many times and remembers it only in a familiar order. Recalling the event out of sequence can shake out details that might otherwise be hidden. For example, the investigator can say, "Let's try something a little different. I'd like you to tell me the story again, but this time I'd like you to start from the end of the crime and work your way back to the beginning." Another approach might be, "Let's start at the point where he drew the

varied retrieval   one way an interviewer can assist a witness to use their memory effectively—for example, the subject may be asked to try and recall the details of the event in a different order or from a different perspective; this can help to stimulate a subject's memory and trigger recollections of an event that they might not otherwise have been able to recall

gun and work back from there to the beginning and then forward from there to the end."

Another way that additional information can be elicited from witnesses is by encouraging them to "activate" all their senses when describing an event. When asked to describe something they experienced, the majority of people will focus on what they saw and to a lesser extent what they heard, but they will not normally include as much detail about what they experienced through their sense of smell, touch, or taste. An interviewer may be able to elicit additional information from an assault victim, for example, by asking him to think about the sensation that he experienced when the suspect grabbed him around the neck. The victim may then recall that the suspect had very rough skin on his hands, long ragged fingernails, and smelled strongly of alcohol. The interviewer is more likely to elicit this type of additional information from a witness if he or she "activates," or draws the witness's attention to, all of their senses when asking for a description of an experience.

Having the witness recall the event from a *different perspective* can be especially helpful if the witness appears fixated on a particular aspect of the event ("All I remember is looking at that big silver gun"). Asking the witness to adopt, for example, the perspective of one of the bank tellers looking at the suspect from behind the counter might help to elicit additional details as the witness concentrates on the scene and probes his or her memory. As we mentioned earlier, however, the investigator must be careful to ensure that the witness does not misinterpret such instructions and that he or she clearly understands that they are not to guess about what they think the teller "might have seen"; they are simply to think about the event from another perspective in order to jog their memory and report only those things that they actually witnessed.

These strategies can have the added benefit of assisting an investigator to determine the strength and reliability of a witness's statement. For example, it is very difficult for witnesses who are manufacturing some or all of their stories to ostensibly recall a fabricated version of an event from a different perspective or in an order other than the one they followed the first time they recounted the event.

Step Six: Summary and Review

In the summary phase of the interview, the investigator, using his or her notes as a guide, summarizes and reviews all the relevant information that the witness provided. The purpose of this stage is to satisfy the interviewer that his or her understanding of the witness's statement is complete and correct. It also gives witnesses a final opportunity to review their memory to ensure that they have told the investigator everything they can recall.

It is important for the investigator to go through this stage slowly in order to give the witness time to listen, think, and respond. Witnesses should be told that, if they remember something new or if the investigator's summary is not accurate, they should interrupt the investigator and tell them so. If the witness offers additional pieces of information, he or she should be allowed to freely recall them, after which the witness should be probed in the same manner as that described in the earlier stages of the ECI process.

When the summary and review process is complete, and before the investigator moves on to the final stage of the interview, the investigator should ask the witness whether he or she can think of *any* other information that may be relevant and that may assist the investigator. If the witness replies with a comment like, "No, that's about it" or some similar phrase, the investigator must use his or her judgment to determine whether there is actually anything more that the witness can reasonably add or whether the witness is simply using a common expression to conclude a conversation. What is most important is to give witnesses the opportunity to tell the investigator everything that they can about the event and to allow them to clarify anything that they might have said. Giving them this opportunity ensures that the information they have given the investigator is as complete and accurate as possible; it also gives witnesses the opportunity to "adopt" their statements. In doing so, witnesses confirm that their statements are what they said; that they are satisfied with the contents of the statement; and that they believe the statement represents an accurate account of the event as they recall it. Giving witnesses this opportunity prevents them from claiming at some later point that what they said was not what they *meant* to say or that the investigator misinterpreted what they said during the interview. Such an approach makes the interview fair in both practice and appearance.

Step Seven: Closure

After their review of hundreds of police interviews, Fisher, Geiselman, & Raymond (1987) found that investigators simply stopped their interviews after they ran out of questions, with little thought given to the effect that this might have on the witness. The closure stage of the interview is an opportunity to leave a positive final impression with the witness; it is also the investigator's last opportunity to gather information that may not be directly relevant to the interview contents—for example, is the witness going on any holidays; are there any trips coming up; how is the witness coping; do they know how to get in touch with you if they recall anything new?

Investigators will want to ensure that they have all of the witness's personal and business contact information. They will also want to leave witnesses with their business card. They may want to ask witnesses whether they have any holidays or business trips coming up or whether they will be available in the coming weeks or months should any investigative followup be required. Investigators should tell witnesses that, if they recall anything further in the coming days, they should feel free to contact them; this is far more likely to happen if the investigator states it explicitly and indicates a genuine interest in hearing from the witness should they recall anything new. The investigator should always thank the witness for their participation and ensure that they are coping well. Some witnesses can be profoundly affected as a result of witnessing a criminal act, and the investigator should ensure that such witnesses are given appropriate referrals to victim witness assistance programs or similar social agencies. Remember, the interview may be over, but the criminal justice process is just beginning. A witness who believes that he or she was given the best opportunity to recall the event and was treated with interest and respect is more likely to agree to further participation in the case if required

Differences in Witness Statements

Investigators must be aware that if they conduct more than one interview with a witness, subsequent statements can (and probably will) differ in some respects from the original statement—and this will be an issue that the defence counsel is certain to focus on in court in an attempt to make the witness appear less reliable. For example, the defence may note: "Mr. Smith, in your initial statement to Detective Jones you said the offender was a white male, about 20 years old, with a scruffy beard. But in your second interview, you described him as a white male, 20 years old, with sandy-coloured hair, and you didn't mention a beard at all. Which one of these descriptions is correct?"

Investigators who decide to conduct a second or subsequent interview with a witness must become thoroughly familiar with the witness's original statement so they are able to recognize any differences or inconsistencies that might arise and be prepared to deal with them. In the example above, the investigator could address the differing suspect descriptions by simply reading the first description of the suspect to the witness after she had finished giving her second description, and asking her to reconcile the differences. The witness may confirm that "yes" the suspect did in fact have a beard, but she simply forgot to mention it in her second description. If the matter subsequently progresses to trial, the court would have to determine what, if any, effect such a difference would have on the evidentiary value of the witness's description.

and will more likely be an effective witness if the matter under investigation proceeds to trial.

Followup Interviews

One strategy for eliciting new information from a witness is to conduct a followup interview at a later date. From a psychological perspective, good theory and good data support the notion that people are likely to remember at least a few new details about an event by repeatedly engaging in the recall process (Turtle & Yuille, 1994). Take, for example, a witness who remains severely shaken by a crime for several hours after it occurred, so that he or she is unable to provide all the information that is potentially available in memory. It makes sense in this case to elicit the basic facts of the event and then arrange a time for a more in-depth interview. But even in less dramatic circumstances, conducting another interview can be beneficial. A different setting, a different interviewer, or different instructions or strategies might lead to the recollection of new details. If specifics regarding, for example, the offender's appearance, a vehicle, or a weapon are important to the case, it is possible that the relevant details can be elicited the second or third time around.

It is not unusual for people to forget details they previously remembered and to remember details they previously forgot to mention. Details recalled by a cooperative witness on repeated occasions should be treated as a cumulative whole, as long as there are no serious inconsistencies. When a witness explicitly contradicts information from the initial interview while recalling the event a second time, a bigger problem exists. We discuss this outcome in Chapter 5, Detecting Deception, regarding the use of statement analysis to detect deception. The possibility of natural, honest imperfections in memory retrieval from one recall attempt to another, however, should not prevent an investigator from conducting a second interview, if a second interview is deemed potentially worthwhile.

KEY TERMS

closed question

cognitive economy

cognitive interview (CI)

context reinstatement

disclosure

encoding specificity

enhanced cognitive interview (ECI)

free recall

hypnosis

KGB caution

misleading post-event information

open-ended question

repressed memories

statement

varied retrieval

will say

witness compatible questions

FURTHER READING

Bull, R., Valentine, T., & Williamson, T. (Eds.). (2009). *Handbook of psychology of investigative interviewing: Current developments and future directions.* West Sussex, UK: Wiley.

Canada, Department of Justice Canada, *Disclosure reform—Consultation paper* (2004). http://www.justice.gc.ca/eng/cons/ref/ref.pdf.

Fisher, R., & Geiselman, R.E. (1992). *Memory-enhancing techniques for investigative interviewing: The cognitive interview.* Springfield, IL: Charles C. Thomas.

Kocsis, R.N. (2009). *Applied criminal psychology: A guide to forensic behavioral sciences.* Springfield, IL: Charles C. Thomas.

Loftus, E., Doyle, J., & Dysart, J. (2008). *Eyewitness testimony: Civil and criminal* (5th ed.) Charlottesville, VA: Lexis Law Publishing.

Milne, B. Professor Becky Milne explains the cognitive interview. http://www.open2.net/eyewitness/becky_milne.html.

Snook, B., & Keating, K. (2011). A field study of adult witness interviewing practices in a Canadian police organization. In *Legal and criminological psychology, 16*(1), 160-172. Pre-print version online. http://www.mun.ca/psychology/brl/publications/Snook_Keating_2010_LCP.pdf.

REVIEW QUESTIONS

TRUE OR FALSE

F   1. Asking leading questions is an excellent technique for witness interviews.

T   (2.) The cognitive interview technique has been criticized because it tends to inspire false confessions.

T   3. The Crown is obligated to give the defence copies of all statements obtained through its witness interviews.

F   4. Inability to remember the details of an event is often due to the decay of memory cells caused by drug abuse.

F   5. Various commissions of inquiry into wrongful conviction cases have concluded that the interviewing of witnesses is a skill that requires no special training.

T   6. Today, most if not all statements taken during the course of any significant criminal investigation are recorded in their entirety, preferably in both video and audio.

T   7. Witnesses speak more freely when a relationship of trust, or rapport, exists between them and the police and when they believe that the police will value what they have to say and will give them a fair opportunity to tell their story.

T   8. Preparation on the part of investigators can enhance the quality of a witness interview.

F   9. Police should use police jargon and technical terms when taking a statement from a witness because it leaves a lasting impression of professional conduct with the witness.

F   10. Police should not encourage a witness to recall events out of sequence or from a different perspective because it tends to limit the witness's ability to recall events accurately.

T   11. The Crown may use a witness's statement to assess the credibility of the witness and to determine whether the statement proves or assists in proving a fact in issue.

F   12. If a witness statement is recorded (video and audio), it is not necessary for the police officer to make any notes of the interview.

MULTIPLE CHOICE

1. According to psychologist Endel Tulving, a subject's ability to recall the details of an event is enhanced when
   a. the subject is interviewed in a hypnotic state.
   b. the subject is treated with courtesy and respect.
   c. the physical and psychological conditions present during the interview match those present during the recalled events.
   d. a and b.

2. Treating all witnesses, including potential suspects, with equal respect is important because
   a. who is and who is not a suspect may not be clear at the beginning of an investigation.
   b. intimidation by investigators may lead to a suggestion that the witness's testimony was not voluntary.
   c. establishing a respectful rapport with the witness has been shown to inspire fuller communication.
   d. all of the above.

3. The theory of misleading post-event information suggests that
   a. learning the details of someone else's memories of an event can influence one's own memories of the same event.
   b. "repressed" memories are as reliable as regular memories.
   c. the older a memory is, the less vulnerable it is to distortion.
   d. all of the above.

4. Allowing the witness to relate his or her memories in a free recall manner is important because
   a. it reduces the likelihood that the investigator's views on the incident will influence the witness's account.
   b. it encourages the witness to reinstate the event context in his or her own mind.
   c. it allows the witness to volunteer details that might not come up in response to specific questions.
   d. all of the above.

SHORT ANSWER

1. On occasion, it may be helpful to have a witness recall an event from a different perspective, especially if the witness appears to be fixated on a particular aspect of an event—for example, "All I remember is looking at that big silver gun." Why must investigators exercise caution when using this technique? *could lead witness to make inferences about what they might have seen*

2. It is important for an interviewer not to "jump in" during pauses in a witness's free recall of events, but to encourage the witness to resume their account. Explain why this is important, and describe some techniques that an investigator could use in such a situation.

3. Explain how asking a witness a "closed" question can contaminate the testimony of that witness at trial. *putting ideas into their minds, suggesting what actually happened*

4. Explain the meaning and significance of "witness compatible" questions.

CASE STUDY

After reviewing John Smith's witness statement below, produce a properly formatted statement for Cheryl, the convenience store clerk. The statement should include facts similar to those provided by John and should reflect Cheryl's recollection of the entire incident. Use your imagination in creating the details.

DATE: 23 March 2011
LOCATION: Residence of John Smith, 223 Henry Street, Hamilton, ON
INTERVIEWER(S):   Ian Interviewer
START TIME: 3:20 p.m.
FINISH TIME: 4:25 p.m.

INTRODUCTION: I am a 28-year-old male residing at 223 Henry Street, Hamilton, Ontario. I am married with two preschool children. I am a steel worker who has worked at Dofasco for the past seven years, and continue to do so.

TESTIMONY: On Thursday, the 22nd of March, 2011, I worked the afternoon shift at the ore docks at Dofasco, which are on Coventry Street in the City of Hamilton. I was relieved by a co-worker at the conclusion of my shift, which ended at 3:00 p.m., and after changing my clothing, I left via the #2 gate on Coventry Street.

I took my usual driving route home, down Coventry onto Main Street and proceeding south toward Henry Street. As is my habit, I stopped at the Mac's Milk convenience store located at the southwest corner of Main Street and Portage Avenue for a loaf of bread and a package of cigarettes. I have lived in my house on Henry Street, approximately two blocks from the store, for nearly six years. I have been in the store hundreds of times and am familiar with the owner and all of the employees.

I arrived at the store at approximately 3:30 p.m. I know the time because, depending on traffic, it takes me about 30 to 35 minutes to get to my residence from Dofasco. Traffic was light that day and I punched my time card out at exactly 3:00 p.m.

On entering the store I knew something was wrong. Cheryl is the clerk during the afternoon shift and she usually greets me with a smile and a cheerful hello when I enter the store. This day she stood staring at the customer directly in front of her and barely gave me a glance as I entered. This made me uneasy, and I wondered what was wrong.

I was about to ask her what was wrong when I noticed tears on her cheeks as she made muffled conversation with the man directly in front of her at the cash register. There was no one else that I could see in the store at the time.

As I approached the front counter where the man was standing he suddenly turned to face me. He had a knife in his right hand and a white plastic bag in his left. I was directly in front of him when he turned and was face to face with him about three feet apart. He looked directly into my eyes, raised the knife to eye level with the point up, and said, "If you don't want to get hurt, get the f*** out of my way." I immediately stepped to my right and he quickly walked by me to the front of the store. Just before exiting onto the street he turned back toward the counter and said, "If you know what's good for you, don't call the cops." He then turned away from the counter and left the store.

The man I saw in the store was a stranger to me and to the best of my knowledge I have never seen him in the neighbourhood. He was approximately 5' 10" tall. I am sure of his height because when he was standing directly in front of me, he was a couple of inches shorter than I am and I am 6' tall. He was thin, perhaps about 140 to 150 pounds. He had a pale complexion, deep-set brown eyes, and dark-brown shoulder-length hair. He did not have a beard but was not clean-shaven. He had about a three or four days' growth of beard and was ragged looking. He was wearing a black leather jacket that looked old and faded. There was a long tear on the left sleeve from the elbow to the cuff. He had on a dirty white or faded gray T-shirt and faded blue jeans, which were torn at the left leg inseam. The right knee was also torn. He was wearing a pair of new or nearly new Nike running shoes. The shoes were white with blue trim and a logo. I did not observe any jewellery on his hands, but he did have a gold chain around his neck that was covered in front by the T-shirt.

When he left the store he turned right and began running south on Main Street. I ran to the window but he had disappeared behind parked cars and traffic. I did not notice it in the store, but he appeared to be limping or at least favouring his right leg when he began to run.

I then turned my attention to Cheryl, who was in a state of shock and still standing behind the cash register. I asked her if she was hurt and she replied no in a sobbing manner. She then stated, "He robbed me." I called 911 and waited for the police to arrive.

I gave my name, address, and telephone number to the police officer who interviewed me briefly at the store and advised him that I am certain I would recognize the man who robbed the store if I ever saw him again.

Witness   _____

Signature   _____

Date   _____

Interviewing Suspects I: Legal Issues and Preparation

3

INTRODUCTION

Over the course of an average career, most police investigators are likely to conduct more interviews with witnesses than with suspects for at least two reasons: (1) in a typical investigation there tend to be more witnesses than suspects, and (2) suspects often refuse to participate in interviews once they are identified. In Chapter 2, Techniques for Interviewing Witnesses, we discussed in detail how to conduct witness interviews. In this chapter and in Chapter 4, Interviewing Suspects II: Approaches and Techniques, we focus on suspect interviews, first by discussing the legal issues involved in interaction with individuals who are detained or arrested, including the enhanced rights of young persons, and then by discussing two specific approaches to conducting interviews with suspects. In this chapter, we also discuss statements made by accused persons and the connection between the admissibility of a statement in court and the circumstances under which it was obtained. The chapter concludes with a general discussion of how to plan for and conduct an interview with a suspect in an effective way. Best practices for suspect interviews are summarized in Figure 3.1 on p. 79.

In this chapter, except where otherwise specified, the term "interview" will refer to the questioning of suspects. (For a discussion of the distinction between an interview and an interrogation, see Chapter 4.)

CHAPTER OBJECTIVES

After completing this chapter, you should be able to:

- Explain the difference between the terms "detention" and "arrest."

- Understand what a person's legal rights are upon arrest or detention under the *Canadian Charter of Rights and Freedoms*, the *Criminal Code*, and case law and the steps that officers must take to ensure that these rights are respected.

- Understand the reasons for a primary and secondary caution and the information that each of these cautions should convey to the suspect/accused.

- Identify the circumstances under which a suspect/accused should be re-cautioned.

- Understand the restrictions that the *Youth Criminal Justice Act* (YCJA) places on police when interviewing young persons and the procedures that investigators who interview young persons must follow.

- Explain the connection between the voluntariness of a statement and its admissibility.

- Identify factors the courts will consider in determining whether a statement made by an accused is admissible or not.

- Explain the different kinds of false confessions and the reasons why individuals give them.

- Explain the steps that investigators should take in planning to interview a suspect/accused and the importance of research and planning.

- Appreciate the importance of creating a complete electronic record of interviews.

LEGAL RIGHTS OF PERSONS WHO ARE DETAINED OR ARRESTED

When an individual is detained or arrested, a set of legal requirements are triggered with which all investigators must comply. These requirements are set out in the Charter, the *Youth Criminal Justice Act* (YCJA), the *Criminal Code*, and Canadian case law, all of which are discussed here. As an investigator, you must understand and respect these requirements. Failure to do so will likely result in any information gained in the course of your encounter with the individual being ruled inadmissible in court, which in turn will hamper the ability of lawyers to prove or disprove certain aspects of the case against the accused.

detention   the suspension of a person's liberty by a significant physical or psychological restraint

Detention is defined as a suspension of an individual's liberty by a significant physical or psychological restraint (*R v. Grant*, 2009). Physical detention is relatively straightforward, and includes situations where a person is handcuffed, locked in a police cruiser, or held in a detention facility. Psychological restraint is deemed by the courts to occur when an individual has a legal obligation to comply with a restrictive demand by an agent of the state (for example, a police officer), or where a reasonable person would conclude that they had no choice but to comply. For example, when a police officer directs a motorist to pull his or her vehicle over to the side of the road, the motorist has a legal obligation to comply with the officer's direction and remain seated in the vehicle; although not physically restrained by the officer, the motorist is not free to simply drive away.

In determining whether a reasonable person would conclude they had no choice but to comply with a directive in a particular situation, the courts will consider:

1. the circumstances as perceived by the individual (this involves consideration of whether the police were making general inquiries or whether they were singling the individual out for focused investigation);

2. the nature of the police conduct (this involves the use of language, use of physical contact, presence of others, duration, and location); and

3. characteristics that are relevant to the individual's particular situation (this involves age, physical stature, minority status, and so on).

arrest   the actual seizure or touching of an individual by an officer with the intent of taking physical control of a person for the purpose of detention; or an announcement by an officer of his or her intent to arrest a person accompanied by an attempt to take physical control of that person

Although police have no general power to detain someone for investigative purposes, in certain circumstances, where it is reasonably necessary to determine what is taking place, they have limited power to briefly detain a person who is not a suspect in a crime and who is not under arrest. This common-law power is referred to as an investigative detention. To exercise this power lawfully, police must have reasonable grounds to suspect that a person is connected to a particular crime and be able to articulate how the circumstances caused them to form this belief.

hybrid offence   also known as "dual procedure" offence; a class of offences that can be prosecuted as either minor (summary) or major (indictable) offences, hybrid offences are considered to be indictable offences until the Crown "elects" how to proceed; examples include impaired driving and theft under $5,000

Arrest is defined as the actual seizure or touching of an individual with a view to detention. An arrest may also take place where an officer announces his or her intention to arrest and *attempts* to take physical control of a person, and/or where the person acquiesces to the officer (Watts, 2007). Pursuant to s. 495(1) of the *Criminal Code*, a police officer may arrest a person whom he or she finds committing a criminal offence or whom he or she believes on reasonable grounds has committed, or is about to commit, an indictable offence (or a **hybrid offence**, which for the

Determining Detention

Whether an individual is considered to be "detained" in a particular set of circumstances is often ultimately determined in court. The 2009 Supreme Court case of *R v. Grant* involved a young adult male who was walking down the sidewalk when he attracted the attention of a number of plainclothes police officers on patrol in the area. One of the police officers exited his vehicle, positioned himself in the young man's path on the sidewalk, and began talking to him, inquiring about his name and address and asking him what was going on. The young man became nervous and started to adjust his clothing, which prompted the police officer to tell him to keep his hands in front of him. The other two police officers then approached the young man, identified themselves, and took up physical positions behind him. Although none of the officers made physical contact with the man, the Court determined that the officers were putting him under their control and effectively removing his choice as to how to respond in the situation, thus constraining his liberty and effectively detaining him.

purposes of arrest is deemed to be indictable). A police officer may also arrest someone he or she reasonably believes is wanted on an outstanding warrant of arrest.

Section 10 of the Charter outlines the rights guaranteed to any individual who is detained or arrested:

10. Everyone has the right on arrest or detention

a. to be informed promptly of the reasons therefor;

b. to retain and instruct counsel without delay and to be informed of that right; and

c. to have the validity of the detention determined by way of *habeas corpus* and to be released if the detention is not lawful.

Section 29(2)(b) of the *Criminal Code* also requires an accused to be informed promptly of the reason for his or her arrest.

Section 24(1) of the Charter authorizes anyone whose rights or freedoms under the Charter have been infringed or denied to seek a remedy from an appropriate court. If the court finds that certain evidence was obtained in a manner that infringed or denied any Charter right or freedom—for example, if evidence was obtained from a person who was not instructed as to their right to retain and instruct counsel, or who was not given a reasonable opportunity to do so—that evidence shall be excluded if admitting it in the proceedings would bring the administration of justice into disrepute (s. 24(2)).

The rights guaranteed by ss. 10(a) and (b) of the Charter are discussed below, as is the right to silence, the importance of police cautions (required by ss. 7 and 11(c) of the Charter and by case law), and the special rights of young persons under the *Youth Criminal Justice Act*.

Note that while the burden of establishing voluntariness (beyond a reasonable doubt) has always been on the Crown, under the Charter the defence bears the burden of proving (on a balance of probabilities) any allegation that a Charter right has been violated. Because not all interactions between the police and members of the public will fit the definition of detention, police may still ask people questions designed to explore a situation in order to gain some general understanding of what may be happening, without necessarily triggering a person's Charter rights related to detention.

The Right to Be Informed of Reasons and Rights

Upon detaining someone, whether for a brief period (as in the case of investigative detention) or for a more lengthy period (such as that following arrest), police must inform the person of both the reason for their detention and the fact that their detention does not oblige them to answer questions posed by the police (*R v. Mann*, 2004). The failure to advise a suspect of his or her Charter rights will almost certainly render any statement that a suspect may subsequently provide inadmissible, and will leave the investigator and the investigation open to criticism by the court.

Two Supreme Court cases, *R v. Black* (1989) and *R v. Borden* (1994), established a link between ss. 10(a) and (b) of the Charter, holding that a violation of an accused's s. 10(a) right can affect the accused's decision whether or not to consult counsel. The court stated that people can only exercise their right to counsel in a meaningful way if they know the extent of the jeopardy in which they have been placed—that is, the risk or consequence they are facing.

The Right to Counsel

right to counsel the right of a person to consult with a lawyer upon arrest or detention, as guaranteed by s. 10(b) of the Charter

Upon arrest or detention, s. 10(b) of the Charter provides individuals with the **right to counsel**. This right is designed to allow individuals to consult with a legal expert in order to be able to make an informed choice about whether to participate in the state's investigation of them. Under s. 10(b) of the Charter, police officers have three duties:

1. Officers must inform all detainees of their right to retain counsel without delay and of the existence and availability of legal aid and duty counsel.

2. Where the detainee has indicated a wish to exercise this right, officers must provide the detainee with a reasonable opportunity to do so (see below).

3. Investigators must refrain from attempting to elicit incriminating evidence from the detainee until the detainee has had a reasonable opportunity to exercise their right to counsel, unless the matter is so urgent that they must proceed with the questioning (*R v. Manninen*, 1987; *R v. Bartle*, 1994).

To continue questioning a detainee otherwise is a serious breach of Charter rights, and any subsequent responses or voluntary statements will typically *not* be admitted into court, unless the court finds the accused was intent on speaking to police.

As can be seen from the list of police obligations above, the right to counsel consists of both an *information* component and an *opportunity* component. To satisfy the information component, investigators must tell any persons whom they detain or arrest:

1. why they are under arrest or detention;
2. that they have the right to consult with a lawyer without delay; and
3. how they can exercise their right to counsel.

As part of the information above, investigators must inform suspects that, if they wish, they can immediately speak with a free lawyer (known as duty counsel) and that, if they cannot afford to pay for a lawyer on their own, they can retain a lawyer at a later time who will be paid by the government through legal aid (*R v. Brydges*, 1990). An example follows:

> A legal aid duty lawyer is available to you without charge. They will provide you with free legal advice and can explain the legal aid plan to you. If you wish to contact a legal aid duty lawyer, I can provide you with a telephone number. The number is 1-800-XXX-XXXX. Do you understand? Do you want to call a lawyer now?

To satisfy the opportunity component of the right to counsel, investigators must ensure that the person has a reasonable opportunity to exercise their right should they choose to do so. This includes providing them with a telephone, a telephone number they can call to speak to duty counsel, and telling them that they can speak to counsel in private. What constitutes a "reasonable opportunity" depends on the circumstances, including the availability of duty counsel in the jurisdiction in question (*R v. Prosper*, 1994). Police are only required to allow a person to speak with a lawyer *once* prior to questioning. During questioning, if the person's jeopardy changes, they must be informed of this and given another opportunity to consult counsel.

The right to retain and instruct counsel is not necessarily violated the moment the police refuse an accused's request to contact counsel—police officers making arrests in potentially volatile situations may be justified in briefly delaying the exercise of an accused's rights until the situation is under control. In *R v. Strachan* (1988), an RCMP officer arrested the accused in his home. At the time, there were two other unknown people in the house, and the officer knew that there were weapons somewhere in the house. Although the accused requested to speak to a lawyer right away, the officer said that he delayed the exercise of the accused's right to counsel until he could get the situation under control. The Court said that because of the volatile situation, the officer was justified in delaying granting the accused his rights until the police had taken care of the unknown variables. Once the accused was arrested, the other individuals had left, and the guns had been found, *then* the accused should have been given his right to counsel.

The courts require diligence—that is, an earnest effort—on the part of the accused in the exercise of the right to counsel. If a detainee is not being reasonably diligent in the exercise of this right, the related duties imposed on the police in a situation where the detainee has requested the assistance of counsel are suspended and are not a barrier to the police continuing their investigation (*R v. Tremblay*, 1987).

Reasonable Opportunity and the Requirement to Be Diligent

The following cases illustrate what the courts have found, in particular circumstances, to either constitute or *not* constitute a "reasonable opportunity" for a suspect to retain and instruct counsel, as well as what they have found to either constitute or *not* constitute "reasonable diligence" on the part of a suspect who expresses a desire to exercise this right.

- In *R v. Ross* (1989), the appellants were arrested and charged with break and enter. They were advised of their right to counsel and, although they attempted to contact their counsel of choice, they were unsuccessful. It was approximately 2:00 a.m. One of the appellants stated that he did not wish to contact a lawyer other than the one he had originally attempted to contact, and was placed in a cell. Shortly thereafter, the appellants were told to participate in a lineup, in which evidence against them was obtained. The Court held that, while the police initially complied with s. 10(b) in advising the accused of their right to retain and instruct counsel, the accused did not receive a "real opportunity" to do so prior to the lineup. There was no compelling reason that justified the police in their decision to proceed with the lineup so quickly; they could have held it later in the day. In this case, the admission of the lineup evidence into the proceedings would have brought the administration of justice into disrepute, and the evidence was therefore excluded. The fact that the appellants did not refuse to participate in the lineup was *not* a waiver of the right to counsel—the very purpose of the right to counsel is to ensure that persons who are accused or detained be advised of their legal rights and how to exercise them; because they were ignorant of their legal position, the appellants were unable to make an informed decision about participating in the lineup. In the words of the Court, "The police cannot be excused for misconstruing and misinterpreting the scope of their duty to provide a reasonable opportunity to retain and instruct counsel."

- In *R v. Smith* (1989), the accused was arrested around 7:00 p.m. and instructed on his right to retain counsel. He said several times that he did wish to speak with counsel, but due to a number of stops made at the request of the accused, he did not arrive at the police station until 9:00 p.m. At that time the accused was given a phone book and a phone, but refused to call his lawyer because he claimed that it was too late at night. The police suggested that he attempt a call in case there was a machine with an alternative number, but he refused. The Court said that because the accused was not making a sincere attempt to exercise his right, the police were justified in continuing to question the accused, and the statements they obtained were admissible. Accused persons do not have unlimited rights under s. 10(b), and cannot use the s. 10(b) right to delay a police investigation.

- In *R v. Eakin* (2000), the appellant was informed of his right to counsel and he indicated his wish to speak to a particular lawyer. He was provided with a telephone book, which he appeared "to thumb through randomly" without locating the lawyer's number. A detective tried unsuccessfully to find the number in the telephone book and went to look for a lawyers' directory, but was unable to locate one. (It was later discovered that the lawyer's name and number were in the phone book, and that he was available at the time.) The police requested duty counsel and ceased questioning; the appellant spoke to duty counsel a short while later and made no objection to this, nor did he make further requests to speak to the lawyer he had wished to consult initially. The appellant subsequently provided hair, saliva, and blood samples. At trial, the appellant argued that he had not been provided with the proper information to allow him to contact his lawyer of choice. The court found that the appellant was both properly informed of his rights and given a reasonable opportunity to exercise those rights; in addition, he appeared to accept duty counsel as an alternative to the lawyer he originally requested. While the police could have made greater efforts to help the appellant locate his preferred lawyer, the appellant himself showed a lack of diligence in his efforts—he made "no earnest attempt" to locate his lawyer and he did not pursue his request.

- In *R v. Richfield* (2003), the appellant, an impaired driver, was arrested at 1:00 a.m. and advised of his right to counsel. The appellant stated that he wished to speak with a particular lawyer. At 1:42 a.m., the arresting officer placed a call to the lawyer the appellant had requested and left a message with a person who was staffing the answering service. At 2:44 a.m.—one hour and 45 minutes after the time of the arrest—the officer's call had not been returned, and he asked the appellant if he wished to speak to duty counsel. The appellant said no, maintaining that he wished to speak only to counsel of his choice; the appellant disregarded further information regarding the purpose of duty counsel and the officer's advice that the appellant make use of this service in the circumstances. Aware of the two-hour period within which a breath sample had to be taken for the prosecution for the evidence to meet the requirements in s. 258(1)(d) of the *Criminal Code*, the officer handed the appellant over to a breath technician, who obtained a sample with the appellant's consent. The appellant argued that the evidence should be excluded, as his right to counsel of his choice was breached. However, the court stated that the appellant was not reasonably diligent in exercising his right to counsel in the circumstances—when informed that his chosen lawyer had not called back, he did not ask to make a further call to his counsel of choice or to another counsel, or choose to consult with duty counsel.

In *R v. Burlingham* (1995), the Supreme Court described three instances in which an accused's s. 10 rights will be found to have been violated:

1. the police continue to question an accused despite the repeated protests that he or she will say nothing without consulting a lawyer;

2. the police belittle the accused's lawyer in an attempt to undermine the accused's confidence in counsel; or

3. the police pressure the accused to accept a deal without first affording the accused an opportunity to consult his or her lawyer.

Accused Who Waive the Right to Counsel

waiver   a decision, communicated clearly by words or actions, to decline the exercise of a particular right

confession   an admission to all of the elements of an offence, including the mental element

A person may waive (give up) their right to speak to a lawyer, but they must do so voluntarily. In addition, for such a waiver to be valid, the person must understand the consequences of giving up their right to counsel. If the **waiver** leads to the police obtaining an incriminating statement or full **confession**, proving that the waiver was unequivocal becomes key to the admissibility of the statement or confession. The standard of proof is very high. In *R v. Bartle* (1994), the Supreme Court established guidelines for accepting a waiver. An effective waiver under s. 10(b) requires that the accused be fully apprised of the information he or she has the right to receive. The mere fact that an accused indicates that he or she does not wish to receive the information does not, in itself, constitute a valid waiver. A waiver is valid only when it is clear that the accused fully understands his or her rights under s. 10(b) and fully understands the means by which those rights may be exercised. *R v. Smith* (1991) established that a trial judge must be satisfied that the accused understood the jeopardy he or she faced when making the decision to dispense with counsel.

An accused's understanding of the jeopardy he or she faces in this context has been the subject of much recent research, most of which focuses on people's ability to comprehend police cautions (Eastwood, Snook, & Chaulk, 2010; Eastwood & Snook, 2010; Moore & Gagnier, 2008; Rogers, Harrison, Hazelwood, & Sewell, 2007; Rogers, Hazelwood, Sewell, Harrison, & Shuman, 2008). It turns out that many people—including but not limited to youth, people with developmental disabilities, and people for whom English (or French, in Canada) is not their first language—do not fully comprehend some of the words and some of the concepts when their rights are delivered by police. Perhaps more important, it is possible that many people *comprehend* their rights, in terms of what the words mean, but don't fully appreciate *why* those rights exist (Basarke & Turtle, 2011). In fact, Saul Kassin's (2005) article on this point is titled, "Does innocence put innocents at risk?" in reference to the finding that most people assume that they don't need a lawyer if *they* know that they didn't do anything wrong. But, of course, innocent people are the *only* ones who are in jeopardy of being wrongfully convicted, so they are the ones who should perhaps be *most likely* to take advantage of their rights. The only jeopardy facing a guilty person in this context is the potential for self-incrimination.

Current research on this issue concerns innocent people's understanding of the risks they face (as small as they might be) if the circumstances in a case conspire to make them a likely suspect, such as being the ex-boyfriend of a recently murdered female, or being a person who matches the description of an offender and is apprehended in the vicinity of a recently committed crime. It is in these situations that the investigation might mistakenly conclude that an innocent person is guilty if, for example, they don't have a good alibi, some physical evidence coincidentally points to them as the culprit, and/or they exhibit signs of nervousness that are interpreted as indicators of deception (see the discussion in Chapter 4, Interviewing Suspects II: Approaches and Techniques, and Chapter 5, Detecting Deception). Yet "lawyering up" is often perceived as a sign of guilt, or at least suspicion, so innocent people might assume that they're making things worse for themselves by invoking their rights. It remains to be seen whether further research and thinking on this issue translate into changes in the way police cautions are delivered.

The Right to Silence

Even before the Charter was enacted in 1982, Canadian courts and common-law courts around the world recognized the impropriety of convicting accused persons on the basis of coerced, self-incriminating statements. Today, protection against self-incrimination is considered by the courts to fall within s. 7 of the Charter, which reads:

> 7. Everyone has the right to life, liberty and security of the person and the right not to be deprived thereof except in accordance with the principles of fundamental justice.

The right against self-incrimination is also protected by s. 11(c), which provides that any person charged with an offence has the right "not to be compelled to be a witness in proceedings against that person in respect of the offence."

Unlike the right to counsel, the **right to silence** has no information component. This means that there is no legal requirement for police to tell a person about their right to silence (*R v. Singh*, 2007), although most standard police cautions do so (see below). The right to silence means that individuals are free to choose whether or not to speak to agents of the state, and the police (as agents of the state) are not allowed to subvert the choice of a person who has been arrested or detained to remain silent. This means, for example, that they cannot place an undercover officer in the cell of a person who has specifically said that they do not wish to speak to police in order to actively elicit information from that person (*R v. Hebert*, 1990).

In Canada, the right to silence is not absolute. While the Supreme Court has acknowledged that a person has the right to remain silent in the face of questioning by police, it has also stated that this right does *not* mean that investigators must stop questioning people who assert their right to silence. In the somewhat controversial decision of *R v. Singh* (2007), the majority of the Court (5:4) said that if a statement is found to be voluntary, there is no s. 7 breach, because a voluntariness inquiry includes consideration of whether or not the accused was denied his or her right to silence. In *Singh*, the accused asserted his right to silence 18 times, but the police continued to question him. Because his statement was made voluntarily, the majority held that the police questioning did not violate s. 7 (see below for a discussion of admissibility and voluntariness).

right to silence the right of an individual not to be compelled to be a witness against himself and to freely choose whether or not to speak to agents of the state, such as police officers

CAUTIONING SUSPECTS

One of the most important police procedures related to interviewing suspects and accused persons is the administration of a caution upon arrest, at the beginning of questioning, and/or at any point where the charges against the accused have changed. The cautioning process is designed to allow police to discharge the obligations imposed on them by case law and legislation such as the Charter. Even if a suspect has not been formally arrested or detained, the courts have advised that an investigator should provide a caution where there are reasonable grounds to believe that the person being interviewed has committed an offence (*R v. Singh*, 2007).

Primary Caution

primary caution warning given by an investigator to a suspect informing him or her that an officer is conducting an investigation into a criminal allegation; that they are a suspect in that investigation; that they do not have to speak to the police, but if they choose to do so the police will make a record of it that may be used against them in court if they are charged with a criminal offence

Because the exact content of a caution will vary, specific wording is not provided here. However, it is clear that a legally sufficient **primary caution** should advise the suspect about the following:

1. the officer is conducting an investigation into a specific criminal allegation (and what that allegation is), and the person is a suspect in that investigation;

2. the nature of each offence that is being investigated, or with which the accused is being charged;

3. the suspect/accused has the right to retain counsel before making any statement, and that free legal advice (including legal aid) is available;

4. the suspect/accused does not have to speak to the police if he or she does not want to; if he or she decides to speak to the police, the police will make a record of whatever is said to them (remember, however, that there is no *duty* to inform suspects of their right to silence); and

5. if the suspect is later charged with a criminal offence, whatever the suspect tells the police can be used against him or her in court.

Police recruits can expect to receive instruction from their police service on the appropriate forms of caution, and should be alert to legal developments that suggest improvements to the cautioning procedure.

In administering the caution, the investigator need not only provide the requisite information, but must also ensure to the best of his or her ability that the suspect has understood the information (if necessary, by arranging for an interpreter) and has been given an opportunity to exercise the right to counsel. In fulfilling these responsibilities, as mentioned above, the police need to provide privacy and access to a telephone so that the accused can call a lawyer. After they have given the primary caution (or the secondary caution, discussed below), it is good practice for investigators to have suspects restate the cautions in their own words, in order to confirm that they have understood them. As with any police/suspect interaction, it is strongly advised that the giving of the caution and the suspect's restatement of it be recorded to prove that the caution was read to—and understood by—the suspect.

Secondary Caution

secondary caution warning given by an investigator to a suspect where the investigator is not the first police officer to have contact with the suspect, advising the suspect that if he or she has had any previous contact with the police regarding the matter under investigation he or she should not be influenced by anything said or done during that contact, and that he or she remains free to decide whether to speak to the investigator

Where the investigator is not the first police officer to have contact with the suspect, there is a danger that the past behaviour of less scrupulous officers or other persons in authority will affect the admissibility of any further statements that the accused chooses to make. For this reason, where an accused has had previous contact with other persons in authority, a **secondary caution** should be given in addition to the primary caution, advising the suspect that, if he has had any previous contact with police officers in regard to the matter under investigation, he should not be influenced by anything that was said or done during that contact (in particular, any threats or promises), and that he remains free to decide whether or not to speak to investigators. For example:

Re-cautioning Suspects

Accused persons who consult counsel after being informed of a particular charge have not necessarily exhausted their s. 10 rights, according to the Supreme Court in *R v. Black* (1989) and *R v. Borden* (1994). If the police alter the charge or add a new charge, the accused must be granted another opportunity to consult counsel. These cases suggest that if an investigating officer begins to suspect that a person has committed additional offences beyond those for which he or she has already been charged, the person should immediately be re-cautioned and given a new opportunity to obtain counsel. If, for example, an officer visits a residence to investigate a report of stolen property and cautions a suspect on the premises with respect to that offence, but a few minutes later notices what appear to be marijuana plants growing under a heat lamp, the officer should caution the suspect again, this time with respect to the marijuana offence.

I wish to give you the following warning: you must clearly understand that anything said to you previously should not influence you or make you feel compelled to say anything at this time. Whatever you may have felt influenced or compelled to say earlier you are not now obliged to repeat, nor are you obliged to say anything further, but whatever you do say may be given in evidence. Do you understand?

In the absence of a secondary caution, it may be difficult for the Crown to prove that the statement was made voluntarily (see the discussion below on admissibility of statements).

ENHANCED RIGHTS OF YOUNG PERSONS

Persons 12 years of age or older but *less than* 18 years of age who come into contact with the police have all of the same legal rights as individuals 18 and older, but because of their unique status in the criminal justice system their rights are enhanced. Section 25 of the YCJA states that a young person has the right to retain and instruct counsel at *any* stage in their interaction with the criminal justice system (in contrast to adults, for whom that right exists only upon arrest or detention), while s. 146 provides a number of special rules that govern the admissibility of any statements made by a young person to a police officer or person in authority. In order for a young person's statement to be **admissible**:

1. it must be voluntary, and
2. the person to whom the statement was made must have explained to the young person in age-appropriate language, before they made the statement, that
   - they were not obliged to make a statement,
   - any statement they do give may be used as evidence against them, and
   - they have the right to consult with counsel and a parent or other person.

admissible   a term normally used to describe evidence that is relevant to a determination of the issues in a judicial proceeding and which is allowed to be considered by a trier of fact in making a decision regarding such issues

Before making the statement, the young person must have in fact been given a reasonable opportunity to consult with counsel, a parent, or adult relative (or other appropriate adult) chosen by the young person.

A young person may waive their right to counsel, but such a waiver must either be recorded or in writing, and must contain a statement signed by the young person that says that they have been informed of their right to counsel and they are choosing to waive it. Section 146(8) of the YCJA holds that in situations where a young person represents themselves to be 18 years of age or older when they make a statement or waiver, or where the person to whom the statement or waiver was made took reasonable steps to determine the age of the young person and believed that they were 18 years of age or older, the court may rule the young person's statement or waiver admissible. A special form (Form 9.1, Statement of a Young Person) is provided under the YCJA, and includes the steps that police must follow when taking a statement from a young person. Officers who are required to take a statement from a young person are advised to prepare themselves by reading the applicable sections of the YCJA and by consulting the Department of Justice Canada website (www.justice.gc.ca) section entitled YCJA Explained (follow the links to Programs and Initiatives, Youth JusticeRenewal, Youth Criminal Justice Act), which contains copies of the related forms, and checklists of the key sections related to the rights and statements of young persons. Officers would also be well advised to read the case of *R v. L.T.H.* (2008), which includes a detailed discussion of s. 146(2) of the YCJA and the requirements that must be met in order for a statement from a young person to be admissible.

Interviews of young persons are different than interviews with adults, and are best conducted by officers who have received special training in both the psychological and legal issues involved.

ADMISSIBILITY OF STATEMENTS

inculpatory   that which establishes or tends to establish a person's guilt

exculpatory   that which clears or tends to clear a person of guilt

If an accused chooses to waive the right to silence and make a statement (whether **inculpatory** or **exculpatory**), no matter how incriminating or valuable to the prosecution an accused's statement may be, if it is shown to have been obtained involuntarily or through some other violation of the accused's legal rights it may be ruled inadmissible. A ruling of inadmissibility is usually the product of carelessness by investigators and is, in most cases, preventable.

For an accused's statement to be admissible, the Crown must demonstrate that the accused:

- was aware of why he or she was being spoken to by the authorities, and the potential jeopardy associated with that;
- had been advised of and understood his or her constitutional rights, and had a meaningful opportunity to exercise those rights; and,
- still chose freely to speak to authorities.

voir dire   a "trial within a trial" to determine the admissibility of evidence, such as a confession given to a police officer or person in authority

The voluntariness of a statement is normally established by a **voir dire**, or a trial within a trial. While an electronic record (discussed below) is the most effective way to prove the voluntariness of a statement, the court may also require that *all* officers who had contact with the accused prior to the taking of the statement—that is, not only the investigators that were present with the suspect in the interview room—be available to testify, in order to determine whether or not they had any conversation with the suspect that may have influenced his or her decision to speak to the police. This is the reason why the secondary caution, discussed above, is so important.

Confession Rule

The **confession rule** is a long-established doctrine of common law, with its roots in such cases as *Ibrahim v. The King* (1914), which holds that no statement made by an accused person to a person in authority—for example, a police officer—is admissible against them unless the Crown can show, beyond a reasonable doubt, that the statement was given voluntarily. This rule is embodied in current Canadian case law in decisions such as *Oickle* (2000) and *Spencer* (2007).

Persons in Authority

Statements made to a person *not* in authority (for example, a friend or a doctor of an accused) are admissible without consideration of their voluntariness, but statements, admissions, or confessions made to a **person in authority** are only admissible if proven by the Crown beyond a reasonable doubt to have been made *voluntarily*. The test to determine who is a "person in authority" is partially subjective—for example, a parent, doctor, teacher, or employer may be found to be a person in authority in certain circumstances, depending on the accused's belief as to the ability of the person to influence the prosecution or investigation of the crime with which they are charged—and partially objective, and was articulated by the Supreme Court in *R v. Hodgson* (1998). In that case, the Court held that a person in authority is a person *who the accused believes on reasonable grounds* is (1) acting on behalf of the state or (2) has influence or control over the proceedings. The subjective component is the accused's *perception* that the statement was given to a person in authority, and the objective component is the requirement that the accused's belief be *reasonable*.

The question of who is a person in authority has produced a great deal of case law, most of which is concerned with what constitutes reasonable grounds. A person's occupation is an important consideration in an accused's perceptions of who is a person in authority. Police officers, Crown attorneys, corrections personnel, and any others involved in the arrest, prosecution, or incarceration of an accused may reasonably be found to be persons in authority, because their ability to influence the prosecution is obvious.

A child's parents or guardians may be persons in authority when the child is a victim of crime. At times, social agency employees such as family counsellors and social workers qualify as persons in authority. The proprietor of a business may be found to be a person in authority in cases involving theft, fraud, or embezzlement within the business, by virtue of the fact that the proprietor may be the one who decides whether the police are notified of the crime.

Persons acting on behalf of a federal, provincial, or municipal branch of government may be found by the courts to be agents of a specific department and thus

confession rule   a long-established doctrine of common law that holds that no statement made by an accused person to a person in authority is admissible against them unless the Crown can show beyond a reasonable doubt that the statement was given voluntarily.

person in authority typically refers to persons who are formally engaged in the arrest, detention, examination, or prosecution of the accused—for example, police officers, prison guards, and Crown attorneys

inducement promise, favour, threat, or representation made to an accused that can be perceived as an effort to coerce the accused into making a confession

persons in authority. Threats, coercion, or **inducements** directed at an accused in the presence of the police by someone who is not a police officer can make that person a person in authority if he or she is found to have acted on behalf of the police, or if his or her conduct was such that the accused could have reasonably inferred that the threats, coercion, or inducements received police consent or acquiescence.

A medical doctor who in his or her professional capacity examines an accused or treats an accused's injury or other physical condition is *not*, according to the courts, a person in authority, and statements made to such a person may therefore be admissible. However, statements made to a psychiatrist during a court-ordered assessment are considered to be induced statements, and therefore generally are inadmissible.

The question of whether or not an undercover police officer is a person in authority is an interesting one, given that a suspect who is unaware of the true identity of an undercover officer might volunteer information that he or she would never disclose to a known police officer. The issue was considered in the 1981 case of *Rothman v. The Queen*. In that case, an accused being questioned by the police refused to make a statement and was placed in the cells. The police then sent an undercover officer into the cells with the accused. Although the accused was suspicious of the undercover officer, the officer was able to convince the accused that he was not a police officer. Inculpatory statements involving narcotics charges were made by the accused to the officer. The court ruled that a *voir dire* was not necessary to judge the voluntariness of the statements, because the accused believed that the undercover officer was not a police officer (and thus not a person in authority). The court also ruled that the undercover officer's deception did not constitute a situation in which the administration of justice had been brought into disrepute. The accused's statements were admitted into evidence against him.

After the passage of the Charter in 1982, a similar set of facts arose in *Hebert* (1990). In deciding *Hebert*, the Court's conclusion about the significance of the Charter protection of the right to silence effectively changed the result in *Rothman*, finding that it is improper for the police to use an undercover agent to elicit a statement that an accused has previously refused to give the police. *Hebert* did not, however, specifically reject the *Rothman* finding that an undercover agent may be a person not in authority vis-à-vis the accused. Recently, in *R v. Grandinetti* (2005), the Supreme Court held that a confession made to an undercover officer was admissible, because the accused did not view the officer as a person in authority, while in other situations, the Court has focused on whether the statement was given *voluntarily*. In *R v. Liew* (1999), the Court held that an accused's confession to an undercover officer did not violate the accused's right to silence because the officer did not actively elicit the information in violation of the accused's right to remain silent.

Thus, because of *Hebert*, if the police use undercover officers to subvert the right to silence, then the Charter will operate to exclude any statements. However, where undercover officers obtain information from an accused in a voluntary manner without attempting to breach the accused's right to remain silent, such statements may be admissible.

Statements "Off the Record"

There are times when an accused may say to a police officer, "I want to tell you something off the record." This indicates that the accused has an expectation of privacy, but the courts have viewed off-the-record statements not from the perspective of privacy, but from the perspective of voluntariness. In *R v. Smith* (1989), the Supreme Court ruled that off-the-record statements are admissible as long as the accused's right to counsel is not violated. The Ontario Court of Appeal in *R v. Moran* (1987) determined that an off-the-record statement made to the police by the accused was admissible because it was voluntary.

False Confessions

Despite many people's intuitive belief that no one would confess to a crime they didn't commit, the problem of false confessions is real. One recent study found that 81 percent of a group of 124 wrongful conviction cases involved false confessions (Drizin and Leo, 2004), while other research has found that in about 25 percent of all DNA exonerations in the United States, innocent people made incriminating statements, gave outright confessions, or pled guilty to crimes they did not commit (Kassin, 2008; Innocence Project, 2010; Uphoff, 2006). In Canada, the issue of false confessions has been the subject of television documentaries (CBC, Disclosure, 2003), and false confessions (such as that of Simon Marshall, a mentally handicapped man who falsely confessed to crimes he did not commit in the late 1990s; he spent five years in jail after being wrongfully convicted, but was subsequently cleared by DNA and awarded $2.3 million by the government of Quebec in 2006) have played an important role in wrongful convictions in this country (Seguin, 2006; *Marshall v. The Queen*, 2005).

The leading Canadian case on the admissibility of confession evidence in Canada is the Supreme Court case *R v. Oickle* (2000). In *Oickle*, the Court identified the five kinds of false confessions, and the interrogation scenarios most likely to produce them:

1. **Coerced–compliant** This is the most common type of false confession. Individuals give this type of confession knowingly, in response to threats or promises. Being told, for example, that it would be better to confess to a lesser charge than to be found guilty of a more serious one could cause an innocent person to make a coerced–compliant false confession.

2. **Stress–compliant** Individuals give this type of false confession knowingly, to escape from what they perceive to be an intolerably intense, punishing interrogation experience, and/or in a situation in which they have been convinced that it is futile to protest their innocence.

3. **Non-coerced–persuaded** Individuals give this type of false confession because, as a result of the use of certain police interrogation tactics, they have become confused, have come to doubt their own memory, and have been temporarily persuaded of their own guilt.

coerced–compliant false confession the most common type of false confession identified in *R v. Oickle* (2000), it is given knowingly by an individual in response to threats or promises

stress–compliant false confession a false confession given knowingly in order to escape from what the person perceives to be an intolerably intense, punishing interrogation, and/or a situation in which someone has been convinced that it is futile to protest his or her innocence

non-coerced–persuaded false confession false confession given as a result of certain police interrogation tactics that have confused a person or caused them to doubt their own memory, and which has temporarily persuaded them of their own guilt

**coerced–persuaded false
confession** false confession that shares the same
characteristics as the
non-coerced–persuaded false
confession, but in which
threats and promises have
also been used

voluntary false confession
false confession given
voluntarily for a variety of
reasons, including mental
illness or a desire for
attention, and not as a result
of the use of police
interrogation techniques

4. **Coerced–persuaded**   This type of false confession shares the characteristics of the non-coerced–persuaded confession, but, in addition, threats or promises have been used.

5. **Voluntary false confession**   In this type of confession, a person who did not commit the crime confesses without any prompting from the police. This often occurs in high-profile cases, for a variety of reasons ranging from mental illness to a desire for attention. For example, in the Jon Benet Ramsay case, John Mark Karr confessed, and was arrested and charged, but the charges against him were dropped when DNA evidence excluded him as a suspect.

Only the first four types of false confessions are relevant to police interrogations, because the fifth is the result of a person coming forward, falsely confessing of his or her own free will, and is not the product of police questioning methods.

Determining Voluntariness

Today, the admissibility of confessions by accused persons is determined according to the approach set out by the Supreme Court in *Oickle*. In *Oickle*, the court noted that false confessions are "rarely the product of proper police techniques" (at para. 45) and stated that, if a confession is produced in certain situations or under certain circumstances, the voluntariness of the confession is difficult to determine. Judges must look carefully at *all* of the circumstances surrounding a confession and how it was obtained and consider the degree to which the following four factors were present:

1. threats or promises;
2. an atmosphere of oppression;
3. an operating mind; and
4. police trickery.

The first three factors are connected with the voluntariness of a statement; depending on the context in which the statement was made, the presence of just one of these three factors to a sufficient degree, or a combination of all three, may be enough to render the statement involuntary. The presence of the fourth factor to a sufficient degree may be enough to exclude a statement based on the fact that the actions of the police reflect negatively on the justice system and have the potential to bring the administration of justice into disrepute.

The four factors are discussed immediately below.

Threats or Promises

The Court in *Oickle* stated that false confessions are likely if the police employ threats or promises before the suspect confesses. Threats or promises, also known as inducements, in the form of words or gestures by a person in authority will make the statements or confession of the accused inadmissible if, whether standing alone or in combination with other factors (such as an atmosphere of oppression or lack of operating mind, discussed below), they are strong enough to overbear the will of the accused. This is based on the notion that the statement or confession must be a product of the accused's free will and not the result of the police having convinced the suspect that making the statement will put him or her in a better position.

Not every police technique to get an accused to confess will be considered an inducement; the courts will look for a *quid pro quo* (which means "something for something") offer by interrogators. If a confession is given in exchange for, or because of, something else (that is, to obtain a benefit or avoid a negative consequence, as opposed to for its own sake), it is more likely to be false—and therefore likely to be inadmissible.

Investigators who employ threats or promises cause a suspect to perceive the "fear of prejudice" or the "hope of advantage." An example of the hope of advantage would be a promise of preferential treatment, where a police officer suggests to a suspect that, in exchange for his confession, the officer will make efforts to see that the suspect faces a lesser charge or receives a more lenient sentence. Similarly, if a police officer offers an accused bail in return for a statement, that offer will likely render the statement inadmissible. An example of the fear of prejudice would be where a police officer threatens to carry out an act (such as hitting the suspect) unless the suspect provides a confession, *and the officer has the capacity to carry out the threat*. Any act of physical violence or torture will always render a statement inadmissible. The threat or suggestion of violence to prompt an accused to give a statement may on its own render a statement involuntary.

Threats or promises do not have to be directed at the suspect alone to be considered coercive—the court has held that threats or promises regarding another person may constitute an improper inducement. For example, a mother who is told that her daughter will not be charged with shoplifting if she confesses to a similar offence is being offered the hope of advantage.

Commenting on the position of an accused before the courts is *not* considered an inducement as long as the police officer states only the facts and does not include an opinion on sentence or release from custody. The courts have held that a police officer who tells an accused person that he or she does not believe what the person is telling them is not engaging in conduct sufficient to make any subsequent statement that the accused person may make to the officer inadmissible unless the accusations of lying are prolonged.

The way in which police phrase questions or statements directed toward an accused may cause the statements to be considered inducements. Comments that hint at the possibility of prejudice (or advantage), such as "It would be better if you told the truth," are problematic. Although such comments may not automatically render a statement inadmissible, they *will* attract the court's scrutiny, because of the possibility that the suspect perceived them as either a subtle threat or as an inducement. By contrast, moral or spiritual promises, or appeals to a person's conscience—for example, promising a suspect that they will "feel better" or gain a "clear conscience" if they confess—are not problematic, because the things that are being promised are not under the control of the police.

Atmosphere of Oppression

Any police interrogation approach that creates an "atmosphere of oppression" increases the likelihood of a false confession because it effectively removes the ability of the suspect to make a meaningful choice about whether or not to speak to the authorities. Actions that contribute to an atmosphere of oppression include the following:

- *Prolonged interrogations.* The courts have held that prolonged interrogations can create an atmosphere of oppression. In this case, the concern is that an oppressive atmosphere may lead to a false confession— that is, an accused may confess in order to escape the horrible conditions rather than confess voluntarily. Although case law has not laid down a precise time limit, interrogations lasting as little as three hours have been called "excessive" by the courts and held to affect the voluntariness of a statement. What constitutes excessive varies from case to case, but when there has not been any apparent adverse treatment or lack of respect for the accused's rights, the courts have been generous in allowing statements gathered during prolonged interrogations into evidence. On the other hand, statements obtained as a result of subjecting the suspect to excessively aggressive questioning over an extended period of time have been ruled inadmissible.

- *Disregard for the dignity and well-being of the accused.* Interview circumstances that jeopardize the dignity and well-being of the accused have been viewed negatively by the courts. Where an accused has made a statement to a police officer after being denied food, water, sleep, use of the washroom, or medical attention, the courts have treated this as a serious violation of basic human dignity and have rejected assertions that the statement was voluntary. Denying clothing to an accused during an interrogation also causes statements to be ruled inadmissible.

  In addition, a harsh custodial or interview environment—that is, one that strips the accused of his or her dignity—can contribute to the creation of an atmosphere of oppression. Basements, locker rooms, and the like can fit into this category.

- *Excessive number of interviewers.* The courts have also considered the presence of an excessive number of police officers during the taking of a statement as a possible ground for a ruling of inadmissibility. Generally speaking, the courts consider two officers an appropriate complement, although the presence of other people essential to the statement-taking process (for example, translators) has been permitted. The number of officers and others interacting with the accused should be kept to a minimum because all of them may be asked to testify about their interactions in order for the Crown to prove that none of them used threats or inducements (see the discussion of *voir dire*, above).

- *Fabricated evidence.* The courts have generally held that confronting a suspect with "entirely fabricated evidence" (for example, suggesting that the crime was caught on camera when it was not) can contribute to the production of a false confession. This action will not automatically result in a statement being ruled inadmissible, but it will be one of the things that the court considers, because of its potential—especially in combination with other factors—to persuade a vulnerable suspect (for example, a person with a developmental disability or a psychological disorder) that he committed the crime, or at least to persuade him that there is no point in claiming that he is innocent.

No Operating Mind

This criterion applies to the cognitive abilities of the suspect rather than to police questioning practices. Even if police investigators proceed properly with respect to all other circumstances, a suspect's statement may not be considered voluntary if it is not the product of an "operating mind." An operating mind means that, at the time the statement was made, the accused had the cognitive ability to understand what was being said to him or her; what he or she was saying; and that it was being said to the police, who could use it to his or her detriment. The determination of the presence or absence of an operating mind is made by the trial judge during a *voir dire*. Shock, acute mental illness, or intoxication by drugs or alcohol may make a person incapable of understanding the consequences of his or her actions, the nature of a police caution, or the right to counsel. Individuals who are functioning at a reduced mental capacity (for example, at that of a young child) may also be said not to possess an operating mind.

In cases of intoxication, the accused's coherence on being questioned by the police is the criterion on which the judge bases his or her decision. That an accused was intoxicated at the time of questioning does not necessarily exclude a confession or statement made to the police. The judge must determine whether the intoxication was such that the accused was incoherent when the confession or statement was made. Determining admissibility is therefore predicated not on the presence or absence of intoxication, but on the severity of the effects of that intoxication. A confession or statement made by an accused who is so intoxicated as to be incoherent will probably be ruled inadmissible.

Police Deceit or Trickery

This criterion is aimed at maintaining the integrity of the criminal justice system. While the Court clearly says that deceit and trickery are acceptable tools that the police can use when questioning suspects, it is equally clear when it says that in a society governed by the rule of law there must be limits on the use of such techniques. Those limits are determined by what is referred to as the "community shock test." Quite simply, any use of deceit or trickery by the police to obtain a confession that would shock the community—for example, an officer pretending to be a chaplain or a legal aid lawyer, or an officer injecting truth serum into a diabetic suspect while telling him it was insulin—will likely result in a confession being ruled inadmissible.

PLANNING FOR A SUSPECT INTERVIEW

As we discussed in Chapter 2 regarding witness interviews, while some experienced investigators may express a preference for spontaneity and instinct in choosing interview questions, a more advisable approach is to go into the interview with as much background information as you are able to acquire in the time that is available to you and at least a rudimentary plan that outlines the areas that must be covered, the critical questions that must be asked, and some sense of the order in which they can be asked most effectively. Conducting a suspect interview with authority and confidence normally requires a plan of attack; interviews conducted by investigators who believe that they can simply enter the interview room and "wing it" will rarely turn out well.

Wherever possible, interviews with suspects and accused persons should be conducted in a quiet environment free of distractions or where distractions are kept to a minimum.

Conducting Background Research

Because they tend to occur far less frequently than witness and victim interviews, suspect interviews are an area in which the typical investigator tends to be the least experienced and the most anxious. This makes careful preparation *especially* important. The most important thing an investigator can do to prepare for a suspect interview is research. As when interviewing a witness or victim, the investigator must take the time to become thoroughly familiar with the case and all its existing evidence (both statement and physical). In addition, the investigator must try to learn as much as possible about the individuals involved in the case. The following are questions that you should attempt to answer (though the time that is typically available will likely not permit you to answer them all):

- Does the suspect have a criminal record and/or any convictions for offences similar to the one under investigation?

- Does the suspect's name come up in any other police reports or records of police contact and, if so, under what circumstances? Have you spoken to investigators who may have dealt with the suspect previously to learn as much as you can about the suspect?

- Is there any evidence linking the suspect in any way to the scene of the crime? For example, shortly after the robbery you are investigating occurred, was the suspect stopped for speeding while driving his car a block away from the scene? Or did the suspect's car receive a parking ticket near the park where the sexual assault took place? Was the suspect captured on video surveillance leaving the apartment building where the murder occurred? Did the suspect leave anything behind (fingerprints, DNA) that could link him to the crime scene?

You must also review the evidence that has already been collected in the course of the investigation, including photographs, video, seized property, and victim and witness statements. If the investigator conducting the interview is not the officer who arrested the suspect (often the case in larger police services), the investigator should speak with the arresting officer(s) to learn as much as possible about the suspect. What conversations did the officers at the scene have with the suspect before he was brought into the police station? Did the suspect make any statements upon arrest? How did the suspect behave when he was arrested; what was his attitude and demeanor? Is there any other relevant information available to the investigator that was not included in the arrest reports?

The investigator must have a solid knowledge of the existing evidence in order to be confident that he or she can put the suspect's statement into context and determine whether it is consistent with what is already known and which areas of the statement need to be further explored. Nothing causes an investigator to lose credibility faster in a suspect interview than not being familiar with the evidence.

Planning to Create a Complete Electronic Record

Although there is no statutory requirement for police to record suspect interviews, Canadian courts have expressed a clear preference for recorded—and preferably video-recorded—statements of both suspects *and* witnesses (*R v. Oickle*, 2000; *R v. Moore-McFarlane*, 2001; *R v. Roks*, 2007; *R v. Ahmed*, 2002). Video-recorded statements allow the decision-maker to observe with his or her own eyes the context in which the statement was made and thus make more accurate determinations regarding inducements, atmosphere of oppression, and operating mind.

Recent Canadian case law seems to place an onus on investigators planning to conduct an interview with a suspect to give some thought to the need to create an electronic record of the interview and to choose a location where recording equipment is available. In *R v. Moore-McFarlane* (2001), the court stated that the "completeness, accuracy, and reliability" of the (electronic) record had everything to do with its inquiry into and its assessment of the circumstances surrounding the taking of the statement. The court also noted that it would be difficult for the Crown to prove voluntariness beyond a reasonable doubt where proper recording procedures are *not* followed.

The case of *R v. Ahmed* (2002) made it clear that if police have arrested and/or called a suspect into a police station or anywhere else for the purpose of conducting an interview or interrogation where recording equipment is available but they deliberately fail to record the suspect's statement, although not fatal, the statement is likely to be found involuntary. In *R v. Khan* (2010), the court noted that where recording facilities are readily available, but the police deliberately set out to interrogate a suspect in custody without attempting to make a reliable record, the resulting non-recorded interrogation will inevitably be deemed "suspect."

Failure to consider the Canadian courts' clearly expressed preference for electronically recorded suspect statements significantly increases the likelihood of unrecorded statements being ruled inadmissible. Investigators can increase the likelihood that a suspect's statement will be deemed admissible by ensuring that (1) suspects' legal rights are duly respected, and (2) *all* police contact with suspects is thoroughly documented. In the unlikely event that an investigator *cannot* record a suspect interview despite making best efforts to do so (for example, in cases where the equipment fails or the subject refuses to be recorded), the investigator would need to take extensive contemporaneous notes to account for both the content of the statement and the circumstances in which it was taken. Even with this documentation, however, in the light of existing Canadian case law, such a statement would likely face a substantial legal challenge.

Suspects Who Are Not in Custody

Whether or not a suspect has been arrested and is in custody will have an impact on planning an interview. If the suspect has been arrested, finding a place for the interview does not pose a problem—the suspect can simply be escorted to the appropriate police interview room. On the other hand, a suspect who has not been arrested has the same right to refuse to attend a police station or to be interviewed as does any other person.

When asking a suspect to attend a police station voluntarily, the investigator should both specify that he or she wants to conduct an interview and indicate the offence about which the suspect is to be questioned. Failure to ensure that a person is aware of their status as a criminal suspect, and of their concomitant legal rights, will (as discussed above) leave the prosecution open to claims that the suspect's statement was involuntary.

Deciding on the Number of Interviewers and Formulating a Plan

The good cop–bad cop interview ploy has become a staple of crime novels, television shows, and movies. The scenario involves two police officers interrogating a suspect in a police station interview room. One officer adopts an adverse approach, ranting and raving in his interaction with the suspect, while the other remains quiet and unassuming. At some point the quiet officer—the "good cop"—either asks the "bad cop" to leave the room or steps between the bad cop and the suspect. The good cop appears to take the suspect's side by reproaching the bad cop. The suspect then comes to believe that salvation lies in cooperating with the good cop and provides a full confession.

Although this scenario makes for good television, a suspect of even average intelligence will likely see through the ruse and may become insulted, thereby strengthening their resolve to say nothing. If the suspect becomes frightened and confesses, his or her lawyer will undoubtedly be advised of these "bullying" tactics, leading to a move to have the confession ruled inadmissible on the grounds of "threat or inducement." Moreover, if the statement was video-recorded, the use of the tactic will be readily apparent to anyone who views it.

Although the good cop–bad cop tactic is largely the stuff of fiction, there are a number of good reasons for having two investigators present during a suspect interview. Where two officers are involved in questioning a suspect, you have two opportunities for one of them to establish a bond with the suspect, thus possibly increasing the chances of obtaining a statement. It may be necessary for the two investigators to alternate asking questions, until it becomes apparent who has the stronger connection with the suspect. However, once this has been determined, the officer with the stronger connection should become the primary questioner, while the other officer assumes the secondary role, taking notes with which to guide the latter phase of the interview.

It is critical that the two investigators discuss the approach they will take well in advance of the interview. Nothing can lead to a poor suspect interview more quickly than two investigators pursuing two different strategies, interrupting one another, or appearing to stumble through the interview. In particular, in advance of an interview, investigators should determine:

- who is going to start the questioning;
- when and how the two officers will transition between the primary and secondary roles;
- whether the suspect will be shown any evidence such as photographs and, if so, who will show them;
- who will ensure that the recording devices are operating properly (a common problem);
- how the two officers will communicate information to one another during the interview; and,
- how the interview will be concluded.

It is unwise to begin an interview hoping that the above details will simply work themselves out—they seldom do. No one has conducted, or will ever conduct, the perfect suspect interview, but you can lower the chances of conducting a poor one by putting in the necessary work beforehand.

Another advantage of having two investigators in the interview room is that one officer can take notes and carefully observe the suspect while the other takes the lead role in questioning the suspect. Once the lead investigator has completed their primary questioning, the second investigator can take over and follow up on anything the first investigator may have missed or anything that may have been discussed but requires further clarification.

Requests for Others to Be Present During the Interview

Sometimes, a suspect may request that a friend or relative be present during the interview. Except in the case of a youth (where the request to have a lawyer and/or adult present *must* be honoured), it is generally not advisable to comply with such a request.

The presence in the interview room of a person other than the investigator(s) and the suspect can create a significant distraction. Questions put to a suspect to clarify a statement may provoke interaction between the suspect and the other person; further, the other person will sometimes interject and interrupt the flow of the interview. Such a situation is conducive neither to the effective elicitation of information from the suspect nor to the creation of an atmosphere of privacy in which a suspect may decide to confess. The presence of another person in the interview room will also complicate any subsequent *voir dire* proceedings, because that person will become an additional "factor" that the court must consider in determining voluntariness; in addition, the person may be called on to testify. Of course, if you have no other choice (for example, because the suspect refuses to

Effect of Counsel's Advice on Investigators' Duty to Investigate

Some investigators are reluctant to attempt to question a suspect after he or she has consulted a lawyer (and has presumably been advised to exercise his or her right to silence). *This is a mistake*, and results in a wasted opportunity to obtain further information if the accused has decided not to follow the lawyer's advice to remain silent. The Supreme Court case *R v. Sinclair* (2010) confirmed that once the accused has been informed of his or her right to counsel and has been given a reasonable opportunity to exercise this right, police officers are free to question the accused. Section 10(b) of the Charter does not afford the accused the opportunity to re-consult with counsel during an interrogation (except as a result of a change in jeopardy), nor does it require an officer to cease interrogating the accused if they ask to re-consult with counsel. Further, s. 10(b) does not mandate the continued presence of defence counsel during the custodial interview. That said, officers must still keep in mind that the accused always has the right to remain silent and that any statements made during the interrogation must be voluntary, as per *Oickle*. Thus, officers are advised to always proceed with caution, being especially careful to record, preferably in electronic form, everything that is said. There must be no evidence to suggest that the evidence provided was coerced in any way.

A related point concerns instructions from counsel to police, either in person or over the phone, asking police not to question the suspect further. The law places *no* requirement on investigators to follow such requests. Again, there are no disadvantages to attempting to obtain a statement from an accused, even if the statement is composed entirely of lies (in fact, lies that can be shown to be lies can be helpful to the Crown's case). In the case of a statement that the Crown does not feel will strengthen its case, the Crown does not have to seek to have it admitted in evidence (Sherriff, 2003).

Investigators must not automatically assume that because a suspect has spoken to a lawyer the suspect will decline to make a statement. Although the suspect's lawyer will typically advise him or her not to speak to police, the decision ultimately rests with the suspect, and investigators have a duty to investigate criminal allegations. There is no excuse for not attempting to obtain a statement from a suspect within the limits discussed here.

speak unless another person is present), an interview with a support person present is preferable to no interview at all. If a decision is made to allow a support person to be present during the interview, the investigator must ensure that the person is in no way involved in the offence under investigation.

Some suspects may request that a lawyer be present with them in the interview room during questioning. However, investigators are not obligated to honour such a request and may refuse it (*R v. McCrimmon*, 2010; *R v. Sinclair*, 2010); in practice, it is relatively rare for a lawyer to sit in on a suspect interview. Despite the above, some experts are of the opinion that investigators should actually *encourage* counsel's presence during an interview, because if the suspect does make a statement in such circumstances, it is likely to be admissible. If counsel attends in the interview room, the investigator should insist that the suspect, not counsel, answer the questions. If, despite such insistence, counsel essentially takes over and answers the questions on the client's behalf, a wise investigator will occasionally ask the suspect if he or she agrees with what his lawyer is saying. If the suspect appears to "adopt" the answers given by his counsel, this can potentially be used as evidence against the suspect. However, investigators must be aware that absent an adoption of counsel's statement(s) by the suspect, anything said by the lawyer during the interview is *not* a statement that can be offered as evidence against the accused at trial.

DURING THE INTERVIEW

Practice Active Listening

Investigators must remember that the goal of a suspect interview is to elicit information from the suspect. In order to achieve this objective, the interview must be managed to ensure that the suspect—not the investigator—does most of the talking. During an interview, actively listening to what a suspect is saying is at least as important as asking questions. If you talk too much or fail to listen carefully, the suspect may either not provide the information you are looking for, or you may fail to recognize the significance of the information the suspect *does* provide.

Police officers are taught to take control of situations, and often equate control in an interview context with talking. You do *not* need to be talking to be in control of an interview. The deliberate use of silence after a suspect has offered a few words, for example, can often result in suspects offering more than they would have if you had immediately resumed your questioning. The use of verbal "encouragers" (neutral phrases such as "aha," uh hum," "go on") and non-verbal encouragers (eye contact and head nods) can have a similar effect. Resist the urge to talk too much in the early stages of a suspect interview; the more the suspect speaks, the more material you will have to explore in the latter part of the interview. And the more carefully you listen to what is said, the better equipped you will be to explore that information later.

Techniques for Active Listening

The following are some of the most common active listening techniques:

- a sustained effort by the listener to focus their attention on the interviewee;
- the use of silence by the listener following the interviewee's statements or responses;
- observation of the interviewee's body language and expressions of emotion;
- repeating, paraphrasing, or summarizing the interviewee's words to allow them to clarify and/or expand on what they said;
- identifying apparent emotions associated with interviewee's responses (for example, "you seem to be angry about that"); and
- the use of verbal and non-verbal "encouragers" (for example, "uh huh," "go on," eye contact, smiles) to encourage the interviewee to continue talking.

Remember that any notes that you make during the interview process, whether you consider them to be "rough notes" or otherwise, must be submitted to the Crown attorney as part of the disclosure process. As they are with the cognitive interview for witnesses outlined in Chapter 2, the notes taken during a suspect interview are designed to highlight significant issues that will inform your questions during the followup phase of the interview. Do not use your notes to create a verbatim record of the interview—it will be electronically recorded, preferably on video, and, in major cases, on video with a digital audio backup in case of equipment failure.

Be Prepared for What a Suspect Might Say

Suspects may respond in any number of ways to police questioning, but most responses are likely to fall (in no particular order) into one of the following categories:

- the suspect will refuse to say anything at all;
- the suspect will deny responsibility and provide a false alibi;
- the suspect will deny responsibility and provide a full and honest exculpatory account;
- the suspect will deny responsibility but provide one or more true admissions;
- the suspect will make a full and honest confession; or
- the suspect will make a false confession.

If a suspect chooses to respond to police questioning, the suspect is said to be making a "statement." In his or her statement:

denial statement in which a person denies any knowledge of or involvement in the matter under investigation

alibi an excuse, which typically takes the form of a claim that a person was somewhere else when the crime was committed

admission statement that concedes at least one fact that, if true, is relevant to proving the suspect's guilt

1. A suspect may deny any knowledge of or involvement in the matter under investigation; this is called a **denial**, and it can include the offering of an **alibi**, or excuse, which typically takes the form of a claim that the person was somewhere else when the crime was committed. Of course, a suspect's exculpatory statement may be honest or dishonest, which the investigation will ultimately seek to establish.

2. A suspect may deny responsibility but make an **admission**, which is defined as a statement that concedes *at least one* fact that, if true, is relevant to proving the suspect's guilt (Skinnider, 2005); however, this does not necessarily mean that the subject is guilty of the crime. Admissions by a suspect regarding *any* element of the crime are a boon to the investigator and should lead to new lines of questioning. Any admission that links the suspect to the crime (revealing, for example, knowledge of the victim, knowledge of the crime scene location or the location of the proceeds of the crime, or the possession by the suspect of a skill or physical ability necessary for committing the crime) is extremely important to the case, as are any admissions regarding motive (for example, drug addiction, financial difficulties, revenge, infatuation with the victim).

3. A suspect may make a confession—whether honest or false—which at its simplest is defined as an admission to *all* of the elements of an offence, including the mental element, or *mens rea* (Skinnider, 2005). Among all of the possible responses, a confession is regarded as a "uniquely potent" form of evidence, followed closely by eyewitness testimony (Kassin & Neumann, 1997). When a person confesses, they acknowledge that they are guilty of the offence, they provide details of the offence, and they describe the role they played in it.

   A confession can become the central piece of evidence in a criminal case, or it can corroborate other evidence. It also provides reasonable grounds for laying a **criminal information** (the form in which a criminal charge is specified), making an arrest, having an arrest warrant issued for a co-accused or accomplice, or obtaining a search warrant. Even if a confession is eventually excluded at trial, it can still provide reasonable grounds for pre-trial investigative purposes. Because of its powerful effect, police investigators strive to obtain a confession from suspects where possible. There is no criminal case so strong that it cannot be strengthened by an admissible confession. Moreover, a confession may lead to evidence concerning other outstanding cases.

criminal information
official form on which an individual, typically a police officer, sets out under oath a specific criminal allegation(s) against a person

Thinking in advance about the different kinds of responses that a suspect is likely to make during an interview is helpful, because it will force the investigator to consider the evidence from a number of different angles prior to conducting the interview. Hopefully, this will result in the investigator gaining a deeper understanding of the evidence, which will in turn assist him or her to determine how best to respond while the interview is in progress.

Changes to a Suspect's Jeopardy

If during the course of an interview with a suspect an investigator becomes aware that the suspect's jeopardy has changed, the investigator must take certain steps depending on the particular situation. The ability of an investigator to make the right decision regarding whether—and when—to caution or re-caution a person is critically important to the outcome of an investigation, and requires good judgment and a full understanding of the law on the part of the investigating officer.

The following examples illustrate changes in a suspect's jeopardy and the actions that the investigator should take in each situation:

- An investigator is conducting an interview with a person who was not previously a suspect in a crime (for example, a witness); in the course of the interview, the investigator receives new information or the person says something that causes the investigator to believe that the person is now a suspect in the crime under investigation or in another crime. For example, suppose the witness admits to being present at the scene of a shooting and to carrying a firearm, but denies firing a shot. In this case, the investigator must stop the interview, advise the person of their new status as a suspect, advise them of their legal rights pursuant to the Charter, allow them to consult with legal counsel, and caution them before continuing the interview.

- The police are interviewing a suspect with respect to one or a series of offences, and it becomes apparent as a result of an admission by that person that he or she is now a suspect for a different offence or series of offences. Again, in this case the suspect must be informed of the change in status and be given his or her rights once more before questioning continues.

- While questioning an individual regarding an assault, the investigator is notified of the fact that the victim of the assault has died. As in the examples above, because of this change in circumstances the investigator must inform the suspect of the nature of the new investigation and explain the suspect's rights to him or her again.

Where an investigator must caution a suspect or advise the suspect of his or her rights again during an interview, this should be done before the suspect has an opportunity to volunteer any additional information.

KEY TERMS

admissible

admission

alibi

arrest

coerced–compliant

coerced–persuaded

confession

criminal information

denial

detention

exculpatory

hybrid offence

inculpatory

inducement

non-coerced–persuaded

person in authority

primary caution

right to counsel

right to silence

secondary caution

stress–compliant

voir dire

voluntary false confession

waiver

FURTHER READING

Canadian Charter of Rights and Freedoms. (1982). Part 1 of the *Constitution Act, 1982*, RSC 1985, app. II, no. 44. http://laws.justice.gc.ca/en/charter/.

Eastwood, J., Snook, B., & Chaulk, S. (2010). Measuring reading complexity and listening comprehension of Canadian police cautions. In *Criminal Justice and Behavior, 37*(4), 453-471.

Smith, S., Stinson, V., & Patry, M. (2010, August 12). Confession evidence in Canada: Psychological issues and legal landscapes. *Psychology, Crime & Law, 16*, 1-17.

Youth Criminal Justice Act. (2002). SC 2002, c. 1. http://laws.justice.gc.ca/en/Y-1.5/index.html.

FIGURE 3.1   Best Practices for Interviewing Suspects and Accused

1. **Upon detaining or arresting individuals**	Immediately inform them: • of the reason for their arrest or detention; • of their right to retain and instruct legal counsel without delay, including free legal counsel; • of the ways in which they can exercise their right to counsel, which includes giving them the telephone number for duty counsel and telling them that they can speak to counsel in private; and • of the fact that they are not legally required to answer questions posed by the police.

NOTE: Do *not* attempt to obtain incriminatory evidence from a person who has been arrested or detained until you have provided the individual with the above information and the individual has understood the information you have provided. Before you proceed, the individual must have had a reasonable opportunity to consult with a lawyer or must have chosen *not* to consult with a lawyer.

2. **Before conducting an interview with a suspect**	Read suspects the following: • A primary caution, informing them (1) that the police are investigating a criminal allegation (specify) and that they are a suspect; (2) of the nature of each offence/charge; (3) of their right to obtain and instruct counsel (including duty counsel/legal aid); (4) that their statements may be used against them in court; and (5) that they may choose whether or not to speak to police. • A secondary caution, informing them that, regardless of who they may have spoken to previously, the decision whether or not to speak to police is theirs alone.

NOTE: Do *not* conduct an interview or an interrogation until you have read suspects these cautions and checked that the suspect has understood them. You should be aware that this may require an interpreter.

3. **Before taking a statement from a person over the age of 12 but under the age of 18**	• Obtain a copy of Form 9.1 under the YCJA; and • Ensure that you are familiar with, and that you give and receive the necessary cautions and responses required to properly take a statement from a young person.

NOTE: Interviews of young persons are different than interviews with adults and are best conducted by officers who have received special training in both the psychological and legal issues involved.

4. **During an interview with a suspect**	• Ensure that the recording equipment is functioning properly and that you have a backup in case of technical malfunction. • Have a plan to guide you and to ensure that you cover all of important issues; don't "wing it," because this will rarely turn out well. • Pay attention; actively listen to and consider what the suspect has to say; don't go into the interview with a closed mind. • Take short, point-form notes to guide you during the followup phase of the interview. Do *not* try to record the interview verbatim, because it is both nearly impossible to do and distracting to both interviewer and suspect.

NOTE: If a suspect makes an inculpatory statement about an offence other than the one being investigated, or if you receive information that changes the jeopardy faced by the suspect, ensure that you explain the suspect's legal rights to him or her again, that you give the suspect another opportunity to consult counsel, and that you caution the suspect once more before continuing the interview.

REVIEW QUESTIONS

TRUE OR FALSE

F. ___ 1. When asking a suspect who is not under arrest to attend a police station for questioning, the investigator must disclose the offence being investigated.

F ___ 2. Detention and arrest amount to the same thing as it pertains to a person's rights under s. 10 of the Charter.

T ___ 3. The confession rule squarely places the onus on the Crown to prove that a confession made by an accused to a person in authority was a voluntary act on the part of the accused and that the accused was aware of his rights under ss. 7 and 10 of the Charter. The defence bears some responsibility to prove to a lesser degree that the accused's rights were violated.

T ___ 4. Like any other witness, a suspect should be encouraged to provide a free recall account of the events in question.

T ___ 5. A KGB caution informs a witness that their statement will be taken under oath or affirmation; that they are agreeing to tell the truth; and that they could face potential criminal consequences if they knowingly give false information to or attempt to mislead the police during the course of the investigation, which, of course, includes the interview.

F ___ 6. When the police inform a suspect or an accused of his or her right to counsel, they need not advise the accused of his or her right to legal aid if the accused appears to be financially stable and able to pay for the services of a lawyer.

F ___ 7. A person who is only under investigative detention need not be informed of his or her right to counsel or legal aid.

T? ___ 8. Under certain circumstances, a "person in authority" may include a suspect's employer.

MULTIPLE CHOICE

1. A coerced-persuaded false confession can result when

   a. as a result of the use of certain police interrogation tactics, a person becomes confused, comes to doubt their own memory, and is temporarily persuaded of their own guilt.

   b. threats or promises have been used.

   c. an innocent person wishes to protect a loved one whom he or she knows is the guilty party.

   d. both a and b.

2. Where two investigators are going to be present during an interview, they should discuss, well in advance of the interview, how they intend to proceed. In particular, they should talk about such issues as

    a. who is going to start the questioning;

    b. who will be responsible for determining whether the suspect is being truthful;

    c. when and how they will transition between the primary and secondary roles.

    d. both a and c.

3. If, during an interview of a suspect, the investigator believes that the suspect's statement has provided reasonable and probable grounds for arresting the suspect on a criminal charge, the investigator must

    a. advise the suspect of the specific nature of the offence to be charged.

    b. advise the suspect of his or her right to silence.

    c. advise the suspect of his or her right to retain counsel.

    d. all of the above.

4. The obligation or obligations mentioned in question 3 must be fulfilled

    a. before the suspect leaves the police station.

    b. as soon as the reasonable and probable grounds arise.

    c. only if the offence is an indictable offence.

    d. within 24 hours.

SHORT ANSWER

1. A 16-year-old boy admits to his mother at dinner that he stole a vehicle from a neighbour. Would the boy's mother be considered a "person in authority" pursuant to the confession rule and, if so, what affect would this have on the admissibility of the boy's statement?

2. Two adult male suspects are arrested on charges of breaking and entering. They are advised of their rights pursuant to ss. 10(a) and (b) of the Charter. They are also given both primary and secondary cautions. On being cautioned, they advise police that, on instructions from their lawyers, they do not wish to make a statement. The two men are then placed in a police station cell, unaware that an undercover police officer is in the cell next to them, pretending to be asleep. The undercover officer overhears a conversation between the two men in which they make several incriminating statements. Would the officer be considered a "person in authority"? Would it be necessary to hold a *voir dire*? Is the officer's evidence regarding what he overheard likely to be admissible?

3. The police arrest a man on a charge of sexual assault. He is informed of his rights under s. 10 of the Charter, which includes the right to counsel, and is given both a primary and secondary police caution. The man asks to speak to a lawyer and, after having done so, advises the police that his

lawyer has instructed him to say nothing more to the police. However, the police continue to question the man, who says, at least five times, that he has the right to remain silent; however, after approximately an hour of questioning, the man makes an inculpatory statement concerning the sexual assault. Is the man's statement to police likely to be admissible? Provide a case law reference in support of your answer.

4. Police arrest a man on a charge of aggravated assault and inform him of his rights under s. 10 of the Charter, including the availability of free legal advice and a telephone number for legal aid duty counsel. The man is then given a primary and secondary police caution. The police inform the man that they intend to question him regarding the assault and ask him if he wishes to speak with a lawyer. The man indicates that he understands his right to consult counsel, but does not ask to speak to a lawyer. He subsequently provides police with a full, signed confession. At trial, defence counsel argues that the confession should be excluded because police should not have questioned the accused until he had consulted a lawyer. Will the confession be admissible? Provide a case law reference in support of your answer.

5. A 40-year-old woman is arrested for fraud. She is advised of her Charter rights and transported to a police station where she is given the opportunity to speak to a lawyer. An investigator then begins to question her about the offence for which she has been arrested. She subsequently makes a confession to the officer. Would the woman's confession be admissible, given that the officer advised her of her legal rights and allowed her to speak to a lawyer but did not caution her prior to taking her statement? Provide a case law reference for your answer.

6. A 27-year-old man is arrested for the knifepoint robbery of an elderly man. The accused is informed of his Charter rights, allowed to speak to a lawyer, and given both a primary and secondary police caution before being questioned by police. During questioning the accused is reluctant to speak to the investigator. In an attempt to elicit a confession from the accused, the investigator tells him that, because he didn't hurt the elderly man, if he confesses, the investigator will only charge him with theft of the man's wallet and not with robbery. The accused subsequently confesses to the robbery. Will his confession be admissible? Provide a case law reference.

7. A 17-year-old male is arrested as a suspect for a break and enter at a local high school in which a number of laptop computers were stolen and extensive damage was done to the school building. The young person is advised of his rights under s. 10 of the Charter and is given both a primary and secondary caution. The investigator then proceeds to question the young man, saying, "Listen, kid, it would be better for all concerned if you just come clean and admit what you did." The suspect subsequently makes an inculpatory statement to the officer. Would the young person's statement likely be admissible? Provide both a legislative and a case law reference for your answer.

Interviewing Suspects II: Approaches and Techniques

4

INTRODUCTION

The two basic processes that investigators use to obtain information from suspects are interviews and interrogations. Although some experts hesitate to draw a clear line between the two approaches, there are important strategic and philosophical differences between them, and investigators must appreciate the consequences of choosing one over the other:

- A suspect interview is a non-accusatory process in which an investigator seeks to gather the maximum amount of relevant, reliable information from a person who might be involved in the crime, but whose status as an official suspect is as yet undetermined.

- An **interrogation** is an accusatory process, the primary purpose of which is to elicit a confession from a person who is believed to be responsible for the offence under investigation.

This chapter examines two significantly different approaches to conducting suspect interviews: the Reid technique and the PEACE model. The Reid technique consists of an initial interview, which is used to determine whether a person is being deceptive and is likely responsible for the offence under investigation, followed by a highly persuasive interrogation process that aims to produce a confession. In contrast, the PEACE model is an inquisitorial approach that focuses on obtaining as much information as possible from a person during an interview, and then using that information to challenge the person to account for any inconsistencies between his or her recollection of an event versus what is known from other evidence gathered during the investigation.

As mentioned at the outset of this text, our discussion of the different interview/ interrogation models is premised on the assumption that the interviewee is an adult with no known or discernable special circumstances. Interviewing people

---

CHAPTER OBJECTIVES

After completing this chapter, you should be able to:

- Explain the difference between an interview and an interrogation.

- Understand the stages and steps that comprise the Reid technique of interviewing and interrogation.

- Understand the stages in the PEACE model of interviewing.

- Understand what research suggests about the effectiveness of the Reid and PEACE methods and the criticisms that have been made of these methods.

- Understand the importance of being able to articulate the reason for choosing a particular investigative technique and the importance of ongoing professional learning regarding various interviewing and interrogation methods.

interrogation an accusatory process, the primary purpose of which is to elicit a confession from a suspect who is believed to be responsible for the offence under investigation

from specific groups—such as children, persons with developmental disabilities, elderly persons, and persons for whom English is not their native language—typically requires special consideration, additional training, and planning.

THE REID TECHNIQUE

In the 1990s, when formal training in suspect interview techniques became more widely available in Canada, the most common approach taught to police officers was the Reid technique, offered by a private company, Reid and Associates, based in Chicago. Today, the company trains over 20,000 people in North America each year on its method of interviewing and interrogation.

The **Reid technique** originated in the 1940s and '50s, based largely on the work of university law professor Fred Inbau. Inbau began his work in the 1930s at Chicago's Northwestern University, in the law school's Scientific Crime Detection Laboratory, where for five decades he specialized in developing and teaching interrogation techniques, attempting to move them away from a crude, physical approach to a more "psychological" approach that included the use of isolation, trickery, and displays of interrogator confidence. Inbau popularized his techniques in a series of books, beginning with the publication of *Lie Detection and Criminal Interrogation* in 1942.

In 1962, Inbau published *Criminal Interrogation and Confessions*—now the most well-known and influential interrogation text in North America—with John Reid, a former polygraph student of his. By the time the third edition was published in 1986, Inbau, Reid, and a third co-author, Joseph Buckley (now the president of Reid and Associates), had transformed the formerly haphazard approach to interrogation into a nine-step, mostly psychological approach.

Reid technique an approach to questioning criminal suspects that consists of three principal elements: a non-accusatory fact-finding interview; a behavioural analysis interview designed to detect deception; and an accusatory, persuasive interrogation designed to obtain a confession

Stages

The Interview

Reid and Associates have traditionally characterized their process as involving two stages—interview and interrogation. For clarity's sake, we have broken the interview stage into two parts—the fact-finding interview and the behavioural analysis interview (BAI). Although you would begin with the fact-finding interview, you would always conduct *both* the fact-finding interview and the BAI as part of the interview, or first stage of Reid, to determine a suspect's "probable guilt." Then, *if* as a result of the interview, you determined that the person was "probably guilty," you would proceed to the interrogation, or second stage of Reid.

THE FACT-FINDING INTERVIEW: GATHERING INFORMATION AND OBSERVING THE SUBJECT

The first part of the interview stage of the Reid method involves a non-accusatory, fact-finding interview. The purpose of this stage is to establish rapport with the subject and gather some basic investigative information regarding the subject's possible motive, opportunity, and/or means to commit the crime. Subjects are more likely to volunteer this kind of information if asked about it in a non-accusatory manner. Another important purpose served by this stage is that it allows the inves-

Reid at a Glance

The Reid technique includes two types of interviews and an interrogation procedure. These processes, and the method an investigator uses to determine when (or if) to transition from one to the other, are described in the stages outlined below; each stage is described in more detail in the main text of this chapter. The text in parentheses explains the purpose of each stage as identified by Reid and Associates.

1. a. Fact-finding interview (gather and analyse information, form early impressions of the suspect):
   - conducted in any location that is convenient, early in an investigation;
   - non-accusatory, conversational, opportunity to build rapport;
   - information gathering, factual analysis;
   - relatively free-flowing and unstructured;
   - allows investigator an opportunity to observe a person's "normal" behaviour;
   - investigator should take notes.
   b. Behavioural analysis interview (BAI) (form opinion about the person's guilt or innocence):
   - observation of person's non-verbal and verbal responses;
   - use of behaviour-provoking questions;
   - use of baiting questions, confronting an alibi;
   - investigator assesses person's credibility and makes a decision regarding guilt.
2. Interrogation (undo deception, elicit a confession from the suspect):
   - includes nine steps;
   - conducted in a controlled environment and only when the investigator is reasonably certain of the suspect's guilt;
   - purpose is to obtain a confession—that is, "learn the truth" (because the BAI has led them to decide that the suspect is guilty, Inbau et al. equate a confession with "telling the truth"; see Inbau, Reid, & Buckley, 1986, p. 332);
   - accusatory;
   - involves active persuasion;
   - investigator should not take notes until after the suspect has told the truth/confessed and is fully committed to that position.

tigator to get a feel for the subject's "normal"—also referred to as "baseline"—behavioural responses to non-accusatory interview questions, including body language and verbal responses. These observations can be important during the subsequent behavioural analysis stage, because a person's deviation from their baseline behaviour may indicate deception.

THE BAI: ASSESSING CREDIBILITY AND DETERMINING GUILT

In the second part of the interview stage of the Reid method, the investigator uses what Reid and Associates call the **behavioural analysis interview (BAI)** to determine whether, in the investigator's opinion, the suspect is "definitely" guilty of the offence being investigated or whether the investigator can be "reasonably certain"

behavioural analysis interview (BAI) second step of the Reid method, which uses behaviour provoking questions and behavioural observations to detect deception during a suspect interview; used to help an investigator make a decision regarding the suspect's guilt

of the suspect's guilt. It is important to note that the "guilt" referred to here is not *legal* guilt, but guilt *in the opinion of the investigator* (Buckley, 2006). It is only after the investigator has made a determination of "guilt" that he or she can progress to the third stage of the Reid method—the interrogation.

In addition to a consideration of the facts gathered during the fact-finding interview, Reid recommends three methods for determining guilt during the BAI stage. The examples of each below are derived from the Reid text. (For a detailed discussion, see Inbau, Reid, & Buckley, 1986, chap. 5; Inbau et al., 2001; or Inbau et al., 2005, chaps. 7 and 8; for a summary discussion, see Buckley, 2006.)

1. *Observation and evaluation of the suspect's verbal and non-verbal behaviour for indicators of truth or deception.* The investigator is advised to observe non-verbal body movements and position changes, gestures, facial expressions, and eye contact. Specifically, Reid and Associates suggest that investigators look for, among other things, lack of eye contact; slouching or leaning back in the chair; sitting at an angle to the investigator so as not to face him or her directly; rubbing or wringing the hands; touching the nose, ears, or lips; shuffling or tapping of the feet; placing the hands over the mouth or eyes when speaking; hiding the hands by sitting on them; and hiding the feet by pulling them under the chair. These are considered by Reid to be possible indicators of deception.

   In addition, the investigator is advised to note the suspect's verbal responses to his or her questions and to look for (among other things) delayed responses; repetition of the investigator's questions; requests for clarification or repetition of the investigator's questions; the use of incomplete sentences; the use of phrases such as "as far as I know," "I don't recall," "to be perfectly honest," "if I recall correctly," "I swear to God"; excessive politeness; and mumbling or talking softly. These, too, are considered possible indicators of deception by Reid and Associates.

2. *Behaviour-provoking questions.* The BAI is based on asking a suspect "behaviour-provoking" questions designed to evoke behavioural responses. From these responses, Reid and Associates say that the investigator can determine whether the suspect is being truthful or not. There are 15 questions in total (Inbau, 2001, chap. 11). Examples include:

   • *"Do you know why you are here?"* Evasive or vague responses should be viewed with suspicion, while a clear, blunt response is thought to be more characteristic of innocence.

   • "John, we have conducted a thorough investigation and the picture of what happened is becoming clear. If you had anything to do with this, you should tell me." If John responds by saying something like, "You mean, did I do this?" accompanied by one or a number of the non-verbal behaviours referred to in method 1 above, this is thought to be characteristic of guilt. In contrast, if John gives a firm response such as, "I had nothing to do with this!" this is believed to be more consistent with innocence.

- *"John, why do you think someone would do this to Jane?"* If John hesitates, repeats the question, or offers an explanation such as, "Well, I never thought about it," in conjunction with one or a number of the non-verbal behaviours described in method 1, this is believed to be characteristic of guilt. Conversely, if John says without hesitation, " I have no idea why anyone would do this" while maintaining eye contact and leaning forward, this is thought to be more consistent with innocence.

- *"John, who do you think might have done something like this to Jane?"* It is believed that a guilty suspect will not indicate suspicion about anyone else, despite repeated efforts by the investigator to have him do so. This stands in contrast to an innocent suspect, who, after some persuasion, may offer his or her suspicions even if they are based on very little.

3. *Use of baiting questions and dealing with an alibi.* The use of "baiting questions" during the behavioural analysis phase involves asking the suspect a non-accusatory question designed to suggest that evidence exists that implicates the suspect in the offence under investigation. Baiting questions are to be used only after the suspect has made a specific denial. Their purpose is to induce a deceptive suspect to change, or at least to think about changing, a previous denial of guilt.

   For example: "John, is there any reason that you can think of why your car was seen at the same plaza as the bank that was robbed?" Before John can answer the question, the investigator is advised to interject by saying something like, "Look, I am not actually accusing you of anything; maybe you just stopped by at the variety store in the plaza to buy some cigarettes?" If John is innocent and was not there when the bank was robbed, it is believed that he will emphatically deny that his car was anywhere near the plaza. If, on the other hand, John is guilty, it is believed that he will hesitate to answer while he thinks about the possibility that someone could have seen his car near the bank and, if that is possible, he will have to decide whether to offer an explanation or devise a lie.

   In asking questions, investigators must be careful to stick to those that suggest the *possibility* that something happened, as opposed to ones that state a specific circumstance. For example, if John did rob the bank and his car was at the plaza, but he parked around back in the loading area, and the investigator said, "John we have a surveillance photograph of your car parked directly in front of the Hasty Market in the same plaza as the bank. Can you explain how that happened?," John can truthfully deny the possibility of such a photograph because he knows that he entered the plaza using a back road and never drove around to the front parking lot.

   Despite maintaining that the best way to deal with an alibi is through actual investigation, Reid states that there are times when this is not feasible or possible, and in those cases the investigator must rely on interrogation methods alone (Inbau, Reid, & Buckley, 1986, p. 73). These methods include dealing with a general alibi by having the suspect relate all of his or her activities during the period covered by the alibi (that is, list specific times, routes, locations) or by having the suspect list all of his or her activities before, during, and after the alibi period. It is believed that a deceitful suspect will be caught up in the details and unable to give a consistent, complete account of the alibi period. Alternatively, it is believed that a deceitful suspect's memory for the before and after periods will seem to be unusually good, while that for the alibi period will appear unusually poor.

The Nine Steps of Interrogation

If, based on the BAI, an investigator concludes that the suspect is guilty of the offence under investigation, he or she can proceed to the interrogation phase, which consists of nine distinct steps designed to raise a suspect's anxiety level while simultaneously decreasing the perceived consequences of confessing (Inbau, Reid, & Buckley, 1986, p. 332; Leo, 2008, p. 113). The steps are described below.

1. *Direct positive confrontation.* In this step, the interrogator directly confronts the suspect by stating that he or she is believed to be the person who is responsible for the offence under investigation. For example: "John, there is no doubt in my mind that you are responsible for the robbery of the Lucky Gas Mart." The interrogator is advised to observe the suspect's verbal and non-verbal responses to this direct statement. Regardless of the suspect's response, the interrogator will then offer a reason why it's important for the suspect to tell the truth. This is referred to as a transition statement, which will introduce the interrogation theme.

2. *Theme development.* In this step, the interrogator offers a possible reason, or excuse, for the commission of the crime; this involves shifting the blame to another person (victim or accomplice) or circumstance (such as an urgent need by the suspect for money to provide for his family). For example: "John, I know you recently lost your job, and I know how hard it is to provide for a family these days. Is that why you robbed the Lucky Gas Mart? You didn't do it for yourself, John, did you? You did it for your family, didn't you. I am a father, I understand that."

    If the suspect appears to listen to or be considering the suggested **theme**, this is believed to be indicative of guilt. If, on the other hand, he strongly rejects the suggestion, this is thought to be more indicative of innocence.

3. *Handling denials.* A suspect, whether guilty or innocent, can be expected to offer denials during the theme development phase of the interrogation. Step three involves discouraging the suspect from repeating or elaborating on such denials, and directing the suspect back to the moral excuse theme that he or she was offered during step two. For example: "John (*interrogator raises his hand, palm outward, in a "stop" gesture toward the suspect*), we are not going to go there. It is not a question of *if* you did it. I know you robbed the Lucky Gas Mart; that has already been established. What I am trying to figure out now is why it happened."

theme a technique used in the Reid method to provide a "moral excuse" to the suspect for their commission of the offence or to minimize the moral implications of their conduct

Suspects who react strongly to the interrogator's attempts to prevent them from voicing their denials and who attempt to take control of the interrogation to repeat them, are thought to be innocent. In contrast, a guilty person will normally stop repeating the denial, or their denial will become progressively less forceful as the interrogator directs them back to the earlier theme.

4. *Overcoming objections.* This step involves dealing with a suspect's "secondary line of defence" following the denial phase. This is where a suspect offers reasons—often moral, economic, or religious—why he or she "would not" or "could not" have committed the offence. For example: "Officer, I am a churchgoing, family man. I am not the kind of guy that would steal anything, let alone rob a gas mart. I just couldn't do that sort of thing."

   It is thought that, typically, only a guilty person offers these sorts of excuses, especially when they follow the denial phase. These statements are thought to be significant because they are "less bold" than an outright denial and therefore trigger less internal anxiety in the suspect. As in stage three, the interrogator is advised to deal with such excuses by moving the suspect back to the theme established earlier. For example: "John, I don't want to hear any excuses about why you could not have robbed the gas mart. You did it, and we both know you did it. Now, let's get back to figuring out why you did it."

5. *Procurement and retention of suspect's attention.* After the interrogator has successfully dealt with any denials or excuses offered by the suspect and returned him or her to the theme of the interrogation, the suspect may attempt to "mentally withdraw" from, or "tune out," the interrogator. An interrogator who allows this to happen risks losing control of the process and failing to achieve his or her purpose. Useful strategies for getting and keeping a suspect's attention include moving physically closer to the suspect; touching their arm or hand; calling them by their first name; changing voice tone; and maintaining eye contact. For example: "John, are you listening to me? Do you understand what I am saying? John look at me. It is important that we deal with this matter here and now. It is important for you to listen to me when I am talking to you, John, so that we can work our way through this."

6. *Handling a suspect's passive mood.* By this stage of the interrogation the suspect is considering the possible benefits of telling the truth, which may be reflected in non-verbal behaviour (slumped in the chair, looking at the floor, looking depressed, perhaps crying). The interrogator must deal with the suspect's passive mood by concentrating on the essence of the interrogation theme and preparing the suspect for the possible alternatives that will be presented to him in the next step. In step two, the interrogator offered a general reason and excuse to John for robbing the gas mart; in step six, the interrogator must develop this theme by focusing on the key reason for the robbery. For example: "John, in this economy it's hard to pay your bills and put food on the table. The money at the gas mart was just

sitting there in an open cash drawer. The cashier was lazy; he didn't put the money in the safe where it should have been. You could see the money and you couldn't ignore it. The money seemed to be the solution to your problems, John. You were in a very difficult position. You had to do something, John. You had to feed your kids. You told the cashier that you had a weapon, and you told him to give you all the money from the cash drawer because it seemed to be the only solution to a terrible situation."

The interrogator must continue to monitor the suspect's behaviour during this step and to display sympathy and understanding while continually urging the suspect to tell the truth for his or her own good and for the sake of everyone concerned. The interrogator must be careful here to speak only in generalities, to make no threats, or offer any inducements.

7. *Presenting an alternative question.* In this step, the interrogator puts what is called an "alternative question" to the suspect. The alternative question technique requires that the suspect choose between two scenarios, one of which is presented as being more "acceptable" than the other, but both of which are inculpatory. This offers the suspect a way of saving face and begins to "smooth the way" toward the suspect telling the interrogator the truth. For example: "John, did you plan the robbery? Or did it just happen when you saw the money sitting there in the open?" When the suspect chooses one of the two alternative questions, he has, in effect, made an admission, thus incriminating himself, which is a critical step toward obtaining a full confession.

8. *Having the suspect orally relate various details of the offence.* The objective in this step is to develop the admission made in the previous step. As soon as the suspect has chosen one of the alternative questions, the interrogator must immediately reinforce the suspect's choice (for example, "Good, John, that's what I thought"), and then have the suspect commit himself to his choice by discussing the details of the crime ("Now tell me what happened next"). The interrogator must encourage the suspect to describe the various details of the offence, which will ultimately be required to establish his legal guilt. Continuing with our example, such details can include exactly what John did with the money, if he actually had a weapon during the robbery, and, if so, what kind of weapon it was and what he did with it.

9. *Converting an oral confession into a written confession.* In this step, the suspect's "oral confession" from the previous step is converted into a written confession. (See the discussion of Reid's position on recording confessions, below.)

Research and Criticisms

Criticisms of the Reid technique fall into four basic categories: (1) what some consider the lack of evidence showing the effectiveness of Reid; (2) the potential of the Reid technique to produce false confessions; (3) the validity of the BAI; and (4) Reid's advice, traditionally, not to electronically record interviews or interrogations (which, as discussed in Chapter 3, Interviewing Suspects I: Legal Issues and Preparation, is not an acceptable practice in Canada).

Researchers have conducted various studies into the effectiveness of the Reid method and some of the specific techniques on which it relies. While some have come out in support of the method, others appear to cast doubt on its claims. Reid itself claims that an experienced investigator using its method can achieve a success rate as high as 80 percent in obtaining confessions (Inbau et al., 2001, p. 364), and cites studies that point to the superior ability of Reid employees to detect deception (for example, Horvath & Jayne, 1994) as well as others that show high rates of success in detecting deception among a group of individuals trained by a Reid instructor (for example, Blair & McCamey, 2002). Critics, on the other hand, claim that many of the studies on which Reid relies to support its position were not conducted properly and therefore the seemingly favourable results do not present an accurate picture (for example, Vrij, 2008). Furthermore, they suggest that the lack of empirical support for key components of the Reid method, such as the non-verbal model of deception detection, could lead to investigators who use the Reid method being challenged in court (Blair & Kooi, 2004). While a detailed examination of this debate is outside the scope of this text, interested readers may consult the sources listed under the Further Reading heading at the end of this chapter.

Some critics of Reid have pointed to the fact that some aspects of the technique are consistent with risk factors for false confessions. The most common strategies for obtaining a confession fall into two categories: minimization techniques and maximization techniques (Kassin & McNall, 1991). **Minimization** strategies seek to minimize the seriousness of the offence and the perceived consequences of confessing; according to some (for example, Leo et al., 2006), the use of interrogation techniques that imply a promise of leniency in exchange for a confession is the primary cause of false confessions. Minimization techniques involve gaining the suspect's trust by appearing sympathetic and understanding and offering the suspect face-saving excuses (Russano et al., 2005). The investigator might suggest that "Anyone else in the same circumstances might have done the same thing," or that "Everyone makes mistakes." In the example above of John robbing the gas mart, the investigator suggested that John committed the crime for his family, to put food on the table. Whatever excuse the investigator uses, the effect is to suggest to the suspect that his or her actions are somehow less morally blameworthy than they really are because they were the result of some external factor—for example, peer pressure, an accomplice, an accident, spontaneity, or hard times—and thus "not really" the suspect's fault.

minimization interrogation strategy that seeks to minimize the seriousness of an offence and the perceived consequences of confessing

Maximization strategies are essentially scare tactics intended to intimidate suspects by confronting them with unequivocal accusations of their guilt, refusing to listen to denials of responsibility or claims of innocence, presenting fabricated evidence to support the investigator's claim of the suspect's guilt, and exaggerating the seriousness of the offence and the possible consequences of a conviction (Russano et al., 2005). Minimization and maximization techniques are designed to work together to alter a suspect's perception of his or her crime and of the consequences of confessing. Examples of minimization and maximization strategies are found in several of Reid's nine steps of interrogation, including step 1 (direct positive confrontation), step 3 (handling denials), and step 4 (overcoming objections). They

maximization an interrogation strategy that seeks to maximize the seriousness of an offence, exaggerate the strength of the evidence against a suspect, and exaggerate the possible consequences of a conviction

Implications of False Confessions

A false confession has a number of implications for the criminal justice system. It connects an innocent person to a crime that he or she did not commit and expends police resources on the investigation of that person while the actual suspect remains free. It sets in motion a series of "confirmatory biases" that affect the way in which police interpret all other evidence in the case. It can result in the investigation of alternative suspects being called off. And it can lead to ignoring evidence that might prove the false confessor's innocence (Leo et al., 2006).

A false confession has a profound effect on a person's experience in the court system. Leo & Ofshe (1998) found that 73 percent of false confessors whose cases went to trial were wrongfully convicted. Scholars who have studied the impact of a confession on a person's experience in the criminal justice system have found that confession evidence is uniquely potent in its impact and a person who confesses is treated more harshly at every stage of the investigative and trial process. They are more likely to be charged, held in custody prior to trial, pressured to plead guilty, and convicted (Leo et al., 2006).

may be more or less prominent depending on how investigators are applying the Reid method.

Because minimization and maximization techniques are designed to get suspects to confess, they are useful when interrogating suspects who are in fact guilty; however, they can be dangerous in cases where innocent suspects are being interrogated. Although one of Reid's presumptions is that, as a result of the BAI, only guilty suspects will be interrogated, in practice this is not always what happens. Investigators, of course, do not always correctly determine guilt as a result of using the BAI. The effects of emotionally charged, suggestive questioning can be devastating on innocent suspects, as the inquiry into the high-profile wrongful conviction case of Thomas Sophonow demonstrates. The inquiry revealed that the interviewers employed techniques designed to break Sophonow's will so that he would confess, and Sophonow himself testified that the interviewers succeeded in taking his will from him (Sophonow Inquiry, 2001).

Because only suspects whom the investigator is reasonably certain are guilty should be interrogated, in order to make a determination regarding guilt, Reid stresses the need to spend as much time as possible "investigating before interrogating"—that is, gathering information, both prior to and during the initial interview phase, about the offence itself, the suspect or suspects, and the victim or victims (Inbau, Reid, & Buckley, 1986, p. 10). As a tool that plays a critical role in this determination, it is extremely important that the BAI be *effective*. While Reid points to studies that indicate the ability of those using the BAI to detect deception at high rates (for example, Horvath & Jayne, 1994; Blair & McCamey, 2002), critics maintain that the BAI is a tool of questionable validity and point to other studies that support their position. The indicators of deception used in the BAI are based on the idea that liars experience more stress than truth tellers, which exhibits itself in easily recognizable indicators of deception. Deception research, however, indicates that the phenomenon of lying is far more complex than this theory suggests (see the detailed discussion in Chapter 5, Detecting Deception). With respect to a suspect's non-verbal behaviour, Reid maintains that liars are more likely to look away, shift in their chairs, cross their legs, or make grooming gestures; however, recent empirical research suggests that this is simply *not* true. As a result of his own studies and analyses of studies conducted by others, Vrij (2008) has concluded that liars tend to move *less* than truth tellers and that eye contact is simply *not* related to deception. In addition, Vrij found little support for the assumptions that underlie the 15 BAI questions. Other studies have found the success rate of officers who used the BAI criteria to determine whether videotaped suspects were telling the truth or lying to be 51 percent—essentially equivalent to chance (Vrij, Mann, Kristen, & Fisher, 2007)—and that observers who were trained to look for the cues of discomfort that Reid maintains are indicative of deceit were less accurate than observers who had received no training at all in the detection of deception (Kassin & Fong, 1999).

The criticism of Reid with respect to creating an electronic record was more relevant in the past than it is today. Traditionally, Reid maintained that creating an electronic record places too great a burden on police and prosecutors; results in confessions being excluded for technical reasons; and, most important, destroys the atmosphere of privacy necessary to effectively elicit confessions (Inbau, Reid, Buckley, & Jayne 2004, pp. 396-397; Inbau, Reid, Buckley, & Jayne, 2005, chap. 18). For these reasons, Reid advised investigators to convert verbal confessions obtained during non-recorded interrogations into written ones.

In the United States, unlike Canada, the situation with respect to the mandatory recording of interviews and interrogations is somewhat unsettled; certain departments are mandated by law to electronically record interviews and interrogations, and some states have moved to make the recording of interrogations mandatory. However, this requirement does not apply to all or even the majority of investigators across the country. Reid's text *Electronic Recording of Interrogations* (Buckley & Jayne, 2005) addresses the issue for those investigators who must record interviews and interrogations, discussing the benefits and liabilities of doing so, in an American context. Investigators who choose to use the Reid method in Canada *must* ensure that they make every effort to create a complete electronic record of all of their interviews, as we discussed in Chapter 3.

Canadian Courts on the Use of Reid

A number of Canadian court cases have considered the effect of the use of Reid on the admissibility of confession evidence. In some cases, the use of Reid was deemed perfectly acceptable, while in others it was deemed objectionable in the particular circumstances. Given the guidelines in *Oickle* (2000), directing courts to consider the use of Reid, or any questioning approach, in the context of the circumstances particular to each individual case, these results are not surprising.

In *R v. M.J.S.* (2000), decided shortly before *Oickle*, the court ruled that Reid was used to psychologically manipulate the suspect, break his will to resist manipulative suggestions, and cause him to doubt his own memory of the events. As a result, the suspect's statement was ruled inadmissible.

In the cases since *Oickle*, the courts are clearly arrayed along a spectrum with respect to their opinions on the use of Reid and its impact on the admissibility of confession evidence. Some have alluded to the balance that must be struck between individual rights and society's interests in fighting crime. In *R v. L.F.* (2006), the Ontario Superior Court stated that Reid "is not inherently objectionable" and that "the police must be afforded the necessary latitude to perform their responsibilities to society," whereas in *R v. Brinsmead* (2006) the court said that "while the use of [Reid] is not objectionable *per se*, a Court must be extremely vigilant in evaluating the statements that result from the use of these techniques."

Some courts have simply adopted the *Oickle* decision (*R v. Collins*, 2008), while others have conducted more detailed analyses of the impact of Reid in context. In one case (*R v. Minde*, 2003), the court found that the use of deceit, moral and spiritual inducements, and minimization techniques, coupled with the absence of food or refreshment for a number of hours, "created an atmosphere in which the accused had to trade admissions in order to extract himself from the more serious consequences of a murder charge." The court in *R v. Cruz* (2008) looked at earlier cases in which the use of Reid was found to be objectionable (*R v. Minde*, 2003; *R v. M.J.S.*, 2000), but considered them to be simply examples of situations in which Reid contributed to suspect statements being ruled inadmissible. According to the court, *any* police interviewing strategy can result in involuntary statements, and it would be an error—and contrary to the *Oickle* decision—to start with a principle that any use of Reid automatically leads to the exclusion of the statement obtained.

Some courts have recognized the use of certain aspects of Reid, even where it has not been referred to by name. The Court in *R v. Barges* (2005) said that, while Reid had not been specifically identified, it was clear that it had been used and that "[t]he technique as used in this case is objectionable in that where anything is said by the accused, he is often not allowed to finish it, as it appears to be the police perception that he is going to deny, or where he does say something, it is difficult to say what, if any, parts of the preceding monologue he is responding to."

In *R v. Amos* (2009), Reid *was* identified by name, and although it was clear that the investigator had used some features of Reid while questioning the suspect—including positive confrontation, minimization, alternative questions, and deceit—in this case the court had little criticism of the questioning techniques that were used. With respect to the use of deceit, the court said simply that "police must be permitted to outsmart criminals" and the community would not be shocked by this. The court eventually ruled that the suspect's statement was inadmissible, not because of the questioning approach but because of the investigator's failure to properly caution the suspect upon detention.

PEACE model a best practice approach to interviewing victims, witnesses, and suspects developed by police, academics, and lawyers in the United Kingdom during the 1990s that focuses on eliciting the maximum amount of information from a subject and, in the case of a suspect, using that information to challenge inconsistencies between the suspect's account of events and the totality of the evidence

THE PEACE MODEL

Whereas Reid uses deception detection and persuasion processes in an attempt to identify guilty suspects and elicit a confession from them, the **PEACE model** seeks to elicit the maximum amount of information from the suspect in order to use it, along with all the other information gathered during the investigation, to challenge the suspect to explain any inconsistencies that may exist between his or her account of events and the account based on the totality of the evidence. The name "PEACE" is a mnemonic device whose letters stand for the four stages of the model: (1) preparation and planning, (2) engage and explain, (3) account, and (4) closure and evaluation. Although the primary goal of PEACE is not to elicit confessions and admissions from suspects, by following this process PEACE is often successful in doing so. Proponents of the model point to research that indicates that the PEACE model reduces the chances of false confessions and wrongful convictions while being no less effective at eliciting confessions than more persuasive suspect questioning approaches (Snook et al., 2010). In addition, because PEACE does not involve persuasive questioning techniques, false confessions are less likely; the statements produced are therefore more likely to be ruled admissible.

The PEACE model originated in Britain in 1992 following a review, in the 1970s and '80s, of police investigative practices and an examination of the interviewing techniques used by police to elicit confessions. The review found that police questioning approaches involved highly persuasive, manipulative techniques that contributed to wrongful convictions (Milne & Bull, 1999). Following a decade of collaboration between police, academics, and lawyers, the PEACE model emerged. Today, PEACE has been widely adopted in the United Kingdom as a best-practice model for conducting interviews with suspects, victims, and witnesses and is also used in Norway and New Zealand. The four stages of the model are explored in more detail immediately below.

Stages

The following description of the four stages is adapted from Shepherd (2007) and Snook et al. (2010).

Preparation and Planning

In this stage, the interviewer considers how the information obtained from an interview will contribute to the larger, ongoing investigation. The investigator prepares for the interview by learning about the interview subject, making a list of investigative objectives, and making the practical arrangements necessary for conducting the interview. Time is spent developing a timeline of events related to the offence under investigation; preparing a questioning plan based on a review of the existing evidence; creating an outline of how the interview should proceed; and planning for different interview contingencies, such as a suspect who invokes their right to silence and refuses to participate in an interview.

Engage and Explain

In this two-part stage, the interviewer first engages the subject in conversation and then explains what will happen during the interview. In an attempt to establish rapport, the interviewer engages the subject by being personable and professional. The interviewer ensures that the subject understands the purpose of the interview, gives any requisite police cautions in a manner that ensures the subject understands his or her legal rights, and identifies any exhibits that may be referred to in the interview.

The interviewer also explains how the interview is expected to progress and outlines any expectations and ground rules that will be followed. In the case of a witness, this involves telling the witness that they have information that the interviewer requires and will therefore play a central role in the interview; in the case of a suspect, it involves telling the suspect that you, the interviewer, have an open mind, are trying to build a complete and truthful account of the event, and are willing to listen objectively to what the suspect has to say.

Account

How the investigator obtains the interview subject's account of an event depends on whether the subject is cooperative. In the case of cooperative subjects, the enhanced cognitive interview is used (Fisher & Geiselman, 1992). For uncooperative subjects, the conversation management (CM) technique, discussed below, is used (Shepherd, 2007). Regardless of which interview technique is used, the interviewer employs the same general "account" framework, which consists of three substages:

1. *An uninterrupted account.* This involves initially asking open-ended questions that give the subject an opportunity to provide an uninterrupted, or free narrative, account of the event. The open-ended questions are intended to elicit as much information as possible from which the interviewer can identify points of interest to be explored further for accuracy and reliability.

   In this substage, the interviewer should:

   • let the subject do most of the talking, encourage the subject to continue talking, and ask for as much detail as possible;

   • listen carefully and pay attention;

   • give the subject time to listen to, understand, and respond to each question; and

   • help the subject remember by suggesting, for example, "take your mind back to ..." and then giving the subject time to search his or her memory.

   In this substage, the interviewer should *not* interrupt, rush to fill silences, or talk too much. Every question or comment should have a specific purpose.

2. *Clarification.* Clarification of the uninterrupted account (also referred to as a free narrative account) is achieved systematically by asking more open-ended questions (using phrases like "tell me more about ... ," "explain how ... ," "describe what ... ," and so on), in order to explore the accuracy and reliability of the points that were raised during the uninterrupted account.

3. *Challenge.* The challenge stage involves the interviewer asking probing questions (using the familiar who, what, when, where, and how format), then summarizing all the information that has been gathered from the interview on a particular topic. If the subject (either a suspect or a witness) gives an account of an event that is itself inconsistent, or is inconsistent with the evidence or information known to the interviewer, then the subject's account is "challenged" and the subject is requested to explain the inconsistencies. Rather than challenging in an aggressive fashion, the

investigator presents the challenge as an opportunity for the suspect to explain and clarify the discrepancy. The interviewer challenges the suspect on all of the identified discrepancies and inconsistencies.

The above three-substage process is repeated until all the topics that were identified in the subject's free narrative account have been thoroughly examined. The interviewer uses the same three-substage process to question the interviewee about topics that formed part of the interview plan prepared beforehand, but which the subject did not touch on during the initial narrative account. In the case of a suspect, the investigator must be sure to ask whether or not they committed the crime; surprisingly enough, some investigators get caught up in the interview process and forget to ask this question. If the suspect confesses to the crime, their confession should not simply be accepted at face value but should be explored for its consistency, accuracy, and reliability in the same manner as any other account a suspect might give.

Closure and Evaluation

When using the PEACE model, interviewers take a professional and courteous approach to drawing the interview to a close. They ensure that the interview objectives have been met, summarize the main points of the subject's statement, and provide the subject with the opportunity to correct or add to his or her statement. They then explain to the subject what will happen after the interview.

The investigator then considers how the information obtained in the interview fits with the information gathered in the rest of the investigation and considers the effect of any new information on the investigation overall. Interviewers are encouraged to reflect on their interview performance, and investigative supervisors give investigators feedback on their interview skills as part of their routine performance review.

Conversation Management

In the "account" section of the PEACE interview, we mentioned that the **conversation management (CM)** technique is used to interview uncooperative subjects. Uncooperative subjects include persons who remain silent or make "no comment" responses, who are hostile or evasive, or who may be lying (Milne & Bull, 1999). The technique was developed in the 1980s by psychologist Eric Shepherd as a way to facilitate a working relationship with any interviewee, be they a suspect, a witness, or a victim (as any experienced investigator knows, some suspects can be cooperative and some victims or witnesses uncooperative); to encourage a maximum disclosure of information; and to enable the interviewer to capture the maximum amount of detail (Shepherd, 2007). In the case of uncooperative witnesses, the interviewer has to take active control of the interview at an earlier stage than they would otherwise and manage it more explicitly than he or she would in the case of a cooperative subject.

CM has three core elements: reciprocity, RESPONSE, and management of conversation sequence. Each element is discussed in the sections immediately below.

conversation management (CM)   a technique used in the PEACE model to interview uncooperative subjects; developed to facilitate a working relationship with any interviewee

Reciprocity

"Reciprocity" is the idea that if we receive something from another person we must give something back in exchange. An example with which we are all familiar is when someone says "good morning" to us and we feel obliged to say something in return. In an interview with an uncooperative subject, you can invite reciprocity by simply introducing yourself, for example, by saying, "Hello I am Detective Smith, and I understand you are John Jones. I am going to grab a cup of coffee before we get going—would you like one?" Such a gesture is part of trying to form a psychological bond with the subject (similar to rapport). The subject does not have to like you, nor do you have to like the subject; the gesture is simply meant to foster feelings of mutual acceptance and respect on which a professional working relationship can be built. You are treating the subject decently in a difficult situation, which increases the chance of the subject responding to you in a similar manner, or at least decreases the subject's justification for responding to you negatively. Of course, the subject may still respond negatively, but not because of how you, the investigator, treated them in the interview room.

RESPONSE

"RESPONSE" is a mnemonic device that stands for a series of elements that are necessary to producing and maintaining a working relationship between the interviewer and the interviewee:

- respect,
- empathy,
- supportiveness,
- positiveness,
- openness,
- non-judgmental attitude,
- straightforward talk, and
- "equals" talking to each other.

As you can see from both the reciprocity and RESPONSE features of the conversation management approach, the interviewer must take the time to build a positive psychological environment conducive to dialogue; playing the "tough guy" or being verbally abusive may make for dramatic portrayals of detective work on television, but in reality they are unlikely to result in an uncooperative subject wanting to talk to you.

Management Sequence

The management sequence is the management component of CM. In the case of uncooperative interviewees, it involves the interviewer taking a more active role in directing the progress of the interview than would be the case with a cooperative subject. Management of the interview begins before the investigator enters the interview room, by ensuring that thorough preparation has taken place and by remembering that reciprocity and RESPONSE behaviours are critical to the success of the interview. Management of the interview itself involves managing the interview's course, conduct, and content (adapted from Shepherd, 2007, s. 1.4.5):

- Managing the *course* of the interview involves ensuring that it progresses through the various distinct stages (PEACE) of the process and that the objectives of each stage are achieved before moving on to the next one.

- Managing the *conduct* of the interview involves ensuring that the interviewer and the subject are both speaking to and listening to each other, and that any other people in the room (for example, another investigator or a lawyer) know what is expected of them and are not allowed to disrupt the course of the interview.

- Managing the *content* of the interview involves ensuring that the interview aims and objectives (which were established by the interviewer in the preparation phase of PEACE) are achieved by maximizing the amount of information generated on each specific topic and by noting, analyzing, and exploring that information.

For a comprehensive discussion of CM and detailed reviews of both the ECI and the PEACE model, see Shepherd, 2007.

Research and Criticisms

One of the most general criticisms of the PEACE model is that it does not involve making overt attempts to persuade suspects whom the interviewer believes are guilty to confess. However, remember that PEACE emerged as an *alternative* to accusatory questioning models that focus primarily on eliciting confessions from suspects, so such criticisms represent more of a difference in investigative philosophy than they do a criticism of the PEACE model *per se*. While it is true that PEACE

PEACE in Canada

In the light of the problems that some have identified with the Reid method, the question has been posed by some whether Reid is still appropriate for continued use by Canadian law enforcement authorities or whether an alternative model should be considered.

In 2006, retired Chief Justice of Canada Antonio Lamer submitted the results of an inquiry conducted into Newfoundland and Labrador's criminal justice system. The report provided 45 recommendations for improving the administration of justice in the province, which the government committed to implementing. One of Lamer's findings was that two recent wrongful murder convictions had resulted in part from a culture of police "tunnel vision" in the province, where police came to believe they knew who committed a crime even though they lacked sufficient evidence to support their belief. In response to the Lamer Inquiry, in 2010 the Royal Newfoundland Constabulary began delivering a two-week training program in the PEACE model to its officers, becoming the first police force to adopt the system for use in North America.

is focused on information gathering and information challenging and not on overt attempts to elicit confessions, research indicates that the number one reason that people confess is their perception of the strength of the evidence against them (Gudjonsson, 2007). Given the rough similarity in confession rates between countries that use the Reid technique and countries that use the PEACE model (see below), it appears that people's perception of the strength of the evidence against them can be influenced as effectively by using a PEACE challenge approach as by using a Reid interrogation approach.

Another criticism of the PEACE model suggests that it limits the investigator's ability to solve cases in contrast to methods like Reid. For such an assertion to be true, the solution to most cases would have to turn on an investigator's ability to successfully interrogate and secure a confession from a suspect, which it does not. In fact, research suggests that, of those things that are under police control, the factors that impact most significantly on the solution of cases include such things as the timeliness and thoroughness of the detective response, the number of detectives initially assigned to a case, thorough computer checks of all involved parties, and the number of witnesses who are located at the primary scene (Wellford & Cronin, 2000; McEwen, 2009). Moreover, if the fact that PEACE does not include an interrogation component severely limited an investigator's ability to solve cases (that is, by obtaining confessions), a significant *drop* in confession rates in Britain after PEACE was introduced might have been expected, but this did not take place; the confession rate in Britain has remained essentially unchanged since PEACE was implemented (Gudjonsson, 2007), and that rate (60 percent) does not differ greatly from the rate in countries where the Reid approach is widely used (50 percent) (King & Snook, 2009; Gudjonsson, 2007). (Because of possible variability in the way key terms are defined, direct statistical comparisons should be approached cautiously; however, it appears that they don't vary much between PEACE and non-PEACE countries and periods.)

In addition, there are no significant differences in crime clearance rates in Britain compared to the United States or Canada—another difference that might be expected. In 2006, Britain's clearance rate was 28 percent, compared to 36 percent in Canada and 32 percent in the United States (Statistics Canada, 2007; Home Office, 2008; US Department of Justice, 2006). With regard to the US Department of Justice statistics, becauses no overall clearance rate was provided in the publication, a simple (that is, non-weighted) average was determined (31.9 percent), from the seven clearance rates that were provided.

PROFESSIONAL PRACTICE AND DEVELOPMENT

Investigators must retain a healthy degree of skepticism when exercising their discretion to choose which investigative techniques to employ in their professional practice. When considering a particular technique, they should ask themselves what assumptions the technique is based on and whether its claims of effectiveness have been independently verified. Just as practitioners in other professions must stay informed about best practices in their fields of expertise, investigators must keep abreast of developments in the area of police questioning techniques and investigation. One of the ways in which such awareness can be maintained is through ongoing professional education. This should include not only practical instruction in the use of various investigative techniques, but also an examination of the theories on which they are based and a review of any research that has been conducted to determine their validity and efficacy.

Investigators are responsible for making informed choices about their professional practice and understanding the possible consequences that may flow from such choices. The choice of an unproven investigative technique can directly affect the quality of evidence that an investigator is able to gather. Additionally, investigators may be required by a court to articulate the reasons for their choice of a particular investigative technique and justify its use; in such a situation, the choices made by an investigator—and his or her ability to explain why those choices were appropriate—may have an impact on the success or failure of a case.

One of the most relevant observations to emerge from the field of interview research is that many investigators believe their interviewing skills to be significantly better than they really are, which limits their prospects for improvement (Walsh & Bull, 2010). Questioning suspects is a demanding task, regardless of which method an investigator uses. Acknowledging one's limitations, educating oneself about developments in the field, and doing the necessary preparatory work before entering the interview room will help investigators meet the challenge.

Analysis of an Interrogation: David Russell Williams

On February 7, 2010, Detective Sergeant Jim Smyth of the Ontario Provincial Police, Behavioural Sciences Unit, interrogated David Russell Williams (formerly known as Colonel Russell Williams) as part of an investigation into the disappearance of a 27-year-old Belleville woman, Jessica Lloyd. Portions of the interview, which lasted for approximately 10 hours, were shown at Williams's sentencing hearing and have been released for public viewing. As the opportunity to see videotaped confessions of serial murderers is extremely rare, it is recommended that you view the excerpts as part of your study of the material in this chapter; the excerpts may be accessed by searching for "Russell Williams confession" on YouTube (http://www.youtube.com).

One of the first observations a viewer might make regarding the Williams interview is its "gentle" nature. Unlike interrogation scenes portrayed on television and in movies, which are often characterized by intense confrontation and overt attempts at persuasion, this interrogation more closely resembles a psychotherapy session. Smyth speaks quietly to Williams, never raising his voice; he asks Williams how he can help him deal with the issues he is facing; and he remains silent over long periods, allowing Williams to consider the information that has been presented to him and to decide what, if anything, to say in response. The changes in Williams's body language, evident from the beginning of the interview (upright torso, with arms folded across his chest chewing gum, casual demeanour) to the end (torso bent forward, arms on thighs, long gaps in his response times, and so on), are worth noting. Through the process, Williams slowly folds—physically and mentally—before confessing.

While a detailed analysis of the interview footage is beyond the scope of this text—an entire book could be written on the subject—we explore several areas here because they serve as an excellent illustration of the techniques described and recommended in this text. Of course, not all interrogations will go as well as this, but students and investigators would do well to study the "textbook" examples of Smyth's use of the various techniques:

1. *Preparation.* It is evident from Smyth's knowledge of Williams and his background, the details of the offences, the evidence that has been gathered in the investigation to the present time, and the ongoing investigative activity that Smyth had done a great deal of preparation prior to the interrogation. It is also evident that effective communication had taken place—and continued to take place—between members of the investigative team.

2. *Legal rights.* With respect to his legal rights, Williams
   - is told that he is not under arrest;
   - is told that the door to the interview room is not locked, and he can leave at any time;
   - is told that he can call a lawyer at any time;
   - is told that if he wants to call a lawyer he will be taken to a private room where he may consult with a lawyer;
   - is told that everything is being recorded;
   - is told that if he does not have his own lawyer, free legal advice is available to him;
   - is asked if he wants to call a lawyer (Williams responds that he does not want to exercise this right);
   - is told what the investigation is about and informed that the criminal offences being investigated range from first degree murder to forcible confinement, sexual assault, and break and enter; and
   - is told that it is important that he understand that he does not have to talk to the police and is given both a primary and a secondary caution.

3. *Rapport building.* During the first few minutes of the interrogation, Smyth
   - asks Williams to have a seat;
   - asks if he has ever been interviewed by police before;
   - explains that everything that is discussed will be recorded;
   - explains what is going to happen in the interrogation, that the interrogation will be detailed, and that it will take some time;
   - offers to get Williams a coffee;
   - politely asks Williams to take his gum out of his mouth and thanks him for doing so;
   - talks about him giving Williams respect and expecting it in return; and
   - talks about the events under investigation being featured in the news and people being widely aware of them.

   During the interview, Smyth
   a. gently regains Williams's attention when it seems to wander: "Russell listen to me for a second" (18:08:23);
   b. asks Williams, after explaining the evidence against him: "What are *we* going to do?" (18:22:50); and
   c. maintains a low-key approach, at some points asking Williams how he can help him: "Russ, maybe this would help—can you tell me what the issue is that you are struggling with?" (18:25:33); "Russ, is there anything you want from me, anything missing, anything I can shed some light on for you?" (19:11:07).

4. *Use of silence.* Smyth's use of silence is one of the best examples in any publicly available interrogation footage. During the interrogation, there are numerous periods of silence, some in excess of a minute in length. Especially interesting is the two-minute period from 19:40 to 19:42 immediately preceding Williams's confession, which takes place approximately four and a half hours after the interrogation begins. Smyth speaks for approximately 18 seconds in total, and there is more than 100 seconds of silence.

During the two-minute period immediately prior to Williams's confession:

   a. Smyth advises Williams of the unlimited resources available to the investigation. This is followed by *31 seconds* of silence (19:40:01 to 19:40:32).

   b. Smyth advises Williams that he has done the best he can to help him understand what is going on in the investigation and its impact. This is followed by *18 seconds* of silence (19:40:52 to 19:41:10).

   c. Smyth asks Williams if the two of them can talk. Williams responds by saying that he wants to minimize the impact of what has happened on his wife, and Smyth says he would like to do the same thing. Williams asks how this can be achieved, and Smyth responds by advising Williams to tell the truth. This is followed by *29 seconds* of silence (19:41:31 to 19:42:00), after which Williams says "Okay," indicating he is going to reveal what happened.

   d. Smyth asks Williams where Jessica Lloyd's body is. This is followed by *23 seconds* of silence (19:42:03 to 19:42:26), after which Williams asks, "Got a map?" indicating that he is going to reveal the location of the body.

5. *Shaping of the subject's perception of the strength of the case against him.* During the interrogation, Smyth revealed evidence gathered during the investigation, discussed evidence that was still likely to be found, and talked about the unlimited resources behind the investigation in order to effectively shape Williams's perception of the strength of the case against him. The information he revealed included the following:

   • In terms of the investigation, the fact that there were 60 to 70 people working on the investigation, including technical experts; that every request for investigative resources would be granted; that the investigation is costing at least 10 million dollars; and that it is ongoing.

   • In terms of the evidence that had been gathered up to that point, that there was a geographical connection between Williams and the crimes; that there was a tire track match between Williams's vehicle and one found at one of the crime scenes; and that during the interrogation Williams's boot print was compared to a boot print found at one of the crime scenes and was a match.

   • In terms of the evidence that was likely to be found in the ongoing investigation, during the interrogation Smyth revealed that police were searching Williams' cottage, his vehicle, his office, and his wife's house. He emphasized that further evidence would likely be found in those locations and, additionally, that once the postmortem examination of the victim's body was complete there would likely be a DNA match with Williams.

For additional information regarding the Williams interrogation, consult the sources listed under Further Reading.

KEY TERMS

behavioural analysis interview (BAI)
conversation management (CM)
interrogation
maximization

minimization
PEACE model
Reid technique
theme

FURTHER READING

Gudjonsson. G. (2007). Investigative interviewing. In T. Newburn, T. Williamson, & A. Wright (Eds.), *Handbook of criminal investigation* (pp. 466-492). Cullompton, UK: Willan Publishing.

Inbau, F., Reid, J., Buckley, J., & Jayne, B. (2001). *Criminal interrogation and confessions* (4th ed.). Gaithersburg, MD: Aspen Publishers.

Kassin, S. (2006). A critical appraisal of modern police interrogations. In T. Williamson (Ed.), *Investigative interviewing: Rights, research, regulation* (chap. 11, pp. 207-228). Cullompton, UK: Willan Publishing.

King, L., & Snook, B. (2009). Peering inside a Canadian interrogation room: An examination of the Reid model of interrogation, influence tactics, and coercive strategies. *Criminal Justice and Behaviour, 36,* 674-694.

Shepherd, E. (2007). Investigative interviewing: The conversation management approach. Oxford: Oxford University Press.

Snook, B., Eastwood, J., Stinson, M., Tedeschini, J., & House, J. (2010). Reforming investigative interviewing in Canada, *Canadian Journal of Criminology and Criminal Justice, 52*(2), 215-229.

Vrij, A. (2008). The Behaviour Analysis Interview. In *Detecting lies and deceit: Pitfalls and opportunities* (2nd ed., chap. 7, pp. 189-200). Chichester, UK: Wiley.

Russell Williams Interrogation Materials

CBC News, The Fifth Estate. (2010, September 24). Above suspicion: The shocking case of Colonel Russell Williams. From http://www.cbc.ca/fifth/2010-2011/abovesuspicion/.

CBC News. (2010, October 22). Savvy detective praised for Williams confession. From http://www.cbc.ca/canada/story/2010/10/21/f-jim-smyth-russell-williams.html.

CBC News, The Fifth Estate. (2010, October 22). The confession: Inside the interrogation of Russell Williams. From http://www.cbc.ca/fifth/2010-2011/theconfession/.

Ontario Provincial Police. (2010, February 7). Redacted transcript of taped police interview of Russell Williams (128 pages). From http://www.cbc.ca/news/pdf/edited-williams.pdf.

REVIEW QUESTIONS

TRUE OR FALSE

____   1. The Reid technique is used exclusively for the interviewing of witnesses.

____   2. Behavioural analysis includes drawing a conclusion of the truthfulness of the statement made by an accused based on the language used in that statement.

____   3. "I'm a church-going man and not the type of person who would steal money from an old lady" is thought by Reid to be the type of response that a person who is guilty of committing the crime would offer.

____   4. If after making certain admissions during the course of an interrogation, an accused begins to withdraw mentally from the interrogator, it is suggested that the police officer conducting the interrogation move closer to the accused and perhaps touch his hand or arm. This will help regain the accused's attention.

____   5. In the "presenting an alternative question" stage of the Reid Technique, the accused should be asked to choose between two answers, one of which is inculpatory and the other exculpatory.

____   6. The Reid technique does not suggest having the accused convert an oral confession into a written confession because this may harm the relationship between the police officer and the accused.

____   7. Suggesting that any reasonable person might have acted in the same manner as did the accused is an example of a minimization interrogation strategy.

____   8. The indicators of deception used in the BAI are based on the idea that liars experience more stress than truth tellers.

____   9. The police in Canada are mandated by law to videotape and record all interrogations conducted with an accused.

____ 10. In *R v. Amos*, the courts acknowledged that the use of deceit by the police is sometimes acceptable because the police must be permitted to outsmart criminals.

MULTIPLE CHOICE

1. The interrogation phase of the Reid technique consists of nine different steps, which include
    a. direct positive confrontation, theme development, closure, and evaluation;
    b. procurement and retention of suspect's attention and handling a suspect's passive mood;
    c. engagement, explanation, and accounting;
    d. both a and c;
    e. both b and c.

2. Some critics of the Reid method have pointed to the fact that some aspects of the technique are consistent with risk factors for false confessions. The most common strategies for obtaining a confession fall into two categories:

   a. expansion and explanation;

   b. context reinstatement and suspect compatible questioning;

   c. minimization and maximization;

   d. closure and evaluation.

3. The PEACE model seeks to

   a. elicit the maximum amount of information from a suspect;

   b. use deception detection and persuasion processes;

   c. calm the suspect so they will explain their side of the story;

   d. introduce a British investigative technique to North America.

4. One of the most general criticisms of the PEACE model is that

   a. it will not work in a North American context;

   b. it does not involve making overt attempts to persuade suspects whom the interviewer believes are guilty to confess;

   c. the model's emphasis on closure and evaluation can contribute to false confession;

   d. it is not as effective as the Reid technique at detecting deception.

5. Professional investigators must retain a healthy degree of skepticism when choosing which investigative techniques to employ in their professional practice. When considering a particular technique, they should ask themselves

   a. if the technique has been in use for at least 10 years;

   b. whether the technique is used by elite investigative units;

   c. if training in the technique is offered by people who claim to be experts in the field;

   d. what assumptions the technique is based on and whether its claims of effectiveness have been independently verified.

SHORT ANSWER QUESTIONS

1. List three implications of a "false confession" for the Canadian criminal justice system.

2. How do the purposes of an "interview" and an "interrogation" differ?

3. How do the ultimate goals of the PEACE model and Reid technique differ?

4. In a 2010 article published on its website, Reid made the following comments with regard to the PEACE model:

   Essentially the PEACE Model is the initial step in The Reid Technique—a non-accusatory fact finding interview. The difference thereafter is that in the PEACE model they are not allowed to engage in the interrogation process in which the investigator attempts to persuade the suspect to tell the truth about what they did.

As a result the PEACE model severely limits the investigator's ability to solve cases.

Do you agree or disagree with this criticism of the PEACE method? Explain your answer.

Case Study

You are investigating the shooting of a known drug dealer. A suspect who was seen running from the scene of the shooting along with two other unknown males was arrested by uniformed officers and brought into the police station. The two other males escaped. When the suspect was arrested, he was searched at the scene and found to be in possession of a handgun. The suspect is 27 years old, appears to understand his legal rights, does not wish to consult legal counsel, and seems willing to talk to investigators.

1. Choose either the Reid method or the PEACE model as your questioning approach toward the suspect. Explain the ultimate goal of whichever questioning approach you choose.

2. Outline the major stages involved in the questioning approach you will use to interview the suspect.

Detecting Deception

5

INTRODUCTION

"If you didn't do anything wrong, then why are you acting so nervous?" This common question reflects a widespread but erroneous belief that nervousness under questioning is always a reflection of guilt. Paul Ekman, one of the world's leading authorities on detecting deception and the author of a popular book on the subject, *Telling Lies: Clues to Deceit in the Marketplace, Politics, and Marriage* (Ekman, 2009; originally published 1985), coined the term **Othello error** for this belief—a reference to the Shakespearean character's erroneous belief that his innocent wife's fear of being disbelieved was evidence of her guilt. The "Brokaw hazard," another term coined by Ekman, refers to a further widespread but erroneous belief based on journalist Tom Brokaw's comment that he can tell when a person is lying by his or her evasive and convoluted responses to his questions.

Ekman's work alerts us to some of the traps criminal investigators can fall into when they attempt to determine whether they are being deceived. Attempting to detect deception is something that nearly everyone has experienced. Casting a skeptical eye over the language a person uses on an Internet dating site, assessing a salesperson's claims about the virtues of his or her merchandise, or questioning a child about a broken lamp in the living room are all examples of attempts to detect deception in everyday life. But when it comes to evaluating the truthfulness of a suspect or an accused in a forensic context, "commonsense" approaches to detecting deception acquired through daily experience pose at least two problems. First, criminal investigators often have no sure way to judge whether their perceptions are correct; this is known as the "ground truth" problem. Second, the consequences of police misinterpreting an innocent

CHAPTER OBJECTIVES

After completing this chapter, you should be able to:

- Identify the most common approaches that investigators take in an attempt to determine whether someone is being truthful or deceptive.

- Explain the assumptions behind each one of the different approaches to deception detection.

- Identify the valid and invalid non-verbal behaviour (body language) clues associated with deception.

- Describe some of the potential problems associated with attempting to use non-verbal behaviour to make judgments regarding truth or deception.

- Define the term "statement analysis" and explain how statement analysis can be used in criminal investigations.

- Describe some of the different approaches to statement analysis and their respective limitations.

- Describe polygraph testing, the assumption behind it, and the different techniques that polygraph examiners use.

- Explain why the validity and reliability of polygraph testing is an issue.

Othello error the false assumption that a person who who acts nervously is necessarily attempting to cover up guilt

person's actions as those of a guilty offender are much more severe than, say, discovering that a person you met on the Internet is very different from the way they portrayed themselves online.

For the police, then, the stakes are high. Moreover, most police interviewers tend to overestimate their ability to detect deception (King & Dunn, 2010; Vrij et al., 2010), and once an investigator believes that a person is guilty, it can be very difficult to modify that belief, even in the face of potentially exonerating evidence (Leo & Drizin, 2010). So, *are* there reliable methods for detecting deception that criminal investigators can use? That's the question we consider in the remainder of this chapter. As we will see, while each approach to detecting deception has some merit, each also has inherent limitations and significant risks associated with it, which investigators need to understand.

There are two basic approaches to detecting deception:

1. those that examine a person's behaviour, and
2. those that examine a person's words.

behaviour analysis
an approach to detecting deception that focuses on observing and analyzing different aspects of a person's behaviour in an effort to determine whether the person is being truthful or deceptive

statement analysis
a blanket term for various techniques that attempt to analyze the truthfulness of recorded statements by applying formal criteria

The approaches that examine a person's behaviour fall under the general heading of **behaviour analysis** and include non-verbal behaviour analysis (analysis of, for example, facial expressions and eye and body movements), voice stress analysis, and polygraphy. The approaches that examine a person's words fall under the general heading of **statement analysis** and include statement validity analysis (SVA), reality monitoring, and scientific content analysis (SCAN).

BEHAVIOUR ANALYSIS

The idea that an investigator can make accurate judgments about whether a person is being truthful or deceptive by observing their behaviour is a widely held belief among both investigative professionals and the wider public. Perhaps the most common approach investigators take in attempting to judge a person's truthfulness is behaviour analysis. Behaviour analysis is based on the assumption that deception causes stress in the deceiver, which manifests itself in certain distinct, observable behaviours such as reduced eye blink rate; examples of behaviour analysis include the observation of body language, polygraphy, and voice stress analysis. The idea was expressed in the writings of the famous psychoanalyst Sigmund Freud (1900/1965), and it served as the premise for the television program *Lie to Me*, which premiered on the Fox network in 2009. The program features, as its prime character, investigative psychologist Dr. Cal Lightman, who is an expert at detecting deception through the observation of body language and facial "microexpressions." Dr. Lightman and his team of experts are frequently called on by the police to help solve difficult cases. The program and the character of Dr. Lightman are based on real-life university professor Paul Ekman and his many decades of research in the area of body movements and facial expressions. As a result of his research and its publicity, Ekman has become one of the world's leading authorities on the facial expression of emotion. However, as we shall see, the real-life process of trying to detect deception using behavioural clues is much more complicated than it appears on television and the results are not encouraging.

Facial Expressions

Many kinds of animals, including humans, convey a wide range of emotions and messages with their faces. Interest in this subject dates back at least to Charles Darwin and other scholars of his era. Darwin (1872) wrote a fascinating book called *The Expression of the Emotions in Man and Animals*, in which he argued that evolution accounts for the way people and other animals express how they feel. But it was Ekman (1970) who first documented the striking similarities in the facial expressions that virtually all human cultures use to convey particular emotions. Although attitudes toward the appropriateness of expressing emotions in public vary from culture to culture, the facial expressions for a wide variety of emotions—such as fear, surprise, joy, disgust, and sadness—appear to be universal and may even be exhibited by very young infants.

Let's first examine the issue of which facial expressions may indicate deception. According to the **leakage hypothesis**, involuntary physiological processes such as blood pressure, blood flow, and heart rate can betray a person's attempts to deceive when monitored by the polygraph (as we will see in more detail in the sections that follow). This notion of leakage can be extended to involuntary processes that investigators can observe with their own eyes, although some of the most potentially revealing processes are too fleeting to be detected by the unaided eye and can be seen only through the careful analysis of videotaped records.

leakage hypothesis
a theory that suggests that deception can be detected by observing the ways in which a person's physiological responses are inconsistent with his or her spoken words

One of the best examples of such processes is something called a "microexpression," an involuntary and fleeting facial movement inconsistent with what a person is consciously attempting to communicate. Microexpressions are thought typically to last less than a tenth of a second and are therefore difficult to see without the benefit of slow-motion and freeze-frame video technology. Research by Ekman and others shows that such "leaks" can take the form of smiles, frowns, eyebrow raises, and grimaces (for example, Ekman, 2009; Ekman & Friesen, 1974). Thus, for example, a distressed person trying to convey the impression that he or she feels fine can betray distress by producing a microfrown that may be picked up by an observer. However, the observation of microexpressions likely has limited practical value for investigators trying to assess the truthfulness of their subjects in real time, because they occur in only a relatively small proportion of cases, and then only in some portions of the face (Porter & ten Brinke, 2008).

For his original research, Ekman and his colleague Wallace Friesen (1974) employed an innovative procedure in which student nurses were shown videotapes of either a placid beach scene or a gory surgical procedure. The nurses were videotaped as they viewed the scenes, and were asked to describe a beach regardless of which scene they were viewing. This setup resulted in the nurses lying half the time as they tried to convince the camera that a bloody operation was in fact a peaceful beach. The student nurses were motivated to pull off the deception because they were told that a crucial aspect of their job is to convey calm when a person's life might be in peril.

The tapes of the nurses' facial expressions were then shown to research participants, who were asked to judge when the nurses were lying and when they were telling the truth; these participants performed at a rate worse than expected by chance (that is, lower than 50 percent). The reason for such poor performance, according to Ekman, was that while the nurses' facial expressions were "leaking" emotion, the research participants were "taken in" by obvious expressions of emotion (for instance, a simple smile that is not indicative of deceit), while missing more subtle cues (a particular *kind* of smile that is associated with deceit). Ekman's realization that a high degree of precision was required to detect deceit from facial expressions led him to develop the facial action coding system (FACS), which describes the precise measurement and categorization of different facial expressions (see, for example, Ekman, Friesen, & Hager, 2002); to date Ekman has identified 50 different kinds of smiles (Ekman, 2009, pp. 126-127). The now-famous tapes of the nurses' expressions have been used in many subsequent studies (for example, DePaulo, 1992; DePaulo et al., 1996).

The results of the experiment with nurses mirror those of most research on deception detection: the average person is about as accurate in detecting deceit from observing non-verbal behaviour as they would be if they just guessed—that is, about 50 percent. Interestingly, the accuracy rates of people who have been "trained" to detect deception (such as police officers) are also largely around the level of chance. Some might argue that much of the research on deception detection has taken place in laboratory settings, and that detection rates must surely be higher when real criminals attempt to lie to experienced investigators in the field. Certainly, there is some good research showing that as a person's motivation to lie increases, the ability of observers to detect his or her deception also tends to increase. In other words, as the stakes of getting caught go up, the ability to prevent "leaks" goes down (for example, DePaulo & Kirkendol, 1989; O'Sullivan, Frank, Hurley & Tiwana, 2009). So there is some merit to the argument that real-life lie-catchers might fare better than those in a laboratory. However, it appears that the differences between the deception detection results derived from research settings and real-life criminal justice settings are not as great as many people might believe (for example, King & Dunn, 2010).

First, although research settings are perhaps not as emotionally intense as criminal justice settings, the materials and procedures used in the type of research conducted in this area are often very real to the participants. And, as we have mentioned, the types of behaviour people exhibit when expressing or attempting to conceal emotions are similar across individuals and situations. In addition, there is some research evidence showing that while deception detection performance for real police officers in realistic settings can be somewhat *better* than for laypeople in the laboratory, the difference is not as great as many would expect (perhaps about 65 percent compared to about 50 percent; see Mann, Vrij, & Bull, 2004).

Second, although it remains a heated debate, there is little research to suggest that some individuals—whether through intuition, experience, or training—are significantly better than others at detecting deception (Bond Jr. & Uysal, 2007; Vrij, 2008; Stromwall & Granhag, 2002; Aamondt & Custer, 2006; DePaulo & Pfeifer, 1986). Most people appear to hover around a 50 to 65 percent accuracy rate, although a few studies identify groups who appear to perform better than most (Ekman & O'Sullivan, 1991; O'Sullivan & Ekman, 2004; O'Sullivan et al., 2009). For these individuals, O'Sullivan and her colleagues use the term "lie detection wizards," the most famous of whom are some US secret service agents from one of their studies, but, as mentioned, there is significant debate as to whether or not

Factors Affecting Deception Detection Success Rates

When trying to determine just how successful people are at detecting deception, we must consider something known as the **base rate**—in this case, the proportion of people in a particular context who are actually lying—because it plays a major role in such an analysis. Of course, police don't interrogate people at random, but usually have some basis to suspect that a person is involved in a crime—for example, their criminal history, physical evidence, their presence at the crime scene, telling conflicting stories, or evading police. If we assume for the sake of argument, therefore, that after some extensive investigation the majority of people whom investigators end up suspecting of committing a crime are in fact guilty, any deception detection strategy that results in more "lying" conclusions than "telling the truth" conclusions will appear more "successful" at detecting deceivers than a strategy that produces a bias in the other direction. In another context, suppose that the correct answer for 75 percent of the questions on a true/false exam in a college course is "true." If a student were to arbitrarily answer "true" for every question, he or she would get 75 percent on the exam, without necessarily knowing anything about the material. This issue is especially relevant for determining the accuracy of the polygraph, discussed later in this chapter.

A further danger in the criminal context is that as investigators' beliefs about the base rate of deception in the population of questioned suspects goes up, the probability of them wrongly deeming an innocent person guilty (referred to as a **false positive** or **Type 1 error**) also rises. For example, an investigator who concludes that a person is being deceptive when, in fact, he or she is not, has made a positive judgment that deceit exists when it does not. And if such mistakes go undetected, investigators' impressions of their own ability to detect deception will not be adjusted to reflect reality. Furthermore, as time passes, most of us are more likely to remember our successes than our failures, which partially explains the human tendency to be overly confident in many of our abilities, including how well we can detect deception. So, for these and other reasons discussed in this chapter, we must be careful when talking about how "successful" any particular person or group is at the complex task of detecting deception.

base rate   the incidence of a particular behaviour or characteristic in a population

false positive   refers to a situation in which an observer mistakenly believes that a condition is present when, in fact, it is not

Type 1 error   *see* false positive

this might be an artifact of the way the research findings were analyzed. There is also some research suggesting that people who have received training in deception detection display increased confidence in their abilities, yet perform no better—and in some cases worse—than those who have received no training (Vrij, 2008; Granhag & Stromwall, 2004; Mann, Vrij, & Bull, 2004; Kassin & Fong, 1999). This is presumably a result of the fact that much of the available and popular training teaches people to look for stereotypical—but invalid—clues to deception, because when training programs address common myths and educate their students about the findings of deception research, they are able to improve student performance (Porter, Woodworth, & Birt, 2000).

Eye Movements and Neurolinguistic Programming

Other types of facial movements have received considerable attention in criminal investigation circles, and there are some who believe that eye movements in particular can reliably indicate deception. This idea is based on a concept called **neurolinguistic programming (NLP)**, which originated in the 1970s. NLP was developed by Richard Bandler and John Grinder, who wrote about it in self-help books and promoted it as a tool to facilitate communication in a variety of settings (Bandler & Grinder, 1979). It is based on essentially two notions: (1) that different people interpret the world through different sensory categories, and (2) that eye movements are indicative of particular brain processes. The first notion incorporates the idea that some people are alleged to be primarily visual and tend to use phrases such as "I *see* where you're coming from." Other people are alleged to be primarily auditory and use phrases such as "I *hear* what you're saying"; still others are alleged to be primarily tactile and say things such as "I *feel* your pain." Some research suggests that therapists and others can modestly improve their communication skills by being alert to this aspect of a person's conversational style and responding in a like manner.

The two NLP claims that have attracted the most attention from investigators are (1) that NLP techniques (such as pacing and mirroring) can be used to unconsciously develop a strong rapport with another person, and (2) that NLP can enable someone to read and understand another person's mental processes by paying attention to the types of words they use and by watching their eye movements.

With respect to claims that the use of NLP techniques will allow one to covertly build a strong rapport with another person, almost none of the existing studies have found that the use of such techniques confers any significant advantage over more traditional techniques, such as attentive listening (Borum, 2006).

Many criminal investigators have focused their attention on the NLP notion that distinct areas of the brain are associated with distinct types of brain activity, and that our eyes tend to move in the direction of those parts of the brain that are active at the moment. Some investigative trainers maintain that an interrogator can determine how a person is accessing their brain while they respond to certain questions, and can therefore determine whether the person is recalling or, instead, creating an experience (see, for example, Zulawsksi & Wicklander, 1993, p. 155). It is alleged, for example, that because the right side of a right-handed person's brain is primarily responsible for creative thought, when such a person is using his or her imagination to create a lie, the eyes will shift to the right. By the same token, the eyes will allegedly shift to the left when a right-handed person is accessing a genuine memory, as memories are allegedly stored on the left side of the brain. (Despite the fact that many of the claims of NLP are not supported by research, there are some grains of truth to it: the brain *is* divided into two hemispheres, and different areas of the brain do control particular mental and physical processes. However, it does not follow from this that particular eye movements are necessarily indicative of specific types of brain activity, such as recalling a memory.)

In summary, although many experienced criminal investigators are supporters of NLP, the "preponderance of empirical research ... has failed to produce strong evidence for the existence of primary representational systems or for the claimed associations between eye movement patterns and internal mental processing"

---

neurolinguistic programming (NLP) a theory that holds, among other things, that eye movements can indicate deception

(Borum, 2006, p. 27). As well, existing research does not support the hypothesis that eye movements are correlated with deception (for example, Vrij & Lochun, 1997). In the words of Aldert Vrij (2004, p. 313), one of the world's leading authorities on detecting deception, "NLP teachers who claim the opposite therefore are engaged in deceiving their pupils."

Gaze Aversion

There is perhaps no single behaviour that is more frequently mentioned in connection with the detection of deception than the avoidance of eye contact, known as **gaze aversion**. However, scientific research on eye contact and deception indicates that there is no evidence that people avoid eye contact when lying (for example, Sporer & Schwandt, 2007; Vrij, 2004, p. 296; Vrij, 2008, p. 60; Hazlett, 2006).

One problem with the notion that eye contact and deception are linked is that some people naturally tend to avoid eye contact, either because they are shy or feel intimidated, or because eye contact is considered inappropriate (at least in some situations) in their culture. Second, although a person who looks away might be concocting a lie, he or she might also be genuinely attempting to access a memory. Third, some research shows that some accomplished liars consciously maintain eye contact because they are aware that people associate such behaviour with honesty. In summary, investigators must be aware that the current scientific research does not support the notion that one can make reliable judgments about truth or deception by observing eye contact.

gaze aversion in the deception detection literature, refers to the avoidance of eye contact, which is perhaps the most frequently cited non-verbal behaviour commonly thought to be indicative of deception

Body Movements

After eye contact, perhaps the most frequently mentioned behaviour that is believed to be associated with deception is body movement. Individual body movements—for example, foot shaking, hand movement and gestures, grooming activity (such as "lint picking"), or an increase in overall body movement—are frequently cited as cues to deception (for example, Walters, 1996). While body movements may indicate deception, insofar as the anxiety they express may be the result of an attempt to conceal the truth, people can be anxious, and express that anxiety through body movements, for a variety of reasons; in addition, some people are just naturally "fidgety."

Not surprising, but contrary to popular belief about body movements and deception, research indicates that increased body movement (fidgeting) is *not* a reliable indicator of deception. If anything, liars tend to move *less* than truth tellers, not more (Vrij, 2008; Hazlett, 2006; Granhag & Stromwall, 2004; Sporer & Schwandt, 2007). They exhibit fewer arm, hand, finger, leg, and foot movements and use fewer illustrators—that is, hand movements designed to augment what is being spoken, sometimes referred to as "speaking with your hands." However, a sudden change in body movements in response to specific questions or accusations, while not indicative of deception, might be something an investigator will want to explore further in an attempt to determine what is behind the change.

Voice Stress Analysis

As we have seen with some of the other behaviour analysis approaches mentioned above, one must be careful when it comes to using them to detect deceit. Analyzing vocal behaviours in an attempt to detect deception shares the same assumptions as other behavioural analysis approaches, which is that a deceitful person experiences more stress than a truthful one and that stress manifests itself in the form of an observable behaviour.

One of the problems with these assumptions is that some people just naturally exhibit traits that indicate deception in other people. So while it is true that accelerated speech is often associated with lying because it accompanies anxiety, the association is not inevitable. And although pitch does tend to increase when people lie (DePaulo et al., 2003; Granhag & Stromwall, 2004; Vrij, 2008), the stress that an innocent person experiences when trying to convince other people of his or her truthfulness can produce the same result (the Othello error, referred to at the outset of this chapter). Research indicates that despite the claims of accuracy put forward by some individuals who manufacture "voice stress analyzers," this approach to deception detection produces results that are essentially equivalent to chance and cannot therefore be recommended as a reliable approach to separate liars from the truthful (National Research Council (NRC), 2003, pp. 166-168).

Polygraphy

polygraph   an electronic device used to measure the body's physiological responses to questioning

polygrapher   an expert in the administration and analysis of polygraph examinations

The **polygraph** (sometimes called a "lie detector") is used by law enforcement agencies, military organizations, and private corporations around the world. As most people know, it is a machine that records a person's physiological responses to questions posed by a polygraph examiner known as a **polygrapher** (pol-*ig*-ruffer). The *graph* in "polygraph" is from the Greek for "writes"—as in "writing" or recording the physiological responses—and *poly* is from the Greek for "many"—as in the many kinds of responses that the device records. The most commonly measured processes include heart rate, respiration, blood pressure, and galvanic skin response (how much perspiration is on the skin and, therefore, how well it conducts electricity). Other processes can also be measured, such as blood volume and sphincter muscle tension. At one time, an analog device that moved ink-tipped needles across a moving roll of paper was used, but the most common tool now is a digital device that displays the same information on a computer screen and saves the examination results to computer memory for evaluation by a polygrapher.

In Canada, polygraph test results are not admissible as evidence in court (*R v. Béland*, 1987); however, the interview conducted by the polygrapher with the subject is potentially admissible. A polygraph examination can be conducted as part of a police investigation, but only where the examinee willingly submits to the procedure.

As it does for the other deception detection techniques, the leakage hypothesis forms the basis of polygraph testing, the assumption being that a guilty person will betray his or her guilt through measurable changes in physiological processes over which people have little or no conscious control. In other words, if a person knows that he or she is guilty, the assumption is that that knowledge is going to leak out.

One often overlooked aspect of polygraph testing bears a striking similarity to how a cognitive interview is conducted. Virtually every polygrapher will tell you that a crucial component of an effective examination is good rapport between the examiner and examinee. What we rarely see in fictional depictions of polygraph testing is the extensive rapport-establishment phase that precedes use of the machine. The polygrapher typically devotes half an hour to an hour or more establishing rapport before actually hooking up the examinee to the device.

The need for rapport highlights the fact that even a mechanical deception detection strategy cannot rely on technology alone—human interaction is a necessary element. As well as providing an opportunity to gain the examinee's trust and cooperation, the rapport-establishment phase gives the examiner an opportunity to convince the examinee that polygraphy is an effective way to get at the truth. For leakage to occur, the examinee must experience anxiety about withholding the truth, so it is important for him or her to believe in the polygraph's effectiveness.

Stories abound in police circles about the power of this belief, and at least some of them may be based on events from real investigations. In one such story, a suspect is led to believe that a photocopier is capable of detecting lies. As the story goes, the suspect was asked a pivotal question while placing his hand on the glass plate of the machine. Upon "receiving" the suspect's response, the photocopier ejected a piece of paper with the word "lie" on it. The ruse was successful, and the suspect then said something like, "Damn! I thought I could get away with it, but now you know I'm lying." We leave it to you to figure out how such "lie detectors" are apparently capable of such amazing feats.

Polygraph Techniques

THE RELEVANT/IRRELEVANT-QUESTIONS TECHNIQUE

Perhaps the most familiar of the three polygraph techniques is the relevant/ irrelevant questions technique developed by Inbau (1942). At the beginning, the examinee is asked to respond truthfully to mundane or irrelevant questions, such as "Is your name Richard Dawkins?" and "Do you work for Ford of Canada?" Then he or she is asked questions relevant to the case, such as "Did you kill Mary Stewart?" or "Do you know where Mary Stewart's body is now?" The assumption underlying this technique is that an examinee's physiological processes will be much more active in response to relevant rather than irrelevant questions. But this technique runs into the problem that some people are likely to have strong physiological reactions to relevant questions even if they are not guilty of the crime. The control-question technique and guilty-knowledge test discussed below are designed to overcome this problem, at least to some extent.

THE CONTROL-QUESTION TECHNIQUE

In this approach, originally developed by Reid (1947), the examinee is instructed to say "no" to questions for which "no" is clearly the wrong answer. This ostensibly allows the examiner to determine the extent to which an examinee's physiological responses are altered by lying about something that is not part of the investigation. For example, the examinee might be told to answer "no" to the question, "Have you ever broken any rule or law in your life?" It is unlikely that anybody could truthfully answer "no" to that question. The examinee's reactions to that question are then compared with his or her reactions to questions about the case. The possibility still exists that the examinee will respond more vigorously to case-related questions, but this technique is an improvement over the relevant/irrelevant questions technique.

THE GUILTY-KNOWLEDGE TEST

Originally developed by Lykken (1981), this is perhaps the best of the three techniques, although it requires the polygrapher to know specific details of the crime. The guilty-knowledge test assumes that, in addition to the investigators, only the person who actually committed the crime should have knowledge of specific details—for example, (in a homicide) the weapon used, the nature of the injury, and how the body was left—and should thus be the only person to experience strong physiological responses to questions that are consistent with the truth. If, for example, the victim is known to have been killed with an ax and only the police and the real offender know that, then, according to the theory behind this technique, only the real offender should show increased physiological arousal in response to the question, "Was the victim killed with an axe?" as opposed to, for example, "Was the victim killed with a gun/knife/by strangulation?" This technique does the best job of getting around the problem of an examinee reacting simply because of general anxiety about being accused. The examinee might experience an elevated heart rate and so forth throughout the entire examination, but his or her physiological responses will be even more extreme in the face of questions on the true details of the crime.

Reliability of Polygraph Results

Many people view the polygraph as an infallible lie detector. Canadian courts, however, do not have such faith in the device; as has been noted, the Supreme Court, in *R v. Béland* (1987), stated that the results of a polygraph examination used to determine or test a person's credibility are not admissible as evidence in court because the assessment of a witness's credibility is a matter for the trier of fact (judge or jury) to determine, not an expert. A second concern is that, whereas an individual's testimony can be evaluated by a layperson for its credibility, the results of a machine-driven test might carry too much weight with a non-expert judge or jury. The third reason is the issue of reliability. Some have suggested that polygraph results can be admitted into evidence as long as the court is informed about the potential for error in polygraph testing, but research on the accuracy of the polygraph has been deemed too controversial to be admitted.

As frustrating as it might be for some of us to accept, there is no universally agreed on accuracy rate for the polygraph test. Values in the neighbourhood of 95 to 98 percent are commonly offered by proponents of the technique, whereas others offer more conservative estimates in the range of 70 to 85 percent (for a full discussion of the issue, see Vrij, 1998a; NRC, 2003). There are several reasons why it is so difficult to answer this apparently straightforward question. First, there is the issue of what counts as an "accurate" test result. Accuracy estimates are often limited to "hit rates" (the percentage of guilty people deemed guilty by the polygraph test) and ignore the "false positives" (the innocent people who are incorrectly deemed to be guilty). At an imaginary extreme, a test that found every subject guilty would be guaranteed to have a 100 percent hit rate because every guilty person would be detected, but with an obviously high cost in false positives (unless every subject were indeed guilty).

This brings up a related issue regarding the percentage of polygraph subjects who are, in fact, guilty of the crime they are being questioned about, or the base rate in the population (as discussed in the box feature earlier in this chapter). Take, for example, a person who has been identified by witnesses as being in the vicinity at the time of a crime, who has a questionable alibi for the time period in question, who was found with shoes that match prints at the scene, who has committed similar acts in the past, and to whose home a trail of blood leads. Such a person is likely to have a higher probability of being guilty than a person who merely matches a vague description of the offender, or a research participant with a 50 percent probability of guilt as determined by a research study. The point is that a technique that leads to a preponderance of "guilty" results will have a higher hit rate than a more conservative technique if the base rate or prior probability of deception is also high. This distinction is especially relevant when it comes to judging the effectiveness of the polygraph when it is used as a "screening device." In this application, such as looking for a single embezzler out of an entire company of employees, potentially thousands of people can be subjected to a polygraph exam when the probability of any one of them having committed the crime is incredibly low (literally, one out of thousands). Therefore, even a very small error rate for the polygraph can translate into many people being judged deceptive when in fact they are innocent. This is not a commentary on the rate of "deceptive" conclusions arrived at by polygraphers, but an indication of one of the difficulties in establishing and interpreting accuracy rates in general.

A second problem concerns the issue of which technique is used. For example, the guilty-knowledge technique often outperforms the other two techniques, but in many cases it is not an available option because knowledge of the crime details is not limited to the suspect and/or the suspect may not have perceived or remembered the details embedded in the guilty-knowledge questions (Raskin, 1988). Related to this issue is the question of how the results are scored. "Blind scoring" of test results by independent evaluators usually leads to lower estimates of accuracy than those obtained when the person who administered the test is also the person who scores it.

Third, there is the issue of whether tests with simulated suspects should be considered or only those tests conducted in real cases. Real suspects in real cases are likely to display much more intense emotion because of the serious consequences of the test results, which should enable the polygraph test to perform more effectively. A participant in a laboratory study, on the other hand, usually stands to lose only a relatively small amount of money or suffer some other relatively minor consequence. Field experiments with real suspects thus appears to be the obviously better choice, but, in addition to the ethical and logistical problems of doing such research, there remains the problem of determining whether a suspect is actually guilty of the crime—again, the "ground truth" problem. The fact that a person confesses after failing a polygraph test, or after any other interrogation procedure, cannot necessarily be interpreted as "proof" that the test was accurate.

NATIONAL RESEARCH COUNCIL FINDINGS

In what is perhaps the most comprehensive review of the literature to date, the NRC (2003) looked at the scientific basis for the polygraph; reviewed studies regarding polygraph accuracy; and offered an opinion on the validity, reliability, and utility of the polygraph as an instrument for detecting deceit.

With respect to the scientific foundation of the polygraph as a "lie detector," the NRC said that *"[a]lmost a century of research in scientific psychology and physiology provides little basis for the expectation that a polygraph test could have extremely high accuracy"* (NRC, 2003, p. 212; emphasis in the original). With respect to polygraphy itself, the NRC noted that research in the field *"has not progressed over time in the manner of a typical scientific field. It has not accumulated knowledge or strengthened its scientific underpinnings in any significant manner"* (NRC, 2003, p. 213; emphasis in the original).

With respect to the validity of the polygraph (that is, the degree to which it actually measures what it intends to measure), the NRC review emphasized that "[t]he physiological responses measured by the polygraph are not uniquely related to deception" (NRC, 2003, p. 212). Therein lies the central problem with polygraphy. Because the polygraph does not and cannot measure deceit directly, it seeks to do so indirectly by measuring responses that are believed to be associated with deception; however, if these responses are not uniquely related to deception, then exactly what does the polygraph measure?

With respect to the accuracy of the polygraph, the NRC observed that the research indicates that in certain situations the polygraph "can discriminate lying from truth telling at rates well above chance"; however, those accuracy rates can vary widely across different situations. In other words, the research indicates that "sometimes it can, and sometimes it can't." The polygraph is therefore not a reliable approach to detecting deception (reliability being the ability of a test to produce consistent results). Polygraph test results vary significantly depending on how the test is administered, who administers it, and on whom it is administered. This is equivalent to an electrician who has a meter with which to measure the amount of electricity flowing through a wire, but whose meter produces significantly different readings on the same wire at the same time depending on whether he or his apprentice happens to be holding it.

With respect to the utility (that is, usefulness) of the polygraph, however, the NRC concluded that "[p]olygraph examinations may have utility to the extent that they can elicit admission and confessions," but any such utility is completely separate from the issue of validity. In other words, the polygraph cannot detect lies, but if people believe that it can and the polygraph examiner is a sufficiently skilful interviewer, then he or she may be able to elicit an admission or a confession where one might not otherwise have been forthcoming (NRC, 2003, p. 214).

The NRC summarized its review of the polygraph by saying that "[t]here is essentially no evidence on the incremental validity of polygraph testing" (NRC, 2003, p. 214). In other words, it does *not* represent an improvement over other approaches to detecting deception.

"Seeing" into the Brain?

Perhaps the ultimate kind of involuntary "behavioural response" that might be indicative of deception is brain activity. Relatively recent research that exploits cutting-edge neuroscience technology is aimed at determining whether electrical activity and/or blood flow in the brain can be used to determine if a person is lying. Electroencephalographic (EEG) recordings have been used for decades in other contexts, but one researcher in particular has made some fairly extreme claims about how they might be used to detect deception. Lawrence Farwell (for example, Farwell & Smith, 2001) claims a success rate over 90 percent using a specific subset of EEG activity that he calls MERMERs (memory and encoding related multifaceted electroencephalographic responses). The website for his company, Brain Fingerprinting Laboratories, displays his appearances on many TV shows and in many major newspapers, as well as testimonials from at least one US senator and a former FBI investigator. His list of scholarly publications, however, ends in 2001, so it's difficult to determine where the technology stands today.

Functional magnetic resonance imaging (fMRI) is another well established technique used in a variety of diagnostic and research contexts, because it allows us to "see" what's going on in the brain by detecting minute changes in blood flow in specific areas. The title of a relatively recent article by some leading fMRI researchers, however, pretty much sums up the status of this pioneering effort to use the technology in detecting deception, and it is consistent with the status of most of the procedures we discuss in this chapter: "Better than chance, but well below perfection" (Monteleone, Phan, Nusbaum, Fitzgerald, Irick, Fienberg, & Cacioppo, 2009, p. 528).

STATEMENT ANALYSIS

One use of the investigative interview is to create a statement that can be formally analyzed for its truthfulness. Statement analysis is based on the hypothesis (often referred to as the Undeutsch hypothesis, after the researcher Udo Undeutsch who originated the technique) that systematic differences exist between truthful and deceptive accounts provided by witnesses and victims (Porter & Yuille, 1996). According to this hypothesis, a person's description of an event they have experienced will differ from their description of a fabricated event in terms of such criteria as content, quality, and expression, and one can assess these differences systematically by applying a set of criteria to the recorded interview and transcript (Raskin & Yuille, 1989). Statement analysis has a long history in Europe, particularly in Germany, where it has been used since the mid-1950s to assess the credibility of children's statements, typically in cases of suspected sexual abuse (Steller & Koehnken, 1989).

We cannot stress too much the importance of having a good statement as a basis for any analysis. A meaningful analysis of "yes" and "no" responses to a series of closed questions is impossible. Indeed, much statement analysis training focuses on the basics of conducting a good interview and is consistent with the recommendations on which the cognitive interview is based, found in Chapter 2, Techniques for Interviewing Witnesses.

[handwritten margin note: through content, quality, & expression]

There are many varieties of statement analysis. Among the most popular are statement validity analysis (Raskin & Yuille, 1989); criteria-based content analysis (Ruby & Brigham, 1998); scientific content analysis (Sapir, 1987); reality monitoring (Johnson & Raye, 1981); and investigative discourse analysis (Petronio, Flores, & Hecht, 1997). We look at some of these in more detail below.

Statement Validity Analysis (SVA) and Criteria-Based Content Analysis (CBCA)

Statement validity analysis (SVA) is a technique for analyzing children's statements alleging sexual abuse (Raskin & Yuille, 1989). **Criteria-based content analysis (CBCA)** is a major component of SVA. SVA was developed in Germany more than 50 years ago and has been widely used there since the Supreme Court of the Federal Republic of Germany declared in 1954 that SVA must be used to assess the validity of sexual abuse allegations made by children in cases where their uncorroborated testimony is the primary evidence. The assessment is carried out by either a psychologist or a psychiatrist. A similar approach is frequently used in Sweden.

SVA is founded on two premises: first, that a child's account of an event that he or she experienced will differ in content, quality, and expression from a description of a fictitious event, and, second, that the statement's characteristics can be systematically analyzed by applying content criteria. A video recording and a typed transcript of a properly conducted interview are necessary prerequisites to a proper analysis of a child's statement (an audio recording will not capture non-verbal communication, and handwritten notes can produce a distorted record of the interaction). SVA does not simply analyze the content of a child's statement, but also takes into account the child's cognitive abilities and experiences in order to put the statement into context. For example, because an older child may have more general sexual knowledge than a younger child, an account of a sexual event given by the older child may not be as telling in its level of detail as a similar account given by the younger child.

The content criteria applied to the interview transcript in CBCA are classified as follows (Steller & Koehnken, 1989):

statement validity analysis (SVA) a technique for analyzing children's statements alleging sexual abuse that is premised on the belief that a child's account of real-life experiences will differ from his or her account of fictional experiences, and that such differences can be systematically analyzed

criteria-based content analysis (CBCA) a major component of SVA, consisting of 19 different criteria grouped under 5 different headings, that holds that truthful statements will have more of the criteria identified by CBCA than will false statements; *see* SVA

General Characteristics	1. Logical structure
	2. Unstructured production
	3. Quantity of details
Specific Contents	4. Contextual embedding
	5. Descriptions of interactions
	6. Reproduction of conversation
	7. Unexpected complications during the incident
Peculiarities of Content	8. Unusual details
	9. Superfluous details
	10. Accurately reported details misunderstood
	11. Related external associations
	12. Accounts of subjective mental state
	13. Attribution of perpetrator's mental state

Motivation-Related Contents	14. Spontaneous corrections
	15. Admitting lack of memory
	16. Raising doubts about one's own testimony
	17. Self-depreciation
	18. Pardoning the perpetrator
Offence-Specific Elements	19. Details characteristic of the offence

"General characteristics" are those related to the statement as a whole and are assessed without reference to the details of its content. This part of the analysis focuses on whether the statement is logically consistent; the child has given a disjointed account or one in which the facts are arranged in a structured, chronological order; and the child is able to provide a sufficiently detailed account of the incident.

The term "specific content" encompasses the criteria for assessing specific parts of a child's statement for the presence of certain types of descriptions. This part of the analysis focuses on references that have a temporal and spatial connection to the essential facts of the matter under investigation, descriptions of interactions between the child and people referred to in the statement, accounts of conversations in which the speakers can be identified by age-specific vocabularies, and sudden interruptions or complications that bring the narrative to a halt before it reaches its logical conclusion.

"Peculiarities of content" is a label for criteria that enhance a statement's concreteness and vividness. These include such things as unusual but not obviously unrealistic details; details that do not support the alleged incident; descriptions of events that have been misinterpreted by the child but are understood by the interviewer; reports of conversations that refer to events not directly related to the allegation but related to its content; descriptions of how the child felt or of what he or she was thinking during the incident; and descriptions that attribute a particular state of mind or motive to the perpetrator, including descriptions of the perpetrator's affective reactions and physiological state.

"Motivation-related contents" is a label for criteria applicable to the child's motivation in making the allegation. Such actions as spontaneously correcting oneself, admitting gaps in memory, raising doubts about one's own testimony, engaging in self-criticism, and providing a statement that favours the accused are considered in determining the credibility of the child's statement.

"Offence-specific elements" is the term for details that empirical research has found are characteristic of the alleged offence. These details may differ from details that laypeople believe are characteristic of the offence.

In conducting CBCA, the content criteria may be scored either as simply present or absent or they may be rated in terms of their strength in a statement. Rules for combining content criteria, or for determining scores that clearly indicate truth or deception, do not yet exist. Moreover, not all the criteria are of equal value in determining the veracity of a statement. At present, then, an overall judgment of the significance of each criterion and the degree to which the criteria are present in the statement forms the basis for a probabilistic assessment of whether the child actually experienced the events described. Accordingly, while CBCA is rooted in a long history of practical experience and has some empirical support, it is an approach that continues to develop. Additional research is required and, if CBCA is used, it should be used with caution (Vrij, 2008, Koehnken, 2004).

Reality Monitoring

Reality monitoring is not a lie detection technique per se, and is not widely used among criminal investigators. Regardless, it has attracted some attention in the scientific world as a method for trying to differentiate between accounts of perceived and imagined events (Vrij, 2008, chap. 9; Memon et al., 2010), and some researchers (Vrij) have used reality monitoring criteria to detect lies. **Reality monitoring** is used to detect false statements—that is, statements that are the result of either people believing that they have experienced an event when in fact they have not or people claiming to have experienced an event that they are aware they did not experience. The assumption behind reality monitoring is the same as that behind CBCA—that is, that memories based on real-life experiences differ from false or invented memories, and that the presence or absence of certain criteria can help investigators distinguish between the two. No standardized set of reality-monitoring criteria has been established, but Vrij (2008) offers the following list, which overlaps somewhat with CBCA criteria:

reality monitoring
a scientific technique that attempts to detect false statements

1. *Clarity*   Clarity and vividness are expected to be present more often in truthful statements.
2. *Perceptual information*   Sensory information (for example, taste, smell) is expected to be present more often in truthful statements.
3. *Spatial information*   Mention of specific locations is expected to be present more often in truthful statements.
4. *Temporal information*   Explicit time references or sequences are expected to be present more often in truthful statements.
5. *Affect*   Information about the subject's feelings is expected to be present more often in truthful statements.
6. *Reconstruction of the story*   The ability to reconstruct the event described based on the information provided by the subject is expected to occur more often in a truthful statement.
7. *Realism*   Realism and plausibility are expected more often in truthful statements.
8. *Cognitive operations*   This criterion refers to descriptions of inferences that were made by the subject when the event was happening. For example, "It looked to me as though he wasn't sure what to do next." Such descriptions are expected to occur more often in *deceptive* statements.

Criteria 1 to 7 are expected to appear more often in truthful statements, while criterion 8 is expected to appear more often in deceptive statements. The research that has been conducted on reality monitoring to date has found some support for the notion that observers can distinguish between true and false memories using the reality monitoring technique (Vrij, 2008, p. 265; Memon et al., 2010), but the results of research on the ability of reality monitoring to detect deception are mixed (Sporer 2004). Memon reports that a higher number of contextual and external details, and auditory and temporal details, were found in experienced events, and that truthful accounts tended to be longer (Memon et al., 2010). Some experts (Sporer, 2004; Vrij, 2008) feel that reality monitoring has the potential, especially when used in conjunction with CBCA, to assist investigators in judging the veracity of statements. However, until more research is conducted in this area, investigators are advised to be cautious in attempting to use reality monitoring as a deception detection tool.

Scientific Content Analysis (SCAN)

Avinoam Sapir, an ex-polygrapher and code breaker for the Israeli Army, invented the **SCAN** technique and has been offering training courses in this method of deception detection since the 1980s. Many police officers in Canada and the United States have been trained in SCAN through Sapir's company, LSI (Laboratory for Scientific Interrogation, Inc.). Again, the underlying assumption of SCAN is that a statement about something that was actually experienced will differ in quality and content from a statement based on something that was not actually experienced. In order to use the SCAN technique properly, subjects must supply a handwritten statement in their own words to the examiner, because the examination includes, among other things, looking at any corrections made to the written statement by the subject; in practice, many investigators forego this step and simply analyze a printed transcript of a suspect's interview.

In using SCAN, the investigator applies an extensive list of criteria to determine whether the interviewee is being truthful, or uses the examination to identify areas in the statement that raise suspicion and warrant further exploration in a subsequent interview.

Some of the more popularly used SCAN criteria include the following (adapted from Vrij, 2008, chap. 10):

1. *Denial of allegations.* Does the person directly deny the allegation in his or her statement by stating "I did not ..."? It is claimed that truthful people are more likely to include denials in their statements than deceptive people.

2. *Social introduction.* How are the people described in the statement introduced? Does the author say, for example, "We went out of the house," without identifying who "we" are? If so, this is claimed to be the result of the author hiding something or of some tension between the author and the other person. Similarly, shifts between the use of a person's name in one area of the statement and omitting it in others and referring to some people by name and other people by pronouns (for example, "he" or "she") are also thought to be indicative of the author hiding something or of some tension between the author and the person referred to ambiguously.

3. *Spontaneous corrections.* Did the writer of the statement make corrections, such as crossing out things that had been written? Because subjects are told not to cross anything out in their statements, corrections are claimed to be possible indicators of deception.

4. *Lack of conviction or memory.* Is the person vague about certain aspects of their statement ("I think ..." "As far as I can recall ..."), or do they claim to

SCAN   an acronym for scientific content analysis and a statement analysis technique premised on the assumption that a statement about something that was actually experienced will differ in quality and content from a statement based on something that was not actually experienced and that one can differentiate between the two by analyzing a person's statement with reference to specific criteria

be unable to remember certain things? Such features in a statement are grounds for suspicion.

5. *Structure of the statement.* It is claimed that a statement should conform to certain rules of proportionality. A truthful person would apparently use 20 percent of their statement to describe what happened before the event, the next 50 percent to describe the event itself, and the remaining 30 percent to describe what happened after the event. The less a statement conforms to this structure, the more likely it is claimed to be deceitful.

6. *Emotions.* Does the writer describe emotions in their statement? Statements that include descriptions of emotion throughout, and particularly after the climax of the story, are allegedly more likely to be truthful.

7. *Objective and subjective time.* How does the person represent different periods of time in their statement? It is claimed that if someone uses 4 lines to describe an event that took 15 minutes, and then 2 lines to describe an event that took an hour, objective and subjective times do not correspond, and this may be indicative of deceit.

8. *Out of sequence and extraneous information.* Does the writer tell the story of events in chronological order? If they don't, SCAN claims that this may indicate deception. Also, if the writer includes extraneous information in their statement, this could indicate that they are attempting to hide or divert the investigators' attention from other, more relevant information.

9. *Missing information.* Does the person use words that indicate that some information has been left out? Such words include "finally," "later on," "shortly afterward," or "eventually." The use of these and similar words are thought to indicate that the writer is seeking to "skip over" certain periods of time and indicates the possibility of deception.

10. *First person singular, past tense.* What format did the writer use in their statement? It is claimed that truthful statements are written in the first person singular, past tense (for example, "I left the building"), because the writer is describing an event that they experienced in the past. When statements deviate from this format, they are thought to be suspicious. Conversely, in some situations, like a missing child for example, SCAN claims that parents should normally refer to the children in the present tense, and the use of past tense references (for example, "My son *used to* love playing with trucks," as opposed to "My son loves playing with trucks") should raise suspicion.

11. *Pronouns.* Does the writer of the statement use words (in particular, pronouns) that are indicative of possession or responsibility—for example, "I," "my," "he," "his, "they," or "their"? It is thought that if a person does not use such words they may be reluctant to commit themselves to or take responsibility for the actions that are described in their statement. The use of pronouns in a statement is also claimed to indicate something about relationships between people (for example, use of the phrase "my wife and I," instead of "we," might indicate tension or detachment between the author and his wife).

12. *Changes in language.* Are there changes in terminology or vocabulary in a person's statement? It is claimed that changes in language indicate a change in the way the writer is thinking about a particular event. For example, if the writer refers to all the meetings he had with a certain individual as "meetings," except for one meeting, which he refers to as a "get-together," it is likely that the writer perceived this meeting as different from the others. If, in the context of the statement, there is no good reason for such a difference in terminology, this may indicate deception.

There has been relatively little written about SCAN over the past 20 years. A couple of articles lauding the approach have appeared in police publications (Lesce, 1990; Adams, 1996). One article, critical of the approach, was published in a popular magazine (Shearer, 1999). Some academics have offered scathing critiques of SCAN (Leo, 2008), while others state that, given the absence of evidence showing that it works, its continued use by law enforcement is unjustified (Shuy, 1998).

One researcher (Vrij, 2008) devotes an entire book chapter to it; he concludes that there is no evidence to support it, but believes that it may offer some potential as a device for helping to structure interviews. To date, we are aware of only five scientific studies that look at the SCAN approach to detecting deception. (A sixth study on language-based deception, by Bachenko et al., 2008, examined some SCAN criteria, but did not discuss the results for the individual criteria.) Driscoll compared the results of SCAN analysis with polygraph examinations and reported that "the SCAN technique appears to be reasonably accurate" (Driscoll, 1994, p. 86); however, he also found a significant number of truth tellers who were judged to be deceptive and, as a result, he cautioned against putting too much emphasis on the analysis of a written statement. Additionally, his study suffered from a significant limitation—it was not known whether each of the individuals whose statements were analyzed were actually telling the truth or lying (again, the problem of establishing "ground truth"). As a result, little to no confidence can be placed in the results of Driscoll's study (Vrij, 2008, p. 288).

Porter & Yuille (1996) looked at transcribed statements (a departure from the written statements preferred in the SCAN approach), which they examined using three SCAN criteria (structure of the statement; missing information; first person singular, past tense). They found no difference between truthful and deceptive statements with regard to these criteria. In a study performed for the British Home Office, Smith (2001) found that three criteria—denial of allegations, missing information, tense change—differentiated between liars and truth tellers, but that the SCAN criteria that were actually used most frequently by investigators were improper use of pronouns, lack of conviction or memory, and changes in language. Smith found that overall there was a great deal of inconsistency in how investigators applied the SCAN technique, and that investigators who used the SCAN method were no better at detecting deception than experienced detectives with no SCAN training.

Adams and Jarvis (2006) found a positive relation between truth and the inclusion of "unique sensory details" in a statement, as well as a positive relation between deception and "equivocation," "negation," and "relative length of prologue." However, they are cautious regarding claims that the SCAN technique can detect deception. They advise that "if specific attributes of the likelihood of deception are found in a written statement, the next step is to conduct a structured interview with the writer" (Adams & Jarvis, 2006, p. 20). This is significantly different from stating that one can draw conclusions regarding the presence of deception simply on the basis of the presence of certain SCAN criteria. Adams and Jarvis maintain that statement analysis techniques such as SCAN can assist investigators primarily by helping them focus on areas of a statement that may require further exploration.

In his review of the research, Vrij (2008), and on the basis of his own new research (Nahari, Vrij, & Fisher, 2011), Vrij concluded that, as a result of both a lack of scientific evidence that SCAN actually works and the lack of a standardized approach to using it, SCAN cannot be justified as an approach to detecting deceit. However, it may be useful for investigators as a structured approach with which to closely examine the contents of a statement in order to identify areas of potential significance for followup in a subsequent interview or in the investigation at large.

In summary, the empirical research that has been conducted on the use of statement analysis to assess the credibility of statements by adult suspects provides some measured support for the SVA/CBCA and reality-monitoring approaches, but raises concerns about the validity of approaches such as SCAN. Overall, the use of statement analysis to assess the credibility of statements by adult suspects, while showing some promise for investigative purposes, must be approached with caution. Relatively little empirical research has been conducted in this area, and the research that does exist, even where it has identified valid analytical criteria, suggests that our record of reliably applying these methods to the analysis of statements is poor to fair at best (Vrij, 2008; Smith, 2001; Koehnken, 2004; Sporer, 2004).

SO WHAT'S AN INVESTIGATOR TO DO?

Given the limitations that have been identified and the cautions that have been given with regard to the detection of deception, what approach should a front-line investigator take to this complex issue? Knowing what *not* to do is probably the most valuable lesson that an investigator can take away from this chapter's review of approaches to deception detection. An informed investigator must not believe that accurately detecting deception is an easy task. Detecting deception with any degree of accuracy, above chance, is not easy to do in controlled laboratory conditions, and it is not easy to do in real-life investigative settings. An investigator must not simply accept commonsense beliefs about what indicates deception, however common they might be.

Perhaps the most prudent approach an investigator can take is one that is encouraged by Ekman (Frank, Yarbrough, & Ekman, 2006), and which is consistent with the suggestions of other researchers (Porter & ten Brinke, 2010)—that is, to treat significant changes in behaviour (those that depart from the person's norm or "baseline" in response to relevant questions or accusations) as "hotspots." These "hotspots" don't equal deception, but *do* indicate that a person may be experiencing increased emotion or having to think harder than normal. These areas can then be explored further in an attempt to ascertain what is behind them. A prudent investigator will likely use hotspots—in addition to all the other information gathered in the course of an investigation—to assist him or her in forming an opinion about whether or not someone is telling the truth. There are no shortcuts in such decisions.

Although research indicates that the behavioural cues most commonly associated with deception are *not* reliable indicators of deception, certain behavioural cues *have* been shown to be reliably related to deception. However, these are not universal; while many liars will exhibit them—and while liars will tend to exhibit them more than truth tellers—not *all* liars will exhibit them. In other words, there is no "Pinnochio effect" or surefire behavioural indicator of deception that *all* liars will show *all* the time. Avoiding eye contact does not necessarily indicate deception and neither does "fidgeting." An investigator must not seize on every "new" deception detection technique that comes along, even those that are based on scientific research. Moreover, one should not assume simply because science has identified something as a reliable indicator of deception that it will be a simple matter to translate that finding directly into investigative technique. Investigators must not make determinations about truth or deception based on one—or even a few—criteria gained during an interview, but must take into account everything that has been learned during an investigation.

With these caveats in mind, investigators *can* use their observations of people's behaviour and language to assist them in making reasonable judgments about deception by looking for significant and consistent changes to a person's baseline behaviour, especially with reference to what research has shown to be the most reliable indicators of deception. Those indicators are changes in the use of illustrators (generally fewer); reduced blink rate; taking longer to respond to questions; longer and more frequent pauses; a reduced speech rate; an increased voice pitch; vague descriptions; repeated details; lack of contextual embedding; and a lack of reproduced conversations in incidents involving multiple persons (Porter & ten Brinke, 2010).

KEY TERMS

base rate	polygraph
behaviour analysis	polygrapher
criteria-based content analysis (CBCA)	reality monitoring
false positive	SCAN
gaze aversion	statement analysis
leakage hypothesis	statement validity analysis (SVA)
neurolinguistic programming (NLP)	Type 1 error
Othello error	

FURTHER READING

Ekman, P. (2009). *Telling lies: Clues to deceit in the marketplace, politics, and marriage.* New York: W.W. Norton.

Granhag, P., & Stromwall, L. (Eds.). (2004). *The detection of deception in forensic contexts.* New York: Cambridge University Press.

National Defence Intelligence College Press. Free downloadable publications related to interrogation, critical thinking, and crime scene intelligence. http://www.ndic.edu.

Vrij, A. (2008). *Detecting lies and deceit: Pitfalls and opportunities* (2nd ed.). Chichester, UK: Wiley.

Website of the National Academies Press. Free podcasts and downloadable publications related to the polygraph and lie detection. http://www.nap.edu.

Website of Professor Paul Ekman. http://www.paulekman.com.

REVIEW QUESTIONS

TRUE OR FALSE

____ 1. The majority of police officers and criminal investigators tend to overestimate their ability to detect deception or "know when someone is lying."

____ 2. Polygraph examination results are admissible in court when the examination has been conducted by a recognized expert in the field.

____ 3. A voice stress analyzer is a reliable means to detect untruthfulness during a telephone conversation when the machine is operated by a qualified expert.

____ 4. Once an investigator has formed a belief that a suspect is guilty he should not be disuaded by other evidence which may suggest any other possibility.

____ 5. Statement analysis includes the use of a polygraph.

____ 6. Behaviour analysis includes statement validity analysis.

____ 7. Scientific research does not support the contention that observing eye contact is useful and significant in detecting deception.

MULTIPLE CHOICE

1. The benefits of establishing rapport with a polygraph examinee before the polygraph equipment is set up include:

    a. obtaining the subject's trust and cooperation.

    b. asking questions that will serve as controls.

    c. observing the suspect's ability to control his or her physiological reactions.

    d. both a and b.

2. The relevant/irrelevant questions technique in polygraph examinations is flawed because:

    a. the polygrapher may not know which questions are relevant.

    b. the examinee can often tell which questions are relevant.

    c. it is sometimes difficult to create a sufficiently long list of relevant questions.

    d. the examinee may demonstrate a strong physiological response to a relevant question regardless of guilt.

3. Othello error is the term for:

    a. depending too heavily on facial expressions when trying to detect deception.

    b. mistakenly interpreting excessive protests of innocence as an indication of guilt.

    c. carrying out a polygraph examination without first establishing control readings.

    d. assuming that 80 percent of people accused of a crime are indeed guilty.

SHORT ANSWER

1. Imagine that a child's account of a sexual assault is being subjected to SVA. Indicate whether you would expect each of the following occurrences to support or refute the assumption that the child's account is truthful and explain your answer:

    a. The child repeats a slang sexual term supposedly used by the perpetrator, but cannot explain the term's meaning.

    b. The child insists that he or she remembers every detail of the incident.

    c. The child relates the details of the incident in a scattered, disorganized fashion.

2. How reliable is statement validity analysis? What are some of its pitfalls?

3. Why do investigators support polygraph testing if the results are not admissible in court? Can their reasons be justified?

4. How does the "leakage hypothesis" work as it relates to the polygraph?

5. Why are polygraph results not accepted by the courts?

Eyewitness Identifications

6

INTRODUCTION

A common element of many movie and TV crime dramas is the scene in which an eyewitness to a crime stands in a darkened room, peers through a two-way mirror to scan a lineup of rather scruffy-looking individuals with height bars behind them and spotlights in their eyes, and then picks out one of them as the offender, saying something like, "That's him! The one with the beady eyes, second from the left." But for many reasons, contrary to how it's often portrayed on television and in the movies, it is extremely rare for police in Canada to arrange a live lineup in which a suspect and several people who resemble him or her are brought together and shown to a witness this way. Sometimes the appropriate facilities are not available, or the suspect is not in custody. If the suspect is in custody, he or she may be unwilling to participate, the witness may be unwilling to look at him or her again, or the police may want to protect a vulnerable victim from further trauma. In addition, there are no laws, rules, precedents, or policies that require this kind of procedure.

In Canada, therefore, it is much more likely that a witness will instead be asked to look at a number of photographs (or "mugshots") in what's called a photo lineup, photo array, or photo spread. In some cases, police services are also using short video clips instead of photos and, as we discuss later in this chapter, there are some live identification procedures that don't involve the formality of the two-way mirror, spotlights, and height bars. In the United States, it is still common to conduct a formal live lineup, if possible, which goes a long way toward explaining why lineups are so popular in the TV shows and movies we see in Canada.

It is interesting that there is no evidence showing that live lineups of any kind are necessarily better than ones using photos, or that video clips are any different from live procedures

CHAPTER OBJECTIVES

After completing this chapter, you should be able to:

- Describe the kinds of factors that can affect the accuracy of eyewitness identifications.
- Explain the benefits of and the risks associated with lineups as an investigative tool.
- Explain best practices for constructing and presenting lineups, including instructing witnesses.
- Explain the factors that should be considered in selecting distracters.
- Understand the ways in which an officer's behaviour and feedback during a lineup can influence a witness and how the associated risks can be minimized.
- Understand the advantages of using a video camera to record the details of the lineup, including the witness's behaviour.
- Explain how the cold mugshot search and the walkthrough procedure work.
- Describe some techniques for creating likenesses of unidentified offenders, including the Identi-Kit and Photo-Fit techniques, the use of sketch artists, and composites from cold mugshot searches.
- Explain the best practices for photo lineup procedures identified by the Sophonow Inquiry.

or videos, despite the intuitive appeal for accuracy to be higher when a witness can view a suspect from multiple angles as the suspect, for example, moves, walks, talks, and makes different facial expressions. Also, formal live lineups in the United States are often preceded by a photo lineup some days or weeks earlier, so good procedures for photo lineups are important there too, especially because a formal live lineup can exacerbate any problems that might have originated in an earlier photo procedure.

The logic, research, and recommendations regarding lineups discussed in this chapter apply to *all* of these procedures. Note that we are focusing on perhaps the most prototypic eyewitness situations, such as a bank robbery (without a complete disguise), purse snatching, and hit-and-run, where the witness or victim is not familiar with the offender. In some eyewitness cases, the issue might only be to confirm the identity of a person known to be the former partner in a sexual assault case, or a fellow gang-member known to be the person with the street name "Cuddles," and other variations. In other situations, an identification might not be possible at all, perhaps because the offender wore a disguise, the crime took place in complete darkness, or the witness's vision was obstructed (for example, with a blindfold or a bag over the head).

FACTORS AFFECTING THE ACCURACY OF WITNESS IDENTIFICATIONS

Researchers interested in eyewitness evidence issues commonly divide the many factors that can affect the accuracy of a witness's identification into two categories: **estimator variables** and **system variables** (Wells, 1978). Estimator variables include those factors over which police and the Crown typically have little or no control, such as the physical and temporal context of the crime (that is, the lighting, the distance between the witness and the offender, and the crime's duration); the age, gender, and race of the witness and offender; the emotions experienced by the witness at the time of the crime; and the witness's eyesight. These are called estimator variables because their impact on the accuracy of any particular identification can only be estimated.

For example, in general, it might well be the case that more light is better than less, shorter distances are better than longer ones, and a moderate level of arousal or attention is better than a witness who is inattentive or extremely stressed, but the exact influence of these factors is difficult if not impossible to know in a given case, and the factors can interact with one another in an almost endless variety of combinations. Furthermore, even the values of these estimator variables can be difficult to determine because, of course, a major point of eyewitness research, and police officers' experience, is that people's perception of things like distance, speed, time, height, weight, and so on can be notoriously inaccurate. So even if there were an exact relation between, for example, crime duration and eyewitness accuracy, if we don't know that a witness's estimate of a particular crime's duration is accurate, we couldn't use the duration–accuracy relation anyway.

System variables, on the other hand, include those factors over which the justice system has at least some control, such as how police officers are trained on eyewitness issues, how an investigative interview is conducted, the procedures

estimator variables factors, such as a witness's eyesight, that affect the accuracy of an eyewitness identification, but over which the police and the Crown have no control

system variables factors, such as conditions in the lineup room, that affect the accuracy of an eyewitness identification and over which the police and the Crown have some control

used to select members of a lineup, the way those lineup members are presented, the instructions given to the witness, and any technology used to facilitate the process.

Laypersons, film and television writers, expert witnesses, law enforcement personnel, and the rest of the legal system often focus on estimator variables. They can, of course, be extremely important in real cases and are also a focus of much good research on perception and memory, but, for the reasons discussed above, it ultimately becomes a judgment call as to how they might be used to determine the accuracy of a specific witness's memory, her identification of a suspect, and her testimony at trial. So, the more directly relevant, applicable research usually involves system variables, a good knowledge of which can greatly increase the value of eyewitness identification evidence. Because investigators can control system variables to some extent, and because eyewitness researchers have devoted much more attention to system variables for the past 40 years or so, we will focus our attention on this category of factors.

THE PROBLEM OF FALSE IDENTIFICATIONS

Concern over eyewitness memory frailty, and especially false identifications, is one of the factors that prompted legal scholars and social science researchers to look at the identification process in the first place, beginning early in the 20th century. In his 1908 book *On the Witness Stand*, popular Harvard psychology professor and researcher Hugo Munsterberg optimistically claimed that the (then) new discipline of psychology was ideally suited to handling the memory-related issues involved in people witnessing, remembering, and testifying about a crime. Munsterberg tried to convince the legal community that psychology's empirical perspective—in fact, just the empirical data available around the turn of the 20th century—was superior to the existing strategies in use by law enforcement and the courts and that psychology-trained professionals should therefore handle those aspects of criminal investigations and trials.

It is traditional at this point in the historical account of eyewitness research to blame Munsterberg for jumping the gun with his claim, and perhaps especially for his adamant style, because the reaction from the legal community was abject dismissal of his idea. Doyle (2005) describes in entertaining detail how Northwestern University's Dean of Law, Henry Wigmore (1909), actually a supporter of Munsterberg's main point that eyewitness evidence needs to be viewed with skepticism, gleefully roasted him in virtual effigy as a dumbstruck expert witness on human memory in the mock transcript of a mock trial in the *Illinois Law Review*. So, the story goes, Munsterberg's significant star power was greatly diminished, and psychology's attempt to apply its tools of the trade to eyewitness issues suffered a major setback.

In the years following Munsterberg's "undressing" by the legal community, a few books and articles were written on cases in which innocent people were wrongfully convicted, often based on false eyewitness identifications (see, for example, Borchard, 1932; Frank & Frank, 1957), but two major events beginning in the mid-1990s are largely responsible for the significantly renewed interest in the issue. The first was a research project and accompanying publication by the US Department of Justice (1996), *Convicted by Juries, Exonerated by Science*; the other was the creation of the Innocence Project (www.innocenceproject.org), a consortium of mostly law school and journalism students in the United States and Canada who have (at the time of writing) worked to free approximately 250 wrongfully convicted persons from prison. For both the US Department of Justice and the Innocence Project, DNA evidence is the key factor that revealed these miscarriages of justice, as new technology allowed for the testing of sometimes decades-old crime scene evidence that proved that the person convicted of the crime was not the person who left the DNA sample.

In Canada, a major event was the release of a document called the *Report on the Prevention of Miscarriages of Justice* (FPT Heads of Prosecutions Committee Working Group, 2004). Careful analyses of these wrongful conviction cases has revealed several causes, including inadequate defence counsel, prosecutorial misconduct, false confessions, and perjured jailhouse informant testimony. Consistently, however, mistaken eyewitness identification is by far the most common factor, occurring in approximately 75 percent of the cases.

Note that some people are not impressed by the DNA exoneration cases as evidence of innocence. There is a valid argument that just because a convicted person's DNA does not match that from the crime scene, it does not necessarily follow that the person is innocent of the crime. Peter Neufeld, who along with Barry Scheck founded the Innocence Project, coined the phrase "the unindicted co-ejaculator theory" in reference to the argument he has heard many times that perhaps the convicted person had an accomplice who left the DNA sample, but was still somehow involved in the crime. This argument is consistent with a staple of formal logic, which is that "absence of evidence [in this case, the convicted person's DNA] is not evidence of absence [in this case, the convicted person's absence from the crime scene]." However, as Neufeld, Scheck, and others have pointed out over the years (for example, Scheck, Neufeld, & Dwyer, 2000), the prosecution's theory of how the crimes were committed in the DNA exoneration cases claimed that the accused (and then convicted) person acted alone, or with an accomplice whose DNA had been accounted for. So while it's possible that some DNA exoneration beneficiaries might actually have been involved in the crime of which they were originally convicted, the crime must have occurred in a very different way from the case that was brought against them, which by itself can be sufficient ground for an acquittal.

Given the high possibility of error, police officers and prosecutors are usually quite wary about arresting or prosecuting someone solely on the basis of an eyewitness identification, but it does happen. Goldstein, Chance, and Schneller (1989) conducted an extensive survey of prosecutions and estimated that some 77,000 cases founded on eyewitness identification evidence are tried each year in the United States. It is not unreasonable to assume that several such cases are also tried each year in Canada. But even if it is relatively rare to arrest and prosecute someone based solely on eyewitness identification evidence, and even if such evidence is perhaps alarmingly prone to error, it is still an important investigative tool and cannot be discarded without missing opportunities to apprehend and convict guilty persons. Lineups and other identification procedures can, among other things, determine the direction in which an investigation will move, help the police rank suspects according to likelihood of guilt, establish the credibility of witnesses, and perhaps exonerate a suspect so that resources can be directed elsewhere. So, we thus have to make the best of an imperfect situation. Some commentators argue that DNA analysis, surveillance videos, vehicle- and person-mounted cameras, retinal imaging, and other biotechnical developments will eventually replace eyewitness identification evidence, but it is likely that eyewitness identification evidence will remain useful in criminal investigations for the foreseeable future, even if it is ultimately superseded by advanced technologies.

The recommendations in this chapter are aimed at walking the sharpest edge between minimizing the rate of false identifications and maximizing the rate of accurate identifications, using relatively traditional eyewitness lineup procedures designed for the kind of "typical" eyewitness situation described earlier. The overarching principle behind the recommendations is that a witness's identification decision should be based solely on his or her memory of the offender, as opposed to some irrelevant aspect of the lineup such as the position of the suspect's photo, anything irrelevantly distinctive about it, the instructions the witness receives, the way the lineup is administered, and other issues we discuss in detail. The principle cuts both ways, however, because in order for memory to be the basis of the witness's decision, a suspect's photo needs to be at least *somewhat* different from the others in the lineup, otherwise everyone in the lineup would look *exactly* the same, so we provide lots of information about how to adhere to the principle in the most reasonable way under several different circumstances. The recommendations discussed in this chapter are consistent with those supported by the American Psychology–Law Society (see Wells et al., 1998), the Ontario Police College, the Sophonow Inquiry (Cory, 2001), and the US Department of Justice document *Eyewitness Evidence: A Guide for Law Enforcement* (1999), among others, and are formally in effect in many jurisdictions in Canada and the United States.

LINEUPS

Lineup Construction

Suppose that information obtained from an eyewitness, an anonymous tip, a low-resolution security camera, or other source has led an investigator to suspect that Bill Smith is the perpetrator of an assault that occurred three nights ago. Bill is known to the police and has been arrested on previous occasions for similar offences. His past arrest photographs can be obtained by searching the police service's computer database by, for example, name, date of birth, and social insurance number. Once the suspect's photographs have been retrieved, the investigator, or perhaps an "Ident" officer or civilian specialist, will search for photographs of all the people in the database whose physical characteristics—for example, height, weight, age, complexion, hair colour, and tattoos—match those of the suspect. In even mid-sized police services, the database will likely provide dozens or even hundreds of matches, unless the suspect's appearance and/or the description of the offender are distinctive in some way.

The next step is to choose, from the matches the database has provided, a few photographs to accompany our suspect's photograph in the lineup. The other lineup members are usually referred to as **distracters** (or foils, stand-ins, shills, and other similar terms). Surprisingly, the exact number of photographs is not a crucial

distracters lineup members other than the suspect

factor in constructing a good lineup, for reasons we discuss below; in Canada, the most common procedure uses a total of 10 or 12 photos, whereas in the United States it's usually six photos, in what's often referred to as a "six-pack." There is a similar lack of uniformity required regarding the type of photograph (black-and-white versus colour, or even a video clip) as well as the poses of the photographed individuals (profile, straight on, or a "three-quarter" view). The more important factors are that the suspect's photograph or video clip provide a fair representation of his appearance when the crime was committed, as opposed to how he might look after the passage of time or an intentional attempt to change his appearance (for example, by dyeing or cutting his hair, shaving, or growing a beard) and the way the other photos in the lineup are selected, discussed below.

Choosing Distracters

Once police determine a suspect and decide to construct a lineup, as they might around our imaginary Bill Smith, the first consideration in choosing distracters is to ensure that they are not potential suspects themselves. Wells and Turtle (1986) strongly suggest that the photo lineup contain only a single suspect and that all other lineup members be "known innocents" or people who could not have or are extremely unlikely to have committed the particular crime under investigation (for example, they were deceased at the time the crime occurred, already in custody for another offence, are in the mugshot database because they were arrested in the past for multiple bank robberies and the current case involves child molestation, or are from another jurisdiction when it's widely agreed that the offender is local). In fact, this is functionally the definition of a formal lineup, especially in contrast to a "cold search" through potentially hundreds of mugshot photos, as we discuss later in this chapter.

The point of a formal lineup is that if a witness chooses anyone other than the suspect, police know immediately that he or she has made an error. In fact, if the suspect is not the offender (as is the case with the "innocent suspect" discussed below), or even if the suspect *is* the offender but the witness didn't get a good look at him, and/or his appearance in the photograph is very different from how he looked at the time of the crime (and therefore the witness is actually just guessing), this procedure provides a measurable rate of detecting an erroneous identification. For example, if there is one suspect and 11 known-innocent distracters, there is a probability of $^{11}/_{12}$ (or about 92 percent) of detecting an error. If the size of the lineup is increased to one suspect and 19 known-innocent distracters, the probability of detecting an error only rises to $^{19}/_{20}$ (or 95 percent). In the other direction, if a lineup has one suspect and only five known-innocent distracters, like the "six-pack" often used in the United States, the probability of detecting an error is still $^{5}/_{6}$ (or about 83 percent). That's why, as we mentioned above, the exact size of the lineup is not that crucial if it is constructed as described in this chapter (see the information under the heading "Recommended Protocol for Eyewitness Identifications" at the end of the chapter). Of course, it's possible that the witness has also made a mistake even if he or she chooses the suspect, but at least this procedure allows police to adjust their investigation strategy if someone other than the suspect is identified (for example, "Maybe our suspect isn't the guy after all" or "Maybe our

Usage of the Term "Suspect"

At this point, it is important to highlight the use of the term "suspect." The word is usually used in reference to a person who is *thought* to have committed a crime, but sometimes it's used in reference to the person everyone agrees is the actual offender. Most people have been exposed to this confusing distinction by watching popular television programs like *Disorderly Conduct* (or other "police-chase" reality shows), where a video camera mounted in a police cruiser or news helicopter, for example, shows a car driving a long distance at well over the speed limit, sometimes on the wrong side of a divided highway, crashing into other vehicles, with the driver shooting at pursuing police and throwing stolen property or drugs out the window, all while the commentary refers to the driver of the vehicle as "the suspect." Similarly, the news media often report on crime by stating something like "Yesterday, a suspect armed with an assault weapon robbed a bank in the city's west end. The suspect is described as about 6 feet tall with a medium build and long dark hair."

Although we realize that the term "suspect" is often used because the driver in the first example is *thought* to be the offender of a crime that initiated the chase (for example, the *murder* suspect), its use is potentially confusing; referring to this person as just "the driver" would pretty much solve the problem. It makes no sense at all, however, to use "suspect" in the second example—unless there is some doubt as to whether the bank robbery actually occurred. That description is of the offender—the person who actually robbed the bank, not the person who might subsequently be arrested as a suspect in the case (although if the suspect is the actual offender, the description might match him as well).

At the other extreme of confusion on this issue, many of us came to learn the opening line from the original *Law and Order* series: "In the criminal justice system there are two separate but equally important groups—the police who investigate the crimes, and the district attorneys who prosecute the *offenders*"? Clearly, *this* is where the word must be "suspects" or "defendants," unless we want to agree that trials are necessary only to determine how harshly offenders should be punished or that they exist only to give bad guys a chance at a not-guilty verdict by virtue of a legal technicality or a sympathetic jury.

The confusion over the term "suspect" becomes even more problematic when you encounter the phrase "innocent suspect" in the context of a lineup, where the person who the police *think* committed the crime is not the actual offender. This concept is, of course, a mainstay of eyewitness research and eyewitness evidence recommendations, because the greatest danger of a mistaken identification lurks there, especially if the innocent suspect happens to match the description of the offender more closely than other members of the lineup or stands out from the other lineup members in some other way. So keep the meaning of suspect, offender, and innocent suspect terms in mind as you read this chapter and think about what people might really be trying to communicate when they use these words in general.

suspect *is* the offender, but this witness didn't get a good look at him, and is just guessing"), as opposed to spending valuable time and resources investigating whichever photo was chosen by the witness. This is why a lineup is used in the first place, as opposed to just showing a witness one photo of a suspect and taking it from there (a "showup" procedure, discussed below).

If the lineup contains more than one suspect, the likelihood of a false identification rises dramatically. We offer this warning because it is not unheard of for police to include multiple suspects in a lineup, or even an entire gang suspected of involvement in a crime, only one of whom may be the actual perpetrator. We argue, therefore, that the police should not rely on a lineup until they have narrowed their investigation to a single suspect. If police are using lineups early in an investigation—which can be a reasonable strategy to weed out hunches or perhaps identify witnesses or victims who are merely eager to pick *somebody* as the offender in their case—they need to downwardly adjust the weight they assign to any identification decisions. If it is thought that more than one person committed the crime in question, separate lineups for each suspect should be constructed. In a pinch, multiple suspects can be included in one lineup, but the total number of photographs must be increased accordingly. If there are multiple witnesses, each should, of course, be asked to view the lineup separately.

Now, suppose that the database has provided 200 photographs of people whose physical characteristics match Bill Smith's from which 11 photographs need to be chosen. Should the investigator choose the 11 people who look most like Bill? The answer, you may be surprised to learn, is no. As Wells (1993) points out, this "match-to-appearance strategy" can often reduce the probability of accurately identifying a guilty person because the photographs are *too similar* to one another. In fact, Wells argues that the match-to-appearance strategy, taken to its extreme, would ultimately lead to a "lineup of clones," from which even the best witness would have great difficulty making a correct lineup choice.

But mustn't everyone in a lineup look alike? Again, no. No statute, rule of evidence, or judicial decision requires similarity of appearance per se, and, as mentioned, such a procedure can actually lead to an almost useless identification task. Suppose, for example, that our witness has described the offender (who may or may not be Bill Smith) as a white male in his mid-20s with short dark hair, a slight build, and a scary look on his face and also says that the offender was wearing blue jeans and a plaid shirt at the time the crime occurred. Lineup logic requires only that everyone in the lineup match this witness's *description* of the offender, not every aspect of Bill Smith's actual appearance (Turtle, Lindsay, & Isaacs, 1998; Wells, Rydell, & Seelau, 1993; Wells et al., 1998). Eyewitness researchers call this the "match-to-description strategy." It means, for example, that even though Bill might have slightly larger ears than anyone else in the lineup, as long as the witness did not describe the offender as having big ears, Bill's bigger ears do not necessarily bias the lineup against him. What the big ears might do, however, is jog the witness's memory in a way that helps him or her make an accurate identification: "Oh yeah, that's the guy! I forgot about those ears, but now I remember thinking at the time that they were pretty big." That's what Wells (1993) termed **propitious heterogeneity** (or "beneficial variety") working to the advantage of the police, without any legitimate bias against Bill Smith. Of course, if he's the only person in the lineup with *huge* ears, and everybody else has average-sized ears, Bill might stand out from the rest, and even somebody who never saw him before might choose his photo just because it's so different from all the others. However, if the

propitious heterogeneity
dissimilarities within a group of subjects, each of whom matches a particular physical description

lineup includes some people with big ears, some with small ears, and some with average-sized ears (as we would expect if ear size was not specified as a database search criterion), an innocent suspect with big ears is no more likely to be singled out than an innocent suspect with a pointy chin, beady eyes, or other features that fall outside the search criteria.

But suppose the witness *did* describe the offender as having big ears, a visible tattoo, or other distinctive feature. And suppose further that Bill Smith has that same feature. Now we can use the lineup logic we've been discussing to create a fair lineup that doesn't make Bill stand out from the rest, but that still allows for a witness who got a good look at the offender to identify Bill (if in fact he's the guilty party). For decades, police in this situation, trying to do a good job and not make the lineup biased against someone like Bill, took steps to hide the distinctive feature by literally masking it with something like masking tape. They would often then realize that everyone in the lineup would need to have a piece of tape over the same part of their face as Bill's, so that Bill didn't stand out as the only one on that score. But their hard work often backfired, because with this technique they would lose the possibility of the feature serving to trigger the witness's memory for the offender. A common alternative is to sift through the database of photos trying to find other people with the same feature. This is a slight improvement over masking the feature, but still limits its potential as a recognition trigger. Similarly, police sometimes use a technique to create the feature on the other photos, most commonly by copying and pasting it with computer technology, but again with the same limitation.

When constructing a lineup, the best procedure for fairly avoiding a false identification and instead gaining an accurate ID of a guilty person is to apply the match-to-description strategy in a creative way. Using the tattoo example, suppose the witness described it as "some kind of insect tattoo" on the offender's right cheek (facially speaking), and suppose that Bill Smith indeed has a spider tattoo on his right cheek. Instead of looking (potentially forever) for 11 other people with the identical spider tattoo, covering it up, or pasting a copy of Bill's spider on to the other faces, the recommendation is to find people with any kind of insect-looking tattoo—for example, a bee, a scorpion, or a butterfly. At first glance, this might appear biased against Bill, because he's the only one with a spider, but if he is in fact an innocent suspect, the odds are low that his spider is identical to the offender's "insect," so he should be no more likely to be picked out than any other innocent lineup member. If, on the other hand, Bill is the offender, then his spider tattoo might serve as the memory trigger for the witness, even though everybody in the lineup has some sort of insect on his face, as per the description. We've used a rather extreme example to make a point, but the concept applies to more everyday examples too, such as scars, birthmarks, blemishes, facial hair, hairstyles, hair color, piercings, and so on. Photos need only match the description of the offender as provided by the witness, not necessarily the actual appearance of the suspect.

Clothing can also be a significant issue in lineup construction (Lindsay, Wallbridge, & Drennan, 1987). Some police services require that all lineup members be dressed the same, perhaps in some sort of coverall and T-shirt combination or in the ubiquitous orange jumpsuit worn by many prison inmates. But research has shown that clothing can safely be allowed to vary from lineup member to lineup

Testing the Fairness of a Lineup

A convenient and relatively easy strategy for determining whether a lineup is fair or biased is to present it to a number of non-witnesses (such as police service administrative staff or police colleagues unfamiliar with the case) with the description of the offender as provided by the witness who's going to view the lineup. For example, "The offender in this case was described as a white male in his mid-20s with short dark hair, a slight build, and a scary look on his face and he was wearing blue jeans and a plaid shirt when the crime was committed. Who do you think our suspect is?" If, say, 11 of 15 non-witnesses choose Bill Smith, the lineup is probably biased against him. If, however, their choices do not single out Bill as the suspect, but instead they say something like, "How the heck should I know who the suspect is? All of these guys match the description you just gave me!" or they spread their choices fairly evenly across the lineup members, then, in either case, the outcome of the procedure is that bias is unlikely. This "mock witness" procedure has been used for decades by researchers trying to establish which factors affect lineup fairness (Malpass & Devine, 1983; Wells, Leippe, & Ostrom, 1979).

member, as long as the suspect is not the only one wearing the clothes described by the witness and does not stand out in some other obvious way (such as being the only one wearing prison garb). The same is true of the background for the photos. Sometimes police go to great lengths to standardize these backgrounds, but, again, as long as the suspect's photo is not distinct from all the others, it is not enough to bias the lineup. Out of 12 photos, for example, if a few have a concrete wall behind them, a few have brick, and a few have a door, it should convey to the witness that the background is irrelevant.

One related issue that police are concerned about is the extent to which it is prejudicial to use photos that were clearly taken upon a person's arrest or booking into some sort of detention. Again, however, as long as the suspect's photo isn't the only one of this type, it likely isn't a problem. Unlike the relatively innocuous backgrounds just discussed, however, it's possible that if some photos were obviously taken upon arrest, while some are from a yearbook, driver's license, or other source, a witness might infer that only the people in the arrest photos are legitimate possible suspects because they have been arrested before. In this case, even though there might be a total of 12 photos, functionally the lineup might only be as large as the number of obvious arrest photos it contains. We are not aware, however, of any necessity in general to disguise mugshots as something other than what they are, based on some kind of notion that anyone who's been arrested in the past is therefore more likely to be deemed guilty in the present. We assume that most witnesses understand where most lineup/mugshot photos come from.

Another potential problem is posed by so-called default descriptors—characteristics that a witness might not mention because they appear so obvious. For example, if a witness fails to mention that the offender was male, that does not mean that he can be the only male in a lineup of females. Lindsay, Martin, and Weber (1994) show that default descriptors need to be recognized as imposing some reasonable limits on the match-to-description procedure. A main point here is the principle we discussed at the outset of the chapter—that is, lineup construction is not an opportunity to influence a witness's choice toward a particular suspect, but nor is it necessary to "hide" a suspect from being identified when the witness thinks he's the person who committed the crime.

Lineup Presentation

Once the lineup is constructed, the next step is to present it (whether in the form of photographs, video clips, or live subjects) to the witness. The following discussion assumes that photographs are being used, because this is the most commonly used procedure in Canada, but the logic also extends to video clip and live lineups. As we discussed at the outset of this chapter, Canadian investigators will rarely, if ever, become involved in formal live lineups or showup procedures (where just the suspect, or his photo, is presented to a witness without the advantages of a lineup). For additional information on conducting live lineups, consult the recommendations made by the Sophonow Inquiry and in the *Ontario Major Case Management Manual* (2004, p. 35).

Instructions to the Witness

A crucial aspect of lineup presentation is telling the witness that "the person you saw commit the crime (in other words, the offender) may or may not be in the photos you are about to see." This simple warning has been shown to significantly reduce the chances of a false identification without a significant decline in accurate IDs (Malpass & Devine, 1981). This warning communicates to the witness that he or she should not choose the photograph that merely *looks most like* the person he or she saw, but should choose a photograph *only if it is of the person he or she saw commit the crime*. If the witness believes that one of the pictures *must* be of the guilty offender, he or she may engage in a potentially dangerous version of Russian roulette in which an innocent suspect is chosen through a process of elimination.

Note that this is very different from what is commonly, but erroneously, said to witnesses: "The *suspect* in this case may or may not be in the lineup." This recalls our discussion, above, of the correct use of the term "suspect." The problem in this case is that the *suspect* is pretty much always in the lineup—it's just that he may or may not be the *guilty* suspect. This is not merely a "splitting hairs" distinction. An astute defense lawyer could make a legitimate argument that police are knowingly lying to witnesses if they use this wording, because they would have to admit that, in fact, they knew full well that the suspect was in the lineup but told the witness otherwise (for example, "Officer Jones, do you ever show witnesses lineups *without* a suspect in them? If not, why do you routinely instruct witnesses that the suspect may or may not be present?").

Another important instruction is to let the witness know that an expression of confidence is expected. As we discuss below, the presentation of eyewitness identification evidence in court should be based on what transpired during the pre-trial identification procedure, not just on what the witness says in court. In contrast, the current emphasis is often incorrectly placed on the potentially dramatic in-court ID:

JUDGE OR CROWN: Do you see the man who robbed you in the court today and, if so, can you point him out to the court?

WITNESS: Yes [pointing], he's the guy sitting at the defense table/in the prisoner's dock.

JUDGE: Are you certain that's the man?

WITNESS: Oh yes, I'll never forget that scary look on his face.

As we discuss at the conclusion of this chapter, the probative value of the in-court ID procedure has been questioned for decades, including the typically high level of confidence expressed by a well-prepared witness; our recommendation to focus on what happened during the pre-trial identification is a way around this problem. This recommendation is especially helpful when the pre-trial procedure instructions include a request for the witness to provide an expression of confidence, especially because a question eliciting a confidence value is typically asked in court. Confidence values need not necessarily be on a scale from 1 to 10 or expressed as a percentage. Many kinds of comments can suffice—for example, "I'm almost certain that's the guy" or "I really remember those big ears!"

Sequential Versus Simultaneous Presentation

The idea of presenting lineup photographs one at a time (sequentially) instead of the more common practice of presenting them all at once (simultaneously) has been around and in use by at least some police officers for decades. In addition, there are other variations, such as laying out a number of photos and having witnesses turn over ones they think are definitely *not* the offender. But it was Lindsay and Wells (1985) who first formally outlined the logic behind the sequential procedure's apparent superiority and provided data to back up their claim. Since 1985, literally thousands of people have participated in research projects on the advantages of the sequential procedure. Many police services in the United States and around the world have adopted the procedure, which is a standard component of lineup procedures in Ontario. Its rationale arises from the problem we discussed above—namely, that the lineup procedure should include as many aspects as possible to reduce people's tendency to choose the lineup member who merely looks *most* like the actual offender. The sequential presentation of photographs is one way of accomplishing that goal.

relative-judgment strategy
strategy whereby a witness decides whether a subject, as compared with other subjects, looks more or less like the offender seen at the crime scene

The simultaneous presentation of lineup photographs can encourage a witness to use what Wells et al. (1998) call a **relative-judgment strategy** ("Hmm, which of these guys is most similar to the person I saw *relative* to one another?") The sequential procedure, on the other hand, encourages a witness to use an **absolute-judgment strategy** ("Hmm, does this person meet an absolute standard of similarity to the image of the offender I have in my memory?") The sequential procedure is advantageous only if instructions of the following kind are given to the witness:

absolute-judgment strategy
strategy whereby a witness decides whether a subject is the offender seen at the crime scene without reference to other subjects

1. You are going to see a series of photos to determine whether you can identify the person you saw commit the robbery last week. Please keep in mind that the person you saw may or may not be in the photos.

2. You will be shown the photos one at a time and you will not be told how many photos there are. For each photo, please decide, "Yes, that's the person I saw," or "No, that's not the person I saw."

3. If you say no to a photo you will not be able to return to it later, and if you choose a photo you will not be allowed to see any remaining photos.

That final instruction often worries experienced investigators, who fear that the witness will be afraid to pick anybody without having the opportunity to see all the photos. But, that concern is relevant only if a witness is trying to use the relative-judgment strategy we're trying to avoid. On the one hand, any overall reduction in identifications is probably a good thing, because some of the lost IDs are going to be mistakes that were avoided—false IDs of innocent suspects that didn't happen because people's tendency to rely on the relative-judgment strategy was reduced. On the other hand, it's possible that some accurate IDs of guilty suspects might also be lost. At the end of the next section, we discuss a major research study that was undertaken in an attempt to determine how different lineup procedures affect identification decisions in real police cases, including the potential problem of fewer accurate IDs using the sequential technique.

There is one potential logistical barrier to relying on sequential presentations: cost. Some police services have a computer setup that makes it prohibitively expensive to print out individual photographs for sequential lineups. This problem has two solutions. The first is one that several enterprising police services have been relying on for years—printing out a single page of 12 small photographs in typical simultaneous-presentation format, and then cutting up the page into individual mugshots for use in a sequential lineup. The other solution is not to print out any photographs at all, but to construct and present the lineup on a computer. We examine this approach below.

The Double-Blind Procedure

Wells and Luus (1990) draw an interesting comparison between the lineup procedure and a well-conducted psychology experiment. Most people are somewhat familiar with concepts such as self-fulfilling prophecies, experimenter bias, and the placebo effect. These concepts revolve around essentially the same problem: when researchers study other people, there is a risk that asking a question or providing instructions in a particular way, with a particular intonation, or simply subjecting the study group to observation will affect the research results. Researchers have therefore developed strategies to minimize such effects. Wells and Luus (1990) point out that the situation researchers face is strikingly similar to the situation that the police face in trying to determine whether or not one person witnessed another person commit a crime.

A good psychology experiment has several characteristics, but two are especially applicable to establishing a proper lineup procedure. First, the participants in an experiment should not be allowed to learn the hypothesis behind it. If the participants are told, for example, that the experiment is testing a new learning strategy that is expected to be more effective than the old one, they might try to confirm that expectation by not putting as much effort into their experimental encounters with the old strategy. Second, the experiment's designers should not tell the researchers they engage to actually conduct the experiment what the hypothesis is, because those researchers might intentionally or unintentionally influence the behaviour of the participants.

A procedure where both the participants and the researchers conducting the experiment are unaware of the experiment's hypothesis is called a **double-blind procedure.** Many people are also familiar with this concept in the context of randomized clinical trials for new medications, where half the participants receive a placebo instead of the experimental drug (typically, a pill or injection that looks, feels, tastes, etc. like the actual drug), while the other half get the real thing. In addition, the medical researchers evaluating the effects of the drug (if any) typically don't know who got the real thing versus the placebo, so they can't intentionally or (more likely) unintentionally influence the results, perhaps by being subtly more interested in patients who took the new drug, or by conveying what they hope to observe. Asking something like, "Do you feel better these days? Are you sleeping and eating any differently?" can have potentially different effects if the questioner is subtly, unconsciously nodding versus shaking her head—for example, based on her knowledge that the patient either took the new drug or the placebo. In most cases, the researchers aren't looking to "fake the data," but might fall prey to a natural human tendency to "see" what they're hoping to find in order to get a helpful new drug on the market.

The parallels between a psychology experiment or a clinical trial for a new drug and a lineup identification procedure are clear. In a traditional lineup situation, the person conducting the procedure is typically the investigating officer who knows where the suspect is in the lineup. Such knowledge can prompt the officer to provide subtle, unintentional cues that can lead the witness to the desired photograph. A specific, major source of potential problems is any feedback that the officer provides during the procedure. For example, saying "Take your time ma'am" in response to a witness's tentative identification of a photograph the officer knows is not the suspect can subtly lead the witness away from that photograph. Your first reaction might be "Good!" but that assumes the suspect is the offender, which may or may not be true. On the other hand, saying something equally innocuous, such as "What is it about that photo that looks familiar?" when the investigator knows it's the suspect can subtly encourage the witness to choose that picture. Even a subtle change in the inflection of one's voice can have the same results. Researchers have also found that self-reported confidence levels are significantly higher among witnesses who are praised for their efforts. Such witnesses are also more likely to volunteer additional information about the crime, whether it is accurate or not (Wells & Bradfield, 1998). If such a witness has honestly misidentified an innocent suspect, he or she will probably be more confident about that wrong decision than if no praise had been given. Almost three decades of research have shown us that witness confidence can be the greatest influence on whether the witness is perceived as credible in court, when, instead, *accuracy* should be the primary, if not sole, factor.

(Note that we are not referring to intentional attempts to manipulate the lineup procedure. Although it might be tempting to engage in such manipulation to "get criminals off the street," the effort will likely eventually backfire. Positioning a suspect's photograph slightly askew, or holding a set of photographs with one finger

double-blind procedure
an experiment or study in which neither the test subjects nor the test administrators have been advised of the experiment's hypothesis

conveniently pointing toward the suspect's photograph, might secure an apparent identification in the short run, but will ultimately be the case's undoing when the deception is revealed.)

An officer's behaviour and any feedback provided during a lineup, which can be so subtle as to be virtually invisible to both the officer and the witness, can thus have an important influence on the case. Fortunately, the problem is easy to eliminate by using one of at least three alternatives that meet the goal of administering a "double-blind" lineup:

1. Ensure that the officer administering the lineup is unaware of who the suspect is. (Here again, cost is a potential factor; many police services are quick to point out that they cannot afford to divert officers to lineup administrations and pay for their resulting court time. Also, in a small service and/or a high profile case, it might not be possible to find other officers who are not familiar with the case.)

2. Have the investigating officer conduct the lineup, but in a way that he or she doesn't know/can't see which photo the witness is discussing. (This can be accomplished by placing the individual photos in envelopes and then shuffling them before presenting them to the witness, or positioning oneself so that the photos are not visible from that angle.) This way, if the witness says something like, "This guy, number 4, looks a lot like the guy I saw," the officer can only respond with some kind of non-specific comment, such as "Take your time, ma'am" or "What is it about number 4 that you recognize?," not knowing if it's the suspect's photo or a distracter.

3. A lineup can be presented via computer, perhaps without any police officer in attendance, or at least not one looking at what the witness sees on the computer screen.

Some police services already have witnesses view formal lineups on computers. It's easy to transfer a computer-generated lineup to a laptop that can be carried to a witness's home or place of work, where photo lineups are often conducted. Another advantage to computer-based presentations is that investigators can remove themselves from the procedure altogether, thus avoiding the feedback problem mentioned above. The computer can display the photographs in random order; log how much time the witness spends on each photograph; and, in some cases, record the witness's behaviour and speech in an accompanying digital video file.

A major research project, often referred to as the Illinois Pilot Project, was undertaken in an attempt to see how the sequential and double-blind techniques affect eyewitness identification (Mecklenburg, Bailey, & Larson, 2008). The project was a relatively rare, large-scale field experiment involving real police officers and real witnesses in actual cases. The results of the study have been the topic of much heated debate because the authors claim that they show that the "traditional" simultaneous, non-blind procedure for conducting lineups was superior to the sequential, double-blind procedure recommended in this chapter and most other sources, such as the American Psychology-Law Society, the Ontario Police College, and policies in place in many jurisdictions across Canada and the United States (see Wells,

2006; Wells, Memon, & Penrod, 2007). The debate centres on how the project was conducted, with many commentators claiming that the research design was fundamentally flawed and other errors were made, making the results difficult if not impossible to interpret (for example, Schacter, Dawes, Jacoby, Kahneman, Lempert, Roediger, & Rosenthal, 2008; Steblay, 2008; Wells, 2008). Despite this apparent setback, the recommendation to use a sequential, double-blind procedure is still supported by the majority of researchers in the area and has been in place with much success in many jurisdictions for a number of years (for example, Steblay, 2007; Wells, 2006).

Recording the Lineup Procedure: What Has Probative Value?

JUDGE OR OPPOSING COUNSEL: Officer, what did the witness say upon identifying the man on trial here today when you showed her the series of photographs five months ago? How certain did she appear to be about her decision?

INVESTIGATING OFFICER (flipping through notebook): Ah, Ms. Ann Bivalent said something to the effect, "Yeah, that could be ... no, that's definitely him, I think." When I asked her whether she was certain, she said, "Oh yes, now I'm sure that it's him."

The preceding exchange is fairly typical of how the details of an identification procedure are presented in court. The assumption is that there might be some probative value in those details. The term "probative value" refers to the quality of evidence, and its ability to help the trier of fact determine whether the accused is guilty of the crime for which he or she is on trial. Aspects of the identification that can have probative value include how much time the witness takes to make an identification; what the witness says during the procedure; and what, if anything, the officer says in response to the witness's identification. In our view—one with which a number of researchers, legal scholars, and police officers agree—the best way to satisfy the court's interest in these details is to use a video camera to record the details of the lineup itself (which photographs were used in the lineup and the order in which they were presented) and the witness's behaviour. This way, the court can later view everything that happened during the procedure, instead of relying on the incomplete notes and memories of the officers and the incomplete memories of the witness.

OTHER IDENTIFICATION PROCEDURES

The "Cold Search" Through Mugshots

An important distinction exists between a formal lineup, in which the suspect (or the suspect's photograph) is mixed in with a group of innocent distracters, and a witness's search through hundreds of photographs to see whether anybody looks familiar. The latter, a **cold mugshot search**, is used when the police do not have a suspect in mind, but believe that the offender's photograph might be on file or that the witness might be able to identify a photograph or set of photographs of people who resemble the offender, thereby allowing the police to narrow their investiga-

cold mugshot search
witness's search through a collection of police file photographs for the possible offender or offenders

tion. We will address the second of these potential benefits of the cold mugshot search in a later section. For now, consider this scenario: a witness files a complaint regarding an assault by a black female, approximately 30 years old, who has short black hair and was wearing blue pants and a white tanktop. With this limited information, the police have no reason to suspect anyone in particular, so the witness is asked to look through all 465 of the photographs retrieved by the computer that match the offender's description. The witness quickly dismisses most of the photographs, but at number 416 she stops and says, "That's her! Her hair is a little longer in this picture, and she's a little older now, but I'm sure that's her!"

Does this constitute an identification? More often than not, the cold mugshot search will be treated as a preliminary procedure toward identifying a suspect, after which further evidence will be sought to support that suspicion. But if our witness's mugshot selection needs to be treated as a formal identification, it's possible to defend it as such. After all, every one of the photographs matched her description of the offender, there was no way the officer could have influenced her choice (because there was no suspect to begin with), the photographs were viewed sequentially, and there were hundreds of them. In many ways, then, a cold mugshot search can be superior to how traditional lineups are conducted and thus there is no need to follow up with a traditional lineup. A lineup need be conducted only if a new photograph of the suspect is obtained and is deemed to be significantly different from the one selected during the cold mugshot search.

The Walkthrough Procedure

Suppose that the police have a suspect in mind, but don't have a sufficiently recent photograph, don't have the suspect in custody, and don't believe that he will willingly participate in a live lineup. Suppose further that the suspect is known to frequent a particular bar and that his car is spotted in that bar's parking lot. Is it fair to the suspect to ask a witness to go into the bar to attempt an identification? Most police officers, judges, and lawyers say yes, as long as the procedure provides the same protection for an innocent suspect as a lineup would. A courtroom exchange over whether such a procedure was fair might go something like this:

CROWN TO OFFICER: How many people were in the bar at the time?

OFFICER: Approximately 100 to 150.

CROWN: And how many of those people matched the description of the offender? In this case, male, 25 years old, long brown hair, with a moustache?

OFFICER: Approximately 20 to 30.

CROWN: And what did you say to the witness before he entered the bar?

OFFICER: I asked him to walk through the bar to see whether he recognized anyone in there as the person who committed the crime. I told him to remember that the actual offender might or might not be in there, but that if he did see the offender he should come back out and tell us where he is.

CROWN: So you did not accompany the witness into the bar? Why was that?

OFFICER: No, I did not. That was so I would not influence the witness's choice and so that I would not tip off the suspect that we were attempting an identification.

CROWN TO WITNESS: What did you do in the bar?

WITNESS: Well, I walked around for about five minutes and then I saw a guy playing pool who looked like the guy who had hit me two nights before. I watched him for maybe two more minutes and recognized his voice, the way he walked, and some of the words he used. I then left the bar and told the officer outside that the man who attacked me was playing pool at the back table, wearing black jeans, a white T-shirt, a denim vest, and a cap with "Roots" on the front.

CROWN TO OFFICER: How many people in the bar matched that description?

OFFICER: Just one. The accused.

walkthrough procedure identification procedure whereby a witness is taken to a public location (such as a bar) in an attempt to identify a suspect

A **walkthrough procedure** of the kind described in the preceding exchange is usually considered fair and reasonable. What is unacceptable is a procedure in which a suspect is displayed in a way that makes him or her the witness's only realistic choice. Asking a witness two weeks after a crime was committed to look into the back seat of a car where a suspect is being held in handcuffs is not a fair identification procedure. Nor is asking a witness who described a teenaged female offender to look into a waiting room containing two female officers in uniform, two adult female civilians, and a teenaged female. Both situations are examples of a **showup,** known more informally as an "Oklahoma lineup." Although some commentators suggest that showups might be beneficial in exceptional circumstances (Gonzales, Ellsworth, & Pembroke, 1993), the prevailing wisdom is to avoid the procedure at all costs. (See FPT Heads of Prosecutions Committee Working Group, 2004, Section 5, where showups are discussed. The report states that they should only be used in "rare circumstances," such as when a suspect is apprehended near the crime scene shortly after the event.)

showup identification procedure whereby a suspect is brought to a location where a witness has also been brought for the purpose of identifying the suspect

composite sketch likeness of an offender constructed by combining individual facial features described by a witness

Creating Likenesses of Unidentified Offenders

In some cases, the police determine that creating a **composite sketch** of an unidentified offender—a likeness constructed by combining individual facial features described by a witness—can aid their investigation or alert the community to be on the lookout for a particular person. Several techniques are available to create such likenesses, including the Identi-Kit and Photo-Fit techniques. Employing a sketch artist is another way to create a likeness.

Identi-Kit technique identification technique in which drawings of facial features are combined by a witness to generate a composite image of a suspect

Computer Composites

The Smith & Wesson Company created the **Identi-Kit technique** decades ago. It used to consist of hundreds of small transparencies, each with an individual hand-drawn facial feature, which were combined to create an image, and today is available in a computer-based format. The **Photo-Fit technique** is similar, but employs

Photo-Fit technique identification technique in which photographs of facial features are combined by a witness to generate a composite image of a suspect

photographs of actual persons' facial features instead of hand-drawn representations. In either case, the idea is that a witness begins by looking through the collection of numbered variations of the facial features that he or she remembers most clearly. If the witness remembers the offender's nose, for example, he or she peruses the dozens of noses on file until the one that matches the offender's nose is found. This procedure continues until the witness had created a composite likeness of the offender.

The problem is that it doesn't work very well. Research conducted over the past two or three decades has shown that, even under the most favourable circumstances (for example, long exposures to a target face, short retention intervals, low/no stress), facial composites are recognized only about 20 percent of the time by people who know the individual on whom the composite is based (for example, Bruce, Ness, Hancock, Newman, & Rarity, 2002; Frowd, Bruce, Smith, & Hancock, 2008; Frowd, Carson, Ness, McQuiston-Surret, Richardson, Baldwin, & Hancock, 2005; Shepherd, Ellis, McMurran, & Davies, 1978). The main reason for this poor performance has been attributed to the fact that composite techniques require a witness to recall individual facial features without the benefit of the original context in which they were viewed—namely, the offender's entire face. But people don't typically encode the details of individual facial features (for example, "I noticed that the distance between his eyes was a little shorter than the distance between his upper lip and nose") unless those features are unusually prominent. Instead, it is much more likely for people to encode holistic information about a person's appearance, along the lines of "He looked a little like you, officer, only younger and more attractive," or "He looked like the typical businessperson you see downtown" (for example, Bruce & Young, 1998; Frowd et al., 2008). Few people have the ability to express specifically what it was about another person that made that person, for example, attractive or resemble a businessperson unless they are given explicit instructions to encode a face by paying attention to individual facial features (for example, Wells & Turtle, 1988). Instead, investigators with experience eliciting descriptions from witnesses are all too familiar with the response, "His chin [nose, ears, or other facial feature] was average looking, you know."

Sketch Artists

Despite the generally poor quality of composite sketches, a skilled person can sometimes facilitate the Identi-Kit or Photo-Fit procedures by drawing from the witness details of the offender's face that often lead to a particular holistic impression. That skill, however, is usually confined to sketch artists. A good sketch artist working with a cooperative witness who got a good look at an offender can sometimes produce astonishingly accurate drawings. The widely publicized "Scarborough Rapist" sketch in the 1980s, for example, turned out to be an eerily accurate rendition of Paul Bernardo, who was, of course, later investigated regarding the rapes in question. Sketches, however, can potentially mislead both the investigators and the community, who might ignore an otherwise suspicious person because he or she does not match a sketch that is inaccurate for some reason. In addition, if a suspect is subsequently detained, and he doesn't look at all like the composite that was circulating in the case, it can be a challenge for police to explain the discrepancy.

Composites from a Cold Mugshot Search

Given the shortage of talented artists at the disposal of the police, it makes sense to look at one last technique that can be used by almost anyone for generating a likeness of an offender. Earlier in this chapter we discussed the possibility that a witness will look at mugshots and not identify any of them as photographs of the offender, but may identify a few as depicting people similar in appearance to the offender. It is not uncommon for a witness to say something such as, "The guy I saw had hair like this guy, number 45, and this other guy, number 131, has the same kind of eyes—dark brown, almost black." The officer monitoring the mugshot inspection will note the witness's comments and set aside the photographs singled out by the witness. The best possible use of these photographs is to extract, by means of computer image manipulation, the features identified by the witness as being similar to those of the offender and combine them in a computer composite. At first glance this might seem to resemble the Identi-Kit or Photo-Fit procedure, but the key difference is that the facial features are recognized in the context of a real person's entire face, not as isolated noses, ears, or other particular facial features. The resulting image amounts to a more natural, and hence possibly more accurate, representation of the offender's face.

RECOMMENDED PROTOCOL FOR EYEWITNESS IDENTIFICATIONS

The logic and recommendations discussed in this chapter have been incorporated into a number of protocols for eyewitness identification procedures across jurisdictions in Canada, the United States, and around the world. Perhaps most relevant for Canadian investigators, however, are the recommendations arising from the Sophonow Inquiry (Cory, 2001), which are based on extensive research into mistaken eyewitness identification and testimony at the inquiry from key figures in the area, including Elizabeth Loftus and Peter Neufeld. The Sophonow Inquiry includes the following recommendations for a photo lineup procedure (from Lepard & Campbell, 2009, pp. 13-14):

- The "photo pack" should contain at least 10 subjects.
- The photographs should resemble as closely as possible the eyewitnesses' description or, if that is not possible, then they should be as close as possible in appearance to the suspect's photo.
- Everything should be recorded on video or audio, from the time the officer meets the witness, through showing the photos, to the end of the interview.
- The officer showing the photo pack should not know who the suspect is and should not be involved in the investigation.
- The officer should tell the witness that he or she does not know who the suspect is or whether his or her photo is contained in the lineup and should advise the witness that it is just as important to clear the innocent as it is to identify the suspect.

- The photo pack should be presented to each witness separately.
- The photo pack must be presented sequentially and not as a package.
- There should be a form for signatures setting out in writing the comments of the officer and the witness. All comments of the witness must be recorded verbatim and signed by the witness.
- Officers should not speak to witnesses after the lineup regarding their identification or their inability to identify anyone.

Investigators are encouraged to review the above guidelines when preparing to conduct a photo lineup, but should also refer to the procedures and forms used by their police service for specific direction on conducting a photo lineup during the course of an investigation.

Note that the above list includes the key points we've discussed, such as using the match-to-description technique for selecting distracters; sequential presentation of the photos by a "blind" administrator; and recording the entire procedure, including any comments made by the witness. In addition to the points above, as discussed earlier, we support the recommendation that some expression of confidence be requested explicitly from the witness, ideally in the instructions provided at the outset of the procedure. As well, we've discussed in some detail how the recommendation that distracter photos "should be as close as possible in appearance to the suspect's photo" can lead to the problematic "clone lineup"; fortunately, the Sophonow protocol recommends this technique only when the match-to-description option is not available for some reason. We hope that the logic we've discussed in this chapter helps to achieve the appropriate balance between fairness and probative value when selecting photos in this way.

Our main point is that, as with any other type of evidence, the quality of the eyewitness evidence you collect will be affected by the procedures you use to collect it. The procedures suggested in this chapter are based on the results of scientific research, logic, legal considerations, and common police practices already in place. They are designed to provide the best possible eyewitness identification evidence by minimizing the rate of mistaken identifications of innocent people and maximizing the rate of accurate identifications of guilty suspects."

KEY TERMS

absolute-judgment strategy
cold mugshot search
composite sketch
distracters
double-blind procedure
estimator variables
Identi-Kit technique

Photo-Fit technique
propitious heterogeneity
relative-judgment strategy
showup
system variables
walkthrough procedure

FURTHER READING

Cutler, B., & Kovera, M. (2010). *Evaluating eyewitness identification.* New York: Oxford University Press.

Cutler, B., & Penrod, S. (1995). *Mistaken identification: The eyewitness, psychology and the law.* New York: Cambridge University Press.

Doyle, J. (2005). *True witness.* New York: Palgrave Macmillan.

Munsterberg, H., Hatala, M., & Loftus, E. (2009). *On the witness stand: Essays on psychology and crime.* Greentop, MO: Greentop Academic Press.

Scheck, B., Neufeld, P., & Dwyer, J. (2000). Actual innocence: Five days to execution and other dispatches from the wrongly convicted. New York: Doubleday.

Sporer, S., Malpass, R., & Koehnken, G. (1996). *Psychological issues in eyewitness identification.* Hillsdale, NJ: Lawrence Erlbaum Associates.

Thompson-Cannino, J., Cotton, R., & Torneo, E. (2009). *Picking cotton: Our memoir of injustice and redemption.* New York: St. Martin's Press.

REVIEW QUESTIONS

TRUE OR FALSE

_____ 1. Video recordings of both a live lineup and a photo lineup are recommended, where possible, as a means of assisting the court in determining the "probative value" of an eyewitness's identification of a suspect.

_____ 2. The most common factor in wrongful conviction cases is eyewitness identification.

_____ 3. The number of photos used in a photo lineup is not a factor in constructing a lineup; however, it is recommended that between 25 and 30 photos be used.

_____ 4. If the photo lineup contains more than one suspect, the likelihood of a false identification rises dramatically.

_____ 5. It is important that the "innocent distracters" in a lineup be consistent with the description of the offender, but they need not necessarily look exactly like him or her.

_____ 6. Absolute-judgment eyewitness identifications tend to be fairer to the suspect than relative-judgment identifications.

_____ 7. The Identi-Kit technique works because it takes advantage of the typical witness's tendency to form a holistic impression of a person's appearance.

_____ 8. An eyewitness should be instructed to choose the lineup member who looks most like the perpetrator that he or she saw at the crime scene.

_____ 9. A lineup comprising live subjects rather than photographs is the most common police procedure for obtaining eyewitness identifications.

F

F

T

___ 10. A double-blind lineup is one in which all of the subjects are distracters.

___ 11. An efficient way to obtain eyewitness identifications in a crime involving multiple offenders is to include all of the suspects in the same photo lineup.

___ 12. An identification obtained through a cold mugshot search is likely to be less reliable than one obtained by arranging a traditional lineup.

MULTIPLE CHOICE

1. A showup is an unfair way of obtaining an identification because
   a. the suspect is displayed in a way that makes him or her the only reasonable choice.
   b. the witness may be too intimidated by the presence of the suspect to make a valid identification.
   c. the procedure violates the suspect's right to freedom from self-incrimination.
   d. the procedure does not normally allow for simultaneous presentation of lineup subjects.

2. A cold mugshot search is
   a. a photo lineup procedure used to confirm the identity of a deceased suspect.
   b. a procedure for creating a composite sketch of a suspect.
   c. a photo lineup procedure used to confirm the results of a live lineup.
   d. a witness's attempt to identify a suspect by viewing a collection of police file photographs.

3. Examples of estimator variables that might affect an eyewitness's ability to identify a suspect include:
   a. the distance between the witness and the offender, and the lighting available when the crime occurred;
   b. the stress level experienced by the witness at the time the crime occurred;
   c. the age, race, and gender of the witness;
   d. all of the above.

4. Using mock witnesses allows investigators to
   a. determine the accuracy of criteria for searching a photographic database of potential suspects.
   b. judge how well the real witness will hold up under cross-examination in court.
   c. test the fairness of a proposed photo lineup.
   d. give the witness lineup viewing practice before conducting a real lineup.

SHORT ANSWER

1. What is the danger in attempting to prosecute a case in which the only evidence is an eyewitness lineup identification?

2. Why do many researchers advocate a sequential presentation when lineups are conducted?

3. What are the benefits of a double-blind lineup?

Portals of Discovery: Investigative Failures and the Lessons Learned

7

"*If we are uncritical we shall always find what we want—we shall look for, and find, confirmations and we shall look away from, and not see, whatever might be dangerous to our pet theories.*"

Karl Popper

INTRODUCTION

Science has long recognized that the process of making observations, gathering evidence, and acquiring knowledge inevitably includes dealing with the possibility of error—indeed, the recognition of fallibility and the need for built-in error-checking mechanisms is central to the scientific method. The professionalization of investigative work, as discussed at the end of this chapter, demands that we adopt a similarly rigorous approach.

The Irish writer James Joyce called mistakes "the portals of discovery." This chapter examines some of the errors commonly identified in cases of investigative failure to discover what we can learn from them. In the majority of cases, failure resulted primarily from a combination of cognitive biases that we *all* share and institutional pressures that we *all* face; professional incompetence, misconduct, and malice were identified only occasionally. Because these cognitive and institutional factors are common and something that every investigator is likely to encounter, we may not be able to completely eliminate the errors that result from them. We *can*, however, learn more about them and apply various techniques with a view to minimizing their effects.

CHAPTER OBJECTIVES

After completing this chapter, you should be able to:

- Explain the most significant sources of error in criminal investigations.
- Describe what tunnel vision is and how it can affect an investigation.
- Outline some of the cognitive and institutional biases that contribute to tunnel vision.
- Explain why it is difficult to avoid common investigative errors even when you are aware of them.
- Understand the strategies investigators can use to minimize cognitive bias and reduce the risk of developing tunnel vision.

KNOWING THE FACTS AND MANAGING ERROR

The classic 1970s rock song "Take the Money and Run" tells the story of two young people who shoot and rob a man in Texas and the police officer who pursues them. It includes the memorable lyric, "Billy Mack is a detective down in Texas. You know he knows just exactly what the facts is" (Miller, 1976). Every law enforcement officer who investigates a crime, charges someone with an offence, and subsequently testifies in court will face the same task—explaining *how* they know "just exactly what the facts is" (or "are"—which is grammatically correct, but doesn't rhyme with "Texas"). The simple answer, of course, is that they have conducted a thorough, objective investigation in which they made certain observations and collected certain pieces of evidence ("the facts"); this process has led them to form a belief about what the facts are, and to have a certain level of confidence in the validity of that belief. While this process may seem simple, it is actually quite complex. Acquiring reliable knowledge about the world through observation is a demanding task fraught with risks—the greatest of which is believing you are right when you are wrong.

Many people believe that acquiring knowledge is similar to gathering seashells on a beach—you walk along, picking up shells and putting them into your bucket, and the more shells you gather, the fuller your bucket becomes. Similarly, when you are learning about something, the more facts you gather and put into your "bucket," the more knowledge you have. While the "bucket theory" of knowledge, as it is sometimes called (Boland, 2002, p. 1), has some validity—knowledge *does* depend in part on gathering facts—it does not deal sufficiently with the key issue in the production of knowledge—the management of error. As we shall see, it is easy to believe that the more evidence you have in support of your investigative theory, the more likely it is to be correct. But it is the ability to manage for *quality* (and not simply to gather for *quantity*) that is the most difficult part of really learning about something. Valid knowledge does not result simply from adding more confirming evidence in support of what one already "knows," but rather from eliminating possible sources of error.

A number of cognitive biases and institutional pressures reinforce our natural inclination to believe that the more evidence we have in support of a theory, the more likely it is to be correct; they also make the task of interpreting the value of the evidence that one has gathered a difficult one. These factors are discussed in the following sections.

TUNNEL VISION

The famous physicist Stephen Hawking said that "[t]he greatest enemy of knowledge is not ignorance, it is the illusion of knowledge." The illusion of knowledge can contribute to **tunnel vision**, which has been identified as one of the principal causes of wrongful convictions in Canada, the United States, Australia, New Zealand, and the United Kingdom.

Tunnel vision was first discussed in Canada during the Kaufman Inquiry into the wrongful conviction of Guy Paul Morin. Since then it has been dealt with in a number of cases—notably, *R v. Spackman* (2009); *R v. Rahman* (2008); *R v. A.P.* (2008); and *R v. Knox* (2006). Tunnel vision has been defined in various ways, including:

tunnel vision the single-minded and overly narrow focus on a particular investigative or prosecutorial theory, so as to unreasonably colour the evaluation of information received and one's conduct in response to that information

- "the single-minded and overly narrow focus on a particular investigative or prosecutorial theory, so as to unreasonably colour the evaluation of information received and one's conduct in response to that information" (Kaufman, 1998, p. 1136); and

- "an unreasonable lack of objectivity by the police in an investigation, or by the Crown in the related prosecution, that creates a risk of a wrongful conviction or otherwise undermines the reliability of information and evidence available to the Court" (*R v. Spackman*, 2009, at para. D.2.2).

Although there is no single "official" definition of tunnel vision, authorities appear to agree on its principal elements (MacFarlane 2008, p. 34):

- Tunnel vision involves an overly narrow focus on a particular investigative or prosecutorial theory of the crime.
- Tunnel vision has the effect of "colouring" both the evaluation of the gathered information and the investigative conduct in response to that information.

As part of the "colouring process," tunnel vision can lead investigators, prosecutors, judges, and defence lawyers to focus on a particular conclusion and then filter all evidence in a case "through the lens provided by that conclusion" (Findley & Scott, 2006, p. 292). The filtering happens unconsciously, with evidence that will build a case against a particular suspect being filtered in and evidence that tends to point away from the same suspect's guilt being ignored or even suppressed (MacFarlane, 2008, p. 34). Information that supports the conclusion is considered more important, while evidence that is inconsistent is "overlooked or dismissed as irrelevant, incredible, or unreliable" (Findley & Scott, 2006, p. 292). Again, this is typically not a conscious process, but a side effect of how humans often make decisions.

Working with a Working Theory

It is important to emphasize that despite the severe criticisms made of some investigators for focusing too narrowly on a particular theory of a crime during an investigation, being guided by a "theory of the crime" during an investigation is not itself problematic. If an investigator's working theory is based on a comprehensive evaluation of the available evidence, if the investigator draws reasonable inferences from that evidence, and if the investigator remains receptive to the possibility that he or she may have to revise or abandon the theory if it is not supported by the evidence, then a working theory is a perfectly legitimate and defensible investigative tool. In fact, it is difficult to envisage how one could effectively investigate any phenomenon without the use a working theory of some kind to manage the volume of information that one encounters and to make judgments about what is and what is not likely to be relevant. Indeed, "filtering" information for probable relevancy is a necessary, and inevitable, part of the investigative process.

There is no reason for investigators to be hesitant about using a working theory to guide their investigation or tentative about explaining why they did so. On the contrary, assuming that investigators employ the suggested techniques discussed below, under the heading "Staying Out of the Tunnel," a working theory is a useful tool.

The problem of tunnel vision is not associated with any particular group of investigators or investigative agency; rather, it is a potential problem in *all* investigations, as noted in the Sophonow Inquiry (see Cory, 2001), "Tunnel vision," in "Recommendations," under "Investigation of Terry Arnold as a Suspect"):

> Tunnel vision is insidious. It can affect an officer, or, indeed, anyone involved in the administration of justice with sometimes tragic results. It results in the officer becoming so focused upon an individual or incident that no other person or incident registers in the officer's thoughts. Thus, tunnel vision can result in the elimination of other suspects who should be investigated. Equally, events which could lead to identifying other suspects are eliminated from the officer's thinking. Anyone, police officer, counsel or judge can become infected by this virus.

The reason why tunnel vision is so widespread is because it arises out of common human cognitive tendencies and institutional pressures (MacFarlane, 2008). These are explored in the following sections.

Cognitive Biases

To explain how tunnel vision works and why it is so common, psychologists examine what are known as cognitive biases. The term "cognition" refers to various thinking processes such as perception, memory, judgment, and reasoning; the term **cognitive bias** refers to the tendency for humans to make consistent and predictable errors in the way they perceive, recall, interpret, and act on information. Cognitive biases must be distinguished from "bias" as the term is commonly understood—that is, in the sense of cultural, racial, or religious bias. A cognitive bias is *not* the result of an emotional or intellectual choice for or against something, but is rather a natural tendency to make systematic "thinking errors" (Heuer, 1999, p. 111).

As Findley and Scott (2006) make clear, cognitive biases are a function of the way we think; we all use them without being aware that we are doing so. They are best thought of as automatic mental filtering mechanisms that help us cope with and efficiently process the mass of information that bombards us on a daily basis. Our need to use such mechanisms to categorize, interpret, and selectively attend to information can, however, lead us to make serious errors of which we are often totally unaware. And when such errors occur among actors in the criminal justice system, the consequences can be devastating.

Researchers in the 1970s sought to understand how people made judgments under conditions of uncertainty, and what role heuristics and biases play in such judgments (Tversky & Kahneman, 1974). They found that while **heuristics** (rules of thumb) are efficient and usually effective, they lead to biases. For example, as a rule of thumb (heuristic) for judging distance, clarity is generally a useful tool: in a given scene, objects that are nearer are seen more sharply than those that are farther away. However, in poor visibility objects tend to appear blurred, causing distances to be overestimated. The opposite is true when visibility is good. Under these circumstances, following this rule of thumb will cause a bias, or a distortion of judgment. The influence of such biases is extremely difficult to surmount because, much like an optical illusion, "the error remains compelling even when one is fully aware of its nature" (Heuer, 1999, p 112).

cognitive bias
the tendency of humans to make consistent and predictable errors in the way they perceive, recall, interpret, and act on information

heuristics "rules of thumb," or a commonsense guide used in problem solving or investigation; sometimes referred to as an "educated guess" or learning by "trial and error"

Since Tversky and Kahneman's groundbreaking studies, a number of researchers have examined how cognitive biases affect decision making in areas such as intelligence analysis (Heuer, 1999; CIA, 2009) and in the criminal investigation process (Rossmo, 2009; Findley & Scott, 2006; MacFarlane, 2006; MacFarlane, 2008; Ask, 2006); we explore their findings in the sections below. Our discussion illustrates how these natural mental tendencies can and do affect the way in which police, prosecutors, and judges, among others, gather and interpret data. But just because cognitive biases are natural inclinations does not mean that those within the justice system bear no responsibility for trying to mitigate their effects—they *do*. As Findley and Scott (2006) stress, investigators and others must make themselves aware of the existence and effect of these tendencies and adopt strategies designed to counter their negative effects. A number of these strategies are considered later in this chapter.

Confirmation Bias

One of the most significant biases involved in tunnel vision is **confirmation bias**, defined as "the tendency to seek or interpret evidence in ways that support existing beliefs, expectations, or hypotheses" (Findley & Scott, 2006, p. 309). In addition to seeking information that confirms their hypotheses, people tend to *avoid* information that would disprove them, or at least they often don't know where to look for such information.

Psychologist Peter Wason coined the term "confirmation bias" to describe a phenomenon he observed among participants in studies first conducted about 50 years ago (for example, Wason, 1960). In one study, participants were given a series of three numbers {2, 4, 6} and told that they conformed to a rule. The participants were then asked to determine what the rule was by generating their own three-number series and submitting these to the experimenter, who would tell them whether each series fit the rule as they submitted it. The participants were told that when they believed they had discovered the rule, they should announce it to the experimenter. Most participants came up with a theory regarding the rule almost immediately (for example, "add two to the previous number"), but, interestingly, for the most part *they only submitted series of numbers that fit their theory*—for example, the series {8, 10, 12}. They tended not to submit series that could have potentially *disproved* their theory—for example, the series {2, 3, 4}. Had they done so, they would have realized that their theory was not correct—that is, they would have discovered that *any* series of ascending numbers was acceptable (Russo & Meloy, 2008).

Proposing examples that fit with a hypothesized rule may seem to be a perfectly logical way for a person to prove that their hypothesis is true, especially when their examples are shown to be *consistent* with the truth. But *it isn't* the most logical strategy because it actually prevents one from discovering that one's hypothesis is *wrong*. This is the logic behind the common phrase "the exception proves the rule," where "prove" means "to test" the rule, just as in the context of evaluating automobiles, a "proving ground" is another term for a "test track."

Consistent with Wason's findings, subsequent research has consistently shown that people tend to seek information in ways that increase their confidence in prior

confirmation bias
the tendency to seek or interpret evidence in ways that support existing beliefs, expectations, or hypotheses

beliefs or hypotheses, even when they have "no vested interest" in the hypotheses (Findley & Scott, 2006, p. 311). This tendency is illogical for two reasons:

1. it prevents people from discovering that a particular hypothesis is wrong, and

2. it does not provide as strong a confirmation of the truth of the hypothesis as the *failure* of a deliberate attempt to *disprove* the hypothesis would provide.

Findley and Scott (2006) point out that not only are people inclined to seek confirming information, they also have a tendency to *recall* information in a biased way—namely, in a manner that favours information that is consistent with a presented hypothesis or belief. People also tend to give greater weight to information that supports existing beliefs than to information that is contrary to those beliefs. As a result, people tend to require *less* information that is *consistent* with their hypothesis to accept their hypothesis as true, but *more* information that is *inconsistent* with their hypothesis to reject it as false. Moreover, people don't just ignore information that is inconsistent with their previously held beliefs—they often scrutinize it in order to undermine it; thus there is a tendency to regard contradictory information as flawed or irrelevant. Again, these are common human tendencies that have been identified and studied for many decades, including Wason's original research in the 1960s and a flurry of related research in the 1970s and '80s (for example, Gilovich & Douglas, 1986; Lord, Ross & Lepper, 1979). The significance of such tendencies in the criminal justice system, where a person is being judged (whether by police, prosecutors, defence counsel, judge, or jury) and where the initial working hypothesis that is presented to each "judge" is that the accused is guilty—notwithstanding the theoretical presumption of innocence—are clear (Findley & Scott, 2006, p. 314).

In light of the above, it should not be surprising that experiments conducted with police detectives, prosecutors, and judges have shown that their initial hypothesis regarding a crime affects how they interpret subsequent crime-related information (Ask & Granhag, 2005; Rassin, 2010). Ask and Granhag (2005), for example, found that in experiments where a group of students and a group of criminal investigators were read a set of facts based on a preliminary homicide investigation, and their initial hypotheses regarding the crime were then manipulated by providing them with background information that suggested that the prime suspect had a jealousy motive or that there might be an alternative suspect, the students ascribed guilt to the prime suspect only when a potential motive was presented, whereas the investigators ascribed guilt to the prime suspect regardless of the hypothesis—suggesting that they were less sensitive to alternative interpretations of the evidence. Rassin (2010) studied a group of police officers, prosecutors, and judges using the same experimental scenario employed by Ask and Granhag and obtained similar results—the participants' evaluations of the various investigative findings were equally incriminating for the prime suspect whether they were given information regarding a possible alternative suspect or not.

As we mentioned at the outset of this chapter, confirmation bias has been a constant theme in several Canadian judicial inquiries. It was identified as an important factor in the Kaufman Inquiry (1998), the Sophonow Inquiry (Cory, 2001), the Lamer Inquiry (2006), and more recently in the Goudge Inquiry (2008). In the Lamer Inquiry, retired Chief Justice Antonio Lamer made an observation that goes to the very heart of the confirmation bias issue when he remarked, regarding one of the investigative theories held by the police, that "the theory must derive from an objective assessment of the evidence. Here, the evidence was assessed with a view to supporting an unsupportable theory" (Lamer, 2006, p. 257).

Belief Perseverance

The same cognitive tendencies that affect the way in which we gather and interpret information, and that can hinder our ability to rationally and logically assess new information and adjust our hypotheses accordingly, also make us resistant to changing our beliefs in the face of new evidence that critically weakens our initial hypotheses. This phenomenon is known as **belief perseverance**, which refers to the fact that people are naturally reluctant to give up their initial conclusions about something even when the foundation for their initial conclusion has been completely undermined. This is why people are more likely to be *critical* of information that is contrary to their pre-existing beliefs and interpret ambiguous information as *supporting* rather than *weakening* their initial beliefs (Findley & Scott, 2006, p. 314).

The issue of belief perseverance has been clearly illustrated in a number of wrongful conviction cases in both Canada and the United States in which DNA evidence exonerated the defendant, yet investigators and prosecutors persisted in believing that the person was guilty (Findley & Scott, 2006, p. 315; MacFarlane, 2008). A particularly striking example of this occurred during the public inquiry that followed the wrongful murder conviction of Guy Paul Morin, where the lead prosecutor clung tenaciously to his belief that jailhouse informants involved in the case had told the truth, despite being confronted with overwhelming evidence that they had lied. This led the inquiry commissioner to state that the prosecutor suffered from tunnel vision "in the most staggering proportions" (Kaufman, 1998, Vol. 1, p. 490). During the same inquiry, in what was characterized by the press as a "stunning moment," a junior prosecutor recounted a long list of evidence she felt was still compelling and refused to accept the government's finding that Mr. Morin was innocent. Two days later, however, she made an emotional apology for having doubted the validity of Mr. Morin's exoneration (Makin, 2004). Such is the power of belief perseverance.

belief perseverance
people's natural reluctance to give up their initial conclusions about something even when the foundation for their initial conclusion has been completely undermined

Hindsight Bias

Another cognitive bias involved in the phenomenon of tunnel vision is **hindsight bias**, sometimes referred to as the "knew-it-all-along effect" or the "Monday morning quarterback effect," in reference to people's tendency to second-guess football plays from Sunday afternoon NFL games. Research shows that people tend to believe, after an event has happened, that it was inevitable, or that its occurrence was more probable than was originally thought (Findley & Scott, 2006; Fischhoff, 1975). For example, once police decide on the prime suspect in a particular criminal investigation, hindsight bias (or looking back) suggests that the person was the likely

hindsight bias
sometimes referred to as the "knew-it-all-along effect," the tendency of people to believe, after an event has happened, that it was inevitable or that its occurrence was more probable than was originally thought

offender all along; this belief is further strengthened by the tendency to best remember those incriminating facts that support this view. Hindsight bias is a function of how our memories work. When we remember something, we do not simply recall it from our minds fully formed, but we assemble it from fragments of information. Those fragments are dynamic, being constantly refreshed as we take in new information. When we remember an event, it is the refreshed fragments that are recalled, thus making the conclusion appear inevitable, or more probable than we could possibly have known at the beginning. In other words, the result of this after-the-fact judgment process is that "[a] given outcome seems inevitable or, at least, more plausible than alternative outcomes" (Findley & Scott, 2006, p. 317).

Hindsight bias may affect actors in the criminal justice system in a number of different ways. In the case of a criminal suspect, once the police begin to focus on an individual whom they believe is guilty, hindsight bias tends to make it appear to them that their choice of a particular individual as a suspect was inevitable. There is then the tendency to overestimate the degree to which the suspect appeared to be guilty from the beginning and to recall the facts that are most consistent with the investigators' belief in the suspect's guilt.

Hindsight bias can also help explain how the eyewitness identification process can be affected by investigators, which in turn can contribute to tunnel vision. The fact that eyewitness confidence is highly susceptible to feedback is well documented— eyewitnesses who receive feedback that confirms their identification decision ("Good, you picked the right person") often indicate a significant increase in their confidence about the correctness of their identification decision (for example, Wells & Bradfield, 1998). Perhaps even more interesting, however, is that witnesses may also come to have more confidence than they should in their general memory for the entire event. For example, an eyewitness who had a poor view of an offender and/or paid little attention to an event when it occurred will likely have a relatively poor memory for the offender and other details of the crime. But if the witness were to take part in a photo lineup procedure and receive feedback that confirms their identification decision, they may also "remember" the original viewing circumstances as more favourable than they really were and their own memory as better than it really is (Wells & Bradfield, 1998).

There are additional cognitive biases (many of which are variations on confirmation bias, belief perseverance, and hindsight bias) that can affect the quality of people's decision making. Findley and Scott (2006) discuss these in detail, including the **reiteration effect**, outcome bias, and the anchoring effect. Readers are encouraged to learn more about these potential barriers to effective reasoning and decision making in criminal investigations.

Institutional Pressures

In addition to cognitive biases, there are various **institutional pressures** that predispose (MacFarlane, 2008, p. 5) actors within the criminal justice system to develop tunnel vision during criminal investigations. The following can contribute, usually in indirect ways, to the development of tunnel vision during an investigation:

reiteration effect the tendency for people's confidence in the truth of an assertion to increase if the assertion is repeated, independent of whether the assertion is true or false and/or evidence that suggests that the assertion is false

institutional pressure factors that make it more likely that an investigator will develop tunnel vision—for example, pressure on the investigator from their superiors, the victims, and the community to solve a case, as well as limited resources

- *Pressure on police investigators from their superiors, the victims, the community, and the media.*   This factor is especially relevant in high-profile cases (murders, abductions, sexual crimes, and crimes involving children) that create public anxiety and result in pressure on the police to solve the case quickly. These crimes, particularly crimes involving children, can affect investigators emotionally, which can make it difficult for them to remain detached and objective and contribute further to the possibility of developing tunnel vision.

- *Limited resources and a steady volume of crime that must be investigated.*   This combination can place additional pressures on investigators, from both the public and police management, to clear cases. Investigative managers must constantly make decisions about the amount of time and resources that can by allocated to each investigation, which can limit the amount of time an investigator is able to spend investigating alternative suspects. Also, in the case of an investigator who has spent considerable time on an investigation and who is denied the use of valuable investigative resources (such as the use of a wiretap or forensic testing), the investigator may be forced to attempt to build his or her case using resources of lesser quality (such as a jailhouse informant or a tentative eyewitness). Some observers have also argued that the rise of the victims' rights movement has placed pressure on investigators to clear cases, which can contribute further to tunnel vision (Findley & Scott, 2006; MacFarlane, 2008). They maintain that the movement has resulted in pressure on investigators to accept victims' accounts of events too readily, charge the suspect, and leave it to the courts to decide what really happened. For a specific example, see the sexual assault case of *R v. A.P.* (2008).

Taken together, the above pressures can cause investigators to become emotionally attached to a particular theory of a case, which in turn can lead to a shift from an objective search for evidence to an exercise designed to prove that the investigator's preferred theory of the crime is correct. This shift can affect the collection of physical evidence. Decisions about where investigative time and energy is best spent and what type of evidence is most relevant is significantly influenced by one's theory of the crime, and inculpatory *and* exculpatory evidence may have been missed if the preferred theory of the crime turns out later to be wrong.

In addition to institutional factors that can indirectly (implicitly) contribute to the development of tunnel vision, police training is a factor that can make a direct (explicit) contribution. Law enforcement training has typically included little if any instruction on how to recognize and counteract the dangers of tunnel vision, although this has begun to change (see, for instance, Ontario Ministry of Community Safety and Correctional Services, 2004, and the Major Crime Investigative Techniques Course 2009, as discussed in Ross, 2010). Some law enforcement training, particularly in the area of interrogation techniques, actively promotes investigative practices that encourage tunnel vision. At least one pair of researchers has stated that "the very notion of a Reid 'interrogation' ... expressly embraces the foundational problems with tunnel vision—a premature conclusion of guilt, and an unwillingness to consider alternatives" (Findley & Scott, 2006, p. 335). (See Chapter 4,

Interviewing Suspects II: Approaches and Techniques, under the heading The BAI: Assessing Credibility and Determining Guilt, for a discussion of determining guilt.) Investigators must guard against this frame of mind when conducting interrogations and assessing evidence.

STAYING OUT OF THE TUNNEL

Research has shown that investigative failures are the result of numerous factors, including unethical conduct by investigators, and police failure to employ best practices in areas such as eyewitness identification, photo lineup methods, interviewing and interrogation, jailhouse informants, and DNA technology (FPT Heads of Prosecutions Committee Working Group, 2004). Past investigative failures also show clearly that tunnel vision can profoundly affect the lives of those who are drawn into the criminal justice system, and that investigative judgments are susceptible to various biases that necessitate safeguards to counter them (Ask & Granhag, 2005; Ask, 2006).

Some researchers (for example, Snook & Cullen, 2008) have said that recommendations either to fix or prevent tunnel vision are premature and that such recommendations are as likely to fail as they are to succeed because we simply don't know enough about the phenomenon yet. They point out that the term "tunnel vision" has not been precisely defined and that, although it has been the subject of much attention in the courts, to date social scientists have not devoted much research attention to it. In addition, they point out that the phenomenon of tunnel vision has not been studied in cases of investigative success, only failure, and that it may have merit as a positive cognitive strategy that allows investigators to operate effectively in environments where intense time and information pressures are a reality.

Although these points are valid—we do need a more precise definition and more research on how tunnel vision operates in scenarios leading to positive outcomes as well as negative ones—it is clear that certain cognitive processes at work in us all, although helpful in many situations, can make us less receptive to new information in others, ultimately leading to negative consequences. Concrete techniques, however, exist to help investigators manage their information-processing strategies and decrease the likelihood of investigative errors. The two primary steps are:

1. educating investigators about the dangers of tunnel vision, including sensitizing them to its causes and consequences; and

2. teaching investigators techniques they can use to counteract the influences that lead to tunnel vision.

These influences are so deeply embedded in our reasoning abilities and our institutions that simply becoming aware of them, although necessary, is not sufficient. For this reason it has been suggested that "explicit debiasing" techniques are needed to counteract those influences that lead to the development of tunnel vision (Kebbel, Muller & Martin, 2010). To be truly effective, such techniques must become part of routine investigative protocols.

The techniques described below have all been used in the real world by scientists, intelligence analysts, and others to help maintain their receptiveness to information and assist them in managing the risk of error in their investigations (descriptions adapted from Findley & Scott, 2006; MacFarlane, 2008; Rossmo, 2009; Heuer, 1999; CIA, 2009; Kebbel, Muller & Martin, 2010.). Some are simple and easy to apply, while others may take more time to use effectively. Because investigations vary widely in scope, complexity, and seriousness, it will be up to you to decide to what extent the following techniques may be required in a particular investigation to help minimize the effects of cognitive bias and institutional pressures.

1. *Suspend your judgment.* Investigators must consciously attempt to suspend their judgment about a case and resist the impulse to draw conclusions too quickly. They must try to keep an "open mind" as the facts come out, and allow their understanding of the case to be formed and reformed as the evidence emerges. As mentioned earlier, an investigator's initial judgments about the evidence in a case can have a significant influence on his or her final analysis of that evidence.

    Creating a large chart onto which each piece of evidence (physical evidence and witness statements) is placed as it is gathered, and summarizing what each piece does or does not tell you, is one way to avoid hasty judgments. During complex investigations, it has the added benefit of helping you maintain a focus on the "big picture."

2. *Adopt the opposite view (or "counterarguing").* One of the products of confirmation bias is overconfidence in the accuracy of one's own interpretations and conclusions; research suggests that this can be mitigated to some degree by requiring people to articulate the reasons why the opposite of their own position might be true (Findley & Scott, 2006). Investigators should therefore consider the opposite of their currently held position and articulate how the available evidence might support it—a technique known as "counterarguing." Counterarguing also has potential to offset the effects of belief perseverance. It has been suggested that, in order to be really effective, counterarguing should become an established part of every investigative process (Findley & Scott, 2006).

3. *Seek the inconsistent.* To counter our tendency to seek only evidence that confirms our theories, investigators should test their theories by seeking facts that are *inconsistent* with their initial judgements about the case. In the case of a witness's statement or a suspect's confession, for example, investigators should look carefully at statements that are not consistent with other known facts about the case or which cannot be corroborated by other evidence. In the case of a witness who, for example, describes a vehicle seen fleeing the scene of the crime as being a particular make and colour, ask whether other witnesses describe the vehicle differently or whether available video surveillance imagery either disconfirms or corroborates their description. In the case of a suspect's confession, does the confession contain information that is inconsistent with other known details of the offence? Does the suspect claim to have been at a particular place at a certain time that, on the basis of other known evidence—for example, an analysis of the geographic location of the suspect's cellular telephone transmissions—seems unlikely?

Finding the Best Explanation by Eliminating the Worst

Science philosopher Karl Popper (1959) popularized the principle of falsification, which holds that we can never conclude with certainty that a hypothesis is correct, because we may at some point discover evidence that refutes it. However, we *can* conclude with certainty that a particular hypothesis is *false*, and by eliminating false hypotheses we can determine which of the remaining hypotheses provides the *best explanation* of reality. To illustrate this, Popper used the example of a black swan: no matter how many white swans you may have observed in your life, you are not justified in concluding that "all swans are white"—there may be a black swan somewhere that you simply have not observed. However, observing a single black swan *does* allow you to conclude with certainty that the hypothesis "all swans are white" is false.

In a forensic context, because an investigator has made a number of observations consistent with his or her theory of the crime does not mean that the investigator can conclude with certainty that his or her theory is *correct*—it is always possible that some future observation will refute it. The reality of this situation has been painfully illustrated in many wrongful conviction cases where a mass of seemingly irrefutable evidence indicating guilt has been countered by the results of a single DNA test, excluding the suspect and disproving the investigator's theory of the case (for example, Guy Paul Morin, David Milgaard, and Simon Marshall). We must always remember that our investigative theories are, at best, only tentative explanations of the evidence and are subject to both revision and refutation.

4. *Consider the alternatives.* An investigator or an investigative supervisor should posit an alternative theory or theories of the crime and offer evidence and arguments to reject the alternative(s). If the alternatives are fairly and successfully rejected, then confidence in the original theory may legitimately increase. If, however, the evidence supports an alternative theory, that theory must be explored fully until it can either be rejected or replace the original theory. This is an important strategy because research indicates that investigators facing time pressures—a reality in virtually all significant investigations—generate fewer alternative explanations for the crimes they are investigating than those not facing such pressures (Doran, Long, & Alison, 2009).

To apply this technique in practice, investigators can construct a matrix with the individual pieces of evidence listed down the left side of the page and the alternative hypotheses set as column headings across the top. For example, in addition to various others, the far left column might include the following entries: "Joe's DNA found on the victim," "Fred's bootprint found behind the barn," "James's hair found on the victim," and "Victim seen getting into Carl's van." The column headings representing the different hypotheses might read: "Joe did it," "Fred did it," "James did it," and "Carl did it." Within the matrix, investigators can work their way down the items in the left-hand column and assess whether each piece of

A Lesson from the World's Most Famous Detective

Sir Arthur Conan Doyle's master detective Sherlock Holmes recognized the significance of confirmation bias decades before Wason's famous experiments. In *The Adventure of Black Peter* (1904), Holmes is called to assist the police in a difficult murder investigation. While the investigation is progressing, the police, who have gathered evidence consistent with their theory of the crime, arrest a man for the murder. The arresting officer then dismisses Holmes, telling him that his assistance is not required after all and that he may return home to London. Fortunately for the man who was arrested, Holmes does not return home, but completes his investigation and delivers the true culprit into the hands of the police.

In the investigative debriefing that follows, Holmes admonishes the young detective, telling him that he had become so absorbed in pursuing the suspect that fit his theory of the crime that he "could not spare a thought" to the true murderer (Doyle, 1904, p. 553). Holmes teaches the young detective a valuable lesson in the dangers of confirmation bias, leaving the reader with a quotation that remains as relevant for investigators today as it was when he first uttered the words more than one hundred years ago: *"One should always look for a possible alternative and provide against [eliminate] it. It is the first rule of criminal investigation"* (Doyle, 1904, p. 550).

evidence "is consistent, inconsistent or not applicable to each hypothesis" (CIA, 2009, p. 15), concentrating on *disproving* hypotheses rather than proving them. Following their analysis, investigators should add up the pieces of evidence that are consistent and inconsistent with each hypothesis to sort the weakest explanations from the strongest (CIA, 2009). (For a more detailed discussion of this technique, see Heuer, 1999, pp. 95-110.)

5. *Approach with ignorance.* Investigators normally base their theory about a case or a suspect on what they know. At some point, given the knowledge and evidence they have gathered, they conclude that they have reasonable grounds to believe that a particular suspect is responsible for the crime—even if, as is often the case, there are gaps in their evidence and knowledge. The investigator may believe that the gaps that exist simply cannot be filled, or that they can be filled by further investigation after arrest. By taking an approach that focuses on what they do *not* know, investigators can reduce the chances of developing tunnel vision. This approach involves investigators asking themselves what information a "reasonable person" would want to know about a particular case and then building their case around what they don't know, but should. Investigators must then either fill in the gaps in their knowledge or explain why they can't be filled in; they must ask whether the gaps exist because the evidence has not yet been found or because their theory of the case is incorrect.

Taking, for example, the case of a homicide investigation in which a taxi driver was killed, a reasonable person would likely want to know when and where the murder occurred; whether the murder was the result of a robbery or some other motive; whether the killer had been a passenger in the taxi, or whether the driver had been attacked from the outside as he sat in his parked car; and whether the taxi driver had been dispatched to pick up a fare immediately prior to the murder. If the investigator knew that the murder had taken place in the cab, that the driver had not been dispatched to any calls prior to being attacked, and that the driver's money had not been taken, the investigator would want to focus on what he or she does *not* know, and ask *why* he or she does not know it. In this example, given that robbery does not appear to have been the motive (because the driver's money was not taken), one of the significant gaps that the investigator would want to focus on would be motive. If the killer's motive was not robbery, the investigator would want to ask whether the victim knew the killer, who had a personal motive for killing him.

6. *Make it explicit/key assumptions check.* Cognitive biases can be rendered less harmful by making them explicit. Visualization has been suggested as one way of maintaining a realistic picture of the level of uncertainty in a situation (Kebbel, Muller, & Martin, 2010). Using visualization programs or simple charts, an investigator or analyst can keep all relevant information— both confirming and disconfirming—visible and thus cognitively accessible.

    By making their assumptions, chains of inference, and areas of uncertainty visual, investigators are forced to confront them and consider on exactly what basis they know what they think they know. In doing so, they break their theories down into key parts and test the validity of each part. This is referred to as a "key assumptions check" (CIA, 2009, p. 7). The act of making assumptions and judgments of evidence explicit will help investigators clarify the strengths and weaknesses of their case and identify errors or unwarranted assumptions that may not have been obvious previously. Related to this is the role of devil's advocate. The devil's advocate identifies the key assumptions behind a strongly held belief of the investigator or investigative team and assesses the nature of the evidence that supports those assumptions. He or she then selects the assumptions that appear weakest and challenges them, pointing out the flaws and describing how the evidence could support an alternative hypothesis (CIA, 2009).

7. *Stimulate critical discussion.* In larger investigations, the use and management of subgroups dedicated to different tasks (for example, gathering physical evidence and conducting witness interviews) can both help facilitate independent lines of inquiry during an investigation and stimulate critical discussion about the significance of various pieces of evidence to the theory or theories of the case. In the major case management (MCM) model employed by Canadian police services to manage large or serious investigations such as homicides, case managers are encouraged to play the role of "contrarian" as one way to counteract the tendency to come to a conclusion about what the evidence "really means" too rapidly (Lepard & Campbell, 2009).

    The Vancouver Police Department is one example of a police service that assigns an investigator to this role. When a suspect is identified, the

Using the Key Assumptions Check to Test an Investigative Theory

The 2002 Washington, DC sniper case is an example of an investigation in which a key assumptions check would have been effective. Following 13 shootings in the Washington, DC area over two-and-a-half weeks, investigators quickly adopted the theory—on the basis of a series of vague witness accounts and assumptions regarding the typical criminal profile of a serial killer—that the sniper was likely a single, white male with military training, driving a white van. Had investigators employed the key assumptions check, they could have broken down the elements of their theory into its key components and checked the validity of each. This would have helped them avoid making premature judgments, stay receptive to new evidence, and give more serious consideration to evidence that was inconsistent with their key assumptions.

As it turned out, the sniper, John Allen Muhammad, was a black man with military training who committed the crimes while in the company of a teenager and drove a blue Chevrolet sedan. Police subsequently discovered that the suspect's blue vehicle had been checked by patrol officers on more than one occasion in the vicinity of several of the shootings, but had not been stopped because investigators had instructed officers to be on the lookout for a white man driving a white van (CIA 2009; Spinney, 2010; Fagan & Badgley, 2002).

contrarian's role is to turn a sceptical eye toward the evidence that appears to incriminate the suspect in an attempt to test the strength of the evidence and potentially "disprove" it. Carefully assembling alibi evidence is part of this role. This serves two purposes. First, it serves to help eliminate a suspect in a timely manner if he or she is innocent (which helps to conserve scarce investigative resources by redirecting them elsewhere) and, second, if after a critical examination the evidence still appears to support the suspect's guilt, the contrarian plays an important role in helping to eliminate potential defences such as a false alibi (Lepard & Campbell, 2009).

8. *Conduct routine debriefings.* Investigators should conduct routine debriefings after all major crime investigations, and case "autopsies" after all investigative failures. The military conducts routine debriefings after missions to ensure that what people have noticed and learned is evaluated and shared. Sometimes the information gleaned from a debriefing will challenge organizational assumptions; for this reason debriefings must be a routine process—to ensure that such information is not simply ignored. Debriefings should be a routine part of the investigative process so that there is an expectation a debriefing will occur at the conclusion of every significant case (Guterman, 2002).

The Vancouver Police Department has entrenched this practice and conducts facilitated debriefings of major cases as a learning exercise. Reports are prepared that set out the challenges faced by the investigators, what went well, what didn't, and what was learned from the investigation.

The reports are available to all department members via a searchable electronic intranet database (Lepard & Campbell, 2009).

9. *Study investigative failures.* As mentioned, the study of investigative failures can be extremely beneficial because the errors that have occurred in past investigations are typically ones to which we are *all* prone. Although understanding why previous investigations have failed will not guarantee that you will not make the same mistakes, becoming aware of some of the more common errors will help you recognize similar errors should they emerge in your own investigations.

The combination of institutional pressures and cognitive biases increases the likelihood that an investigator will develop tunnel vision. To counteract the effect of such pressures and biases, and to decrease the chances of "entering the tunnel," it is critical that investigators use some sort of error checking mechanism, based on some combination of the techniques described above, as a routine part of their investigative protocol.

THE PROFESSIONALIZATION OF POLICE INTERVIEWING AND INVESTIGATION

For an occupational group to have what is referred to as a "professional practice," on the basis of which they are entitled to claim autonomy and authority for solving specific types of problems, they must have "expert knowledge" consisting of particular competencies, specialized knowledge, and practice; this body of knowledge is generally contained in a professional literature written for practitioners, and mastery of it is key to being recognized as professionally competent (Stelfox, 2007). Examples of professions are medicine, law, nursing, and engineering.

Because much of the specialized knowledge and practice on which criminal investigators depend has developed and is transmitted "on the job," the professional practice typical of other occupations has been slow to develop in policing. Historically, rather than being seen by police as an area requiring specialist abilities, criminal investigation was regarded as simply another aspect of police work, requiring little more than the application of common sense. This view persisted in Canada until the 1990s, when a series of events combined to bring about a change of attitude and cause criminal investigation to be seen as an area of policing in need of its own professional practice (Stelfox, 2007). A series of wrongful convictions and failed investigations resulted in the creation of various commissions of inquiry to examine police investigations, from which emerged a series of recommendations designed to improve police investigative practice. Technological advances have resulted in an expansion in the kinds of investigative specialists and techniques available to assist investigators (for example, crime scene, forensic, intelligence, behavioural, and media), which means that investigators need to know when to use these resources and how to coordinate them for maximum benefit. Legislative and regulatory changes (O. Reg. 3/99, Adequacy and Effectiveness of Police Services; O. Reg. 354/04, Major Case Management) have resulted in officers being required to acquire certain knowledge, skills, and abilities before they can be officially designated as criminal investigators; regulating the way in which certain investigative practices can be employed; and providing investigators with a mechanism for effectively managing major criminal investigations.

In Canada, commissions of inquiry into wrongful conviction cases (see Hickman, 1989; Kaufman, 1998; Cory, 2001; Lamer, 2006; MacCallum, 2006; Lesage, 2007); acquittals of wrongfully convicted persons (for example, Truscott, 2007; Mullins-Johnson, 2007; Sherret-Robinson, 2009; *R v. Henry*, 2010; Hutchinson, 2010); inquiries into the professional practices of some key players in the criminal justice system, such as pathologists (Goudge Inquiry, 2008); and academic studies showing the need for increased investigative training (Snook & Keating, 2010) have led to a sustained scrutiny of criminal justice practitioners. As a result, there is a clear expectation that the lessons of past investigative failures will be learned, and that such knowledge will be used to raise the standards of practice in all fields, including criminal investigation, forensic pathology, and law.

Of the "take-home" lessons that have been gleaned from reviews of past investigative failures, two are of particular relevance to police interviewing and investigation practices. These lessons must be learned by those who will assume the role of major case managers in large investigations (Lepard & Campbell, 2009, pp. 269-293):

1. Managers must be aware of best practices in the area of questioning suspects, which include the avoidance of coercive interrogation approaches.
2. Managers must be aware of how evidence can be misinterpreted as a result of information-processing errors.

Another issue that underscores the need for a further professionalization of criminal investigation is the relatively new legal issue of investigative negligence. Police liability for investigative negligence is an area of law that has developed in Canadian courts over the past decade. It was first recognized in the case of *Beckstead* (1997), and has since been dealt with by the Supreme Court in *Hill* (2007). In that case, the Court said (at para. 36):

> The unfortunate reality is that negligent policing has now been recognized as a significant contributing factor to wrongful convictions in Canada. While the vast majority of police officers perform their duties carefully and reasonably, the record shows that wrongful convictions traceable to faulty police investigations occur. ... Police conduct that is not malicious, not deliberate, but merely fails to comply with the standards of reasonableness can be a significant cause of wrongful convictions.

In *Hill*, the Court allowed that while police may use discretion, hunch, and intuition in their investigative work—as other professionals do in theirs—they must do so "reasonably" (paras. 52 and 54). The Court further established that police owe a **duty of care** to those they investigate and, like practitioners in other professions, they will be held accountable for the exercise of that judgment; where it falls short of the **standard of reasonable care**, police may be found to be **negligent** (para. 73). An investigator need not make perfect decisions, and it is not necessary that investigators be found after the fact to have made the best decision in the circumstances. The standard that must be met is simply the standard "of a reasonable

duty of care legal duty of a police officer to those they investigate to conduct an investigation to a reasonable standard; where such a standard is not met, an officer may be found civilly liable for negligence

standard of reasonable care duty of an officer to exercise reasonable care in the investigation of a suspect, the standard for which is defined by how a reasonable officer would act in like circumstances

negligence legal finding of liability in a civil court where an officer has been found to have acted without due care and concern in conducting an investigation and has failed to meet a reasonable standard of care, as a result of which he or she can be sued

officer, judged in the circumstances prevailing at the time the decision was made" (para. 73). Investigators who fall short of this standard, however, may be found to have conducted a negligent investigation and may be sued.

On the basis of our examination of interviewing and investigation, it is clear that what may have been considered "reasonable" professional practice as little as a decade ago has changed. We now have the benefit of lessons learned from the mistakes of investigators who have gone before us, of the painstaking analyses of investigative failures conducted over the past two decades, and of an expanded body of science-based professional literature. As a profession, we have always had a duty to ensure that our investigative practices were effective and informed by scientific research. While that has often been difficult to achieve in the past, we have never had more knowledge to help us meet that obligation than we do now. Consequently, our obligation to reach for and maintain a higher standard of investigative practice has never been greater.

KEY TERMS

belief perseverance

cognitive bias

confirmation bias

duty of care

heuristics

hindsight bias

institutional pressure

negligence

reiteration effect

standard of reasonable care

tunnel vision

FURTHER READING

Campbell, A. (1996). *Bernardo investigation review: Report of Mr. Justice Archie Campbell.* Toronto: Queen's Printer for Ontario.

Cory, P. (2001). *The inquiry regarding Thomas Sophonow.* The Honourable Peter de C. Cory, Commissioner. http://www.gov.mb.ca/justice/publications/sophonow/index.html.

Findley, K., & Scott, M. (2006). The multiple dimensions of tunnel vision in criminal cases. *Wisconsin Law Review, 2,* 291-397.

Goudge, S. (2008). *Inquiry into pediatric forensic pathology in Ontario.* The Honourable Stephen T. Goudge, Commissioner. Ontario Ministry of the Attorney General, Queen's Printer for Ontario. See, especially, vol. 3: Policy and recommendations, chaps. 15 ("Best Practices"), 17 ("The Roles of Coroners, Police, Crown, and Defence"), and 18 ("The Role of the Court"). http://www.attorneygeneral.jus.gov.on.ca/inquiries/goudge/index.html.

Grisham, J. (2006). *The innocent man.* New York: Bantam Dell. (Novel based on the story of a wrongful murder conviction in Oklahoma; a New York Times Bestseller.)

Heuer, R. (1999). *Psychology of intelligence analysis.* Washington, DC: Centre for the Study of Intelligence.

Innocence Project (2010). *250 exonerated: Too many wrongfully convicted.* An Innocence Project Report on the First 250 DNA Exonerations in the United States. New York: Benjamin N. Cardozo School of Law, Yeshiva University, Innocence Project, Inc. http://www.innocenceproject.org/docs/ InnocenceProject_250.pdf.

Kaufman, F. (1998). *Report of the Kaufman commission on proceedings involving Guy Paul Morin.* The Honourable Fred Kaufman, Commissioner. http:// www.attorneygeneral.jus.gov.on.ca/english/about/pubs/morin/.

Lamer. A. (2006). *The Lamer commission of inquiry pertaining to the cases of Ronald Dalton, Gregory Parson, Randy Druken.* The Right Honourable Antonio Lamer, St. John's: Office of the Queen's Printer. http://www.justice.gov.nl .ca/just/publications/lamerpart1.pdf.

MacCallum, E. (2006). *The commission of inquiry into the wrongful conviction of David Milgaard.* The Honourable Mr. Justice Edward P. MacCallum, Commissioner. http://www.justice.gov.sk.ca/milgaard/DMfinal.shtml.

MacFarlane, B. (2006). Convicting the innocent: A triple failure of the justice system. *The Manitoba Law Journal, 31,* 1-78.

MacFarlane, B. (2008). Wrongful convictions: The effect of tunnel vision and predisposing circumstances in the criminal justice system. Prepared for the *inquiry into pediatric forensic pathology in Ontario.* The Honourable Stephen Goudge. http://canadiancriminallaw.com/articles/articles%20pdf/ Wrongful-Convictions.pdf.

Rossmo, D.K. (Ed.). (2009). *Criminal investigative failures.* Boca Raton, FL: CRC Press.

Snook, B., Eastwood, J., Stinson, M., Tedeschini, J., & House, J. (2010). Reforming investigative interviewing in Canada. *Canadian Journal of Criminology and Criminal Justice, 52*(2), 215-229.

Williamson, T., Milne, B., & Savage, S. (Eds.). (2009). *International developments in investigative interviewing.* Cullompton, UK: Willan Publishing.

Working Group on the Prevention of Miscarriages of Justice of the Federal–Provincial–Territorial Heads of Prosecution Committee, Department of Justice Canada (2004). *Report on the prevention of miscarriages of justice.* http://www .justice.gc.ca/eng/dept-min/pub/pmj-pej/toc-tdm.html.

REVIEW QUESTIONS

TRUE OR FALSE

____   1. Tunnel vision is a broad focus on investigative or prosecutional theories of the crime.

____   2. Being guided by a "working theory of the crime" does not pose a problem during the course of an investigation.

_____ 3. The problem of "tunnel vision" is not associated with any particular group of investigators.

_____ 4. A cognitive bias is the result of an emotional or intellectual choice for or against something.

_____ 5. A confirmation bias is defined as the tendency to seek or interpret evidence in ways that support existing beliefs.

_____ 6. The majority of investigative failures are the result of professional incompetence, misconduct, and malice.

_____ 7. Acquiring reliable knowledge about the world through observation is a demanding task fraught with risks, the greatest of which is believing you are right when you are wrong.

_____ 8. Valid knowledge results simply from adding more confirming evidence in support of what one already knows to be true.

_____ 9. The _key_ issue in the production of knowledge depends on the gathering of facts.

_____ 10. Tunnel vision was first discussed in Canada during the Goudge Inquiry in 2008.

MULTIPLE CHOICE

1. Although there is no single "official" definition of tunnel vision, authorities appear to agree on its principal elements. Tunnel vision

   a. involves an investigator focusing objectively on the available evidence in an effort to narrow down the range of possible suspects in an investigation.

   b. involves an overly narrow focus on a particular investigative or prosecutorial theory of the crime.

   c. has the effect of "colouring" both the evaluation of the gathered information and the investigative conduct in response to that information.

   d. both a and c.

   e. both b and c.

2. As part of the "colouring process," tunnel vision can lead investigators, prosecutors, judges, and defence lawyers to focus on a particular conclusion and then

   a. filter all evidence in a case through the lens provided by that conclusion.

   b. filter evidence consciously based on whether or not it appears to support the guilt of the suspect being investigated.

   c. filter evidence in a case based on its apparent importance in explaining the motive(s) of a particular suspect.

   d. categorize all evidence in an investigation into one of a series of three analytical groups categorized by colour and based on relevance (green—relevant; yellow—possibly relevant; red—not relevant).

3. Some investigators have been severely criticized for focusing too narrowly on a particular theory of a crime during an investigation. Being guided by a "theory of the crime" during an investigation is not itself problematic, providing:

   a. an investigator's theory complies with one of a series of criminological theories that researchers have tested and found to be effective in explaining the causes of criminal behaviour.

   b. an investigator's working theory is based on a comprehensive evaluation of the available evidence and the investigator remains receptive to the possibility that they may have to revise or abandon their theory if it is not supported by the evidence.

   c. an investigator is able to gather sufficient corroborating evidence to prove beyond a reasonable doubt that the theory of the crime they have chosen is the correct one.

   d. an investigator is able to articulate the process they went through in deciding which theory of the crime was the correct one.

4. Psychologist Peter Wason coined the term "confirmation bias" to describe a phenomenon he observed in a psychological study conducted more than 50 years ago, in which participants attempted to discover an unknown rule governing a series of numbers by coming up with a theory regarding the rule and, for the most part, submitting a series of numbers that

   a. fit their theory.

   b. could potentially disprove their theory.

   c. they guessed might fit their theory.

   d. were mathematically consistent.

Short Answer

1. Briefly explain "belief perseverance" and how it can weaken an investigation.

2. How does conducting routine debriefings during and after lengthy and complex investigations aid police services in reducing the number of errors made and the prudent use of their resources.

3. Give a brief explanation for why providing examples that fit a particular hypothesis, while appearing to be a perfectly logical way for a person to prove the truth of that hypothesis, is, in fact, not the most logical way to demonstrate such proof.

4. A series of nine techniques, described in this chapter, are intended to help investigators maintain their receptiveness to information and manage the risk of error in investigations. Choose two of these techniques and explain how they can assist an investigator in managing error and staying receptive to information.

APPENDIXES

Selected Case Law

The following summaries are intended to serve as a guide to some important cases that relate directly to many of the issues discussed in this book. Of course, you should always review the full text of a case before attempting to apply it in your day-to-day police work.

You may find that these cases are not always easy to reconcile with one another—such is the nature of case law. In determining the relative importance of a case, you should take into account the level of the court in which it was decided (cases decided by provincial courts, for example, do not carry as much authority as those decided by the Supreme Court of Canada, which are binding on all lower courts) and the year of the decision (particularly for cases decided before 1982, when the Charter came into force).

RIGHTS OF PERSONS WHO ARE DETAINED/ARRESTED
Right to Silence (Charter, s. 7)

> 7. Everyone has the right to life, liberty and security of the person and the right not to be deprived thereof except in accordance with the principles of fundamental ju stice.

Case	Description
Broyles	An undercover agent must take a passive role when obtaining statements from an accused (for example, when an accused is in a holding cell). The test is whether the exchange between the accused and the undercover agent would have taken place, in the form and manner in which it did, without the intervention of the state or its agents.

[1991] 3 SCR 595, 68 CCC (3d) 308.

Case	Description
Hebert	Section 7 of the Charter accords a detained person the right to remain silent. The opportunity to exercise the right must be a meaningful one, and statements obtained under circumstances violating that right will be excluded. The police obligation to guarantee the right does not apply in the case of voluntary statements made to cellmates, but does apply in the case of police undercover operators who solicit information. Where the right to remain silent has not been guaranteed, the court may exclude evidence whose admission would bring the administration of justice into disrepute. [1990] 2 SCR 151, 57 CCC (3d) 1, 77 CR (3d) 145.
Osmar	Officers posed as members of an organized crime organization and obtained incriminating information from the accused. The court held that this strategy did not violate the accused's s. 7 right to silence from *Hebert*, because the accused was not detained and there was no question of voluntariness, since the accused believed the officers were members of an organized crime organization. [2007] OJ No. 244, 2007 ONCA 50.
Singh	The accused was arrested and asserted his right to silence 18 times. The officers continued to question him. The Court held that there was no violation of the accused's s. 7 right to silence: officers are not required to stop questioning an accused who asserts this right. [2007] 3 SCR 405, 2007 SCC 48.

Right to Counsel (Charter, s. 10(b))

10. Everyone has the right on arrest or detention

a) to be informed promptly of the reasons therefor;

b) to retain and instruct counsel without delay and to be informed of that right; and

c) to have the validity of the detention determined by way of habeas corpus and to be released if the detention is not lawful.

Case	Description

Definition of Detention

Grant

Detention is defined as a suspension of an individual's liberty by significant physical or psychological restraint. The courts will deem an individual to have been psychologically restrained where the individual has a legal obligation to comply with the restrictive demand or where a reasonable person would conclude that he or she had no choice but to comply. In determining whether a reasonable person would have no choice but to comply, the courts will consider: (1) the circumstances as perceived by the individual (this involves consideration of whether the police were making general inquiries or whether they were singling the individual out for focused investigation); (2) the nature of the police conduct (this involves the use of language, use of physical contact, presence of others, duration, and location); and (3) characteristics that are relevant to the individual's particular situation (this involves age, physical stature, minority status).

2009 SCC 32, [2009] 2 SCR 353.

Duties and Rights of Police

Bartle

Officers have three duties under s. 10(b) of the Charter: (1) to inform the detainee of his or her right to retain counsel without delay, and of the availability of legal aid and duty counsel; (2) to provide the detainee with a reasonable opportunity to exercise the right where the detainee has indicated a wish to do so; and (3) to refrain from eliciting evidence from the detainee before the detainee has had a reasonable opportunity to exercise the right.

[1994] 3 SCR 173.

Black

An accused must be re-advised of his right to counsel where the charge or the reason for detention has changed. The accused can only retain and instruct counsel meaningfully if they know the reasons for their detainment.

[1989] 2 SCR 138.

Brydges

Where an accused requests the assistance of counsel, the police have a duty to facilitate contact with counsel and to inform the accused of the existence of duty counsel and the availability of legal aid.

[1990] 1 SCR 190, 53 CCC (3d) 330.

Case	Description
Burlingham	Police are prohibited from belittling defence counsel in an attempt to undermine the accused's confidence in counsel. Further, unless the accused has waived the right to counsel, plea bargains can only take place through or in the presence of defense counsel. [1995] 2 SCR 206.
Cotter	Where s. 10 rights have been explained to an intoxicated person who is interviewed several hours later when sober, the courts have ruled that investigators must advise the suspect of his or her rights anew before any statement is taken. [1991] BCJ No. 42, 62 CCC (3d) 423.
Cuff	Questioning an accused is part of a police investigation; once an accused has been advised of his or her right to retain and instruct counsel and, in fact, has done so, the police are free to continue questioning the accused in the absence of his or her lawyer. There is no continuing obligation to advise the accused of the right to retain and instruct counsel. Although counsel advised the accused not to make a statement to the police in counsel's absence, there was no reason why the police could not continue questioning the accused. [1989] NJ No. 94, 75 Nfld. & PEIR 1 (Nfld. CA).
Elshaw	The police must fulfill their s. 10(b) Charter responsibilities to a detained person before obtaining evidence from that person unless urgency or necessity requires that the evidence be obtained before an opportunity to fulfill those responsibilities arises. [1991] 3 SCR 24.
Manninen	The Charter imposes two implementation duties on police officers under s. 10(b): (1) the police must give a detainee a reasonable opportunity to exercise the right to retain and instruct counsel without delay, and (2) the police must cease questioning or otherwise attempting to elicit evidence from the detainee until he or she has had an opportunity to retain and instruct counsel unless the matter is so urgent that they must proceed with the questioning. [1987] 1 SCR 1233, 34 CCC (3d) 385.
McCrimmon	Where a detainee expresses a desire to consult with a particular lawyer, but ultimately consults with duty counsel, the detainee has exercised his or her s. 10(b) rights. Following the detainee's consultation with duty counsel, police may lawfully interrogate the detainee, and are not required to cease their questioning if the detainee requests to re-consult with counsel. 2010 SCC 36.

Case	Description
Sherwood	At a detainee's request, an officer is required to give the detainee sufficient information concerning the basis for his or her arrest. The purpose is "to enable the detainee when instructing counsel to obtain meaningful advice as to how to exercise his rights." [1991] BCJ No. 4041, 29 MVR (2d) 21 (BCCA).
Sinclair	Section 10(b) of the Charter does not mandate the continued presence of defence counsel throughout the custodial interrogation. In general, if the detainee is informed of his or her right to counsel and given a reasonable opportunity to exercise that right, s. 10(b) has been satisfied. Once the detainee has been informed and had a reasonable opportunity to consult with counsel, police officers are free to interrogate the detainee and are not required to provide further opportunities to consult with counsel, even if the detainee requests it. The detainee may only re-consult if a change in circumstances occurs and the detainee requires legal advice relevant to his or her right to choose whether to cooperate with the police investigation, such as a new procedure involving the detainee, a change in the jeopardy faced by the detainee, or a reason to believe that the detainee may not have understood his or her right to counsel. 2010 SCC 35.

Responsibilities of Accused Persons

Hollis	The accused (once he or she has been properly cautioned) is responsible for expressing his or her wish to speak to counsel. Unless the accused requests counsel, "the police are entitled to proceed with their investigation in the same manner as they would be if the right [to counsel] had been [explicitly] waived." An accused who has been adequately informed of his or her right to counsel under s. 10(b) of the Charter is not obliged to retain and instruct counsel. It is the essence of a right that its exercise must be the result of free choice. It therefore follows that the police are not obliged to assume that the accused will exercise the right to counsel; nor can they be expected to guess whether a decision has been made to exercise or waive that right. [1992] BCJ No. 2066, 76 CCC (3d) 421 (BCCA).

Case	Description
Smith	The duty imposed on police to refrain from questioning an accused prior to the accused's exercise of the right to counsel is suspended where the accused is not reasonably diligent in that exercise. This limit on the accused's right is necessary; otherwise it would be possible for the accused to needlessly delay an investigation with impunity. The burden of proving that it was impossible to communicate with counsel falls on the accused. The main goal of s. 10(b) of the Charter is to ensure fairness in the questioning of suspects by police. [1989] 2 SCR 368, 50 CCC (3d) 308.

Temporary Suspension of Rights

Case	Description
Schultz	In some cases, the police may temporarily deny certain rights to the accused. In *Schultz*, the right to use the telephone was temporarily denied because the police were concerned that the accused would warn his associates of his arrest and they would flee the country. [1991] BCJ No. 2757, 67 CCC (3d) 360 (BCCA).

Waiver of Right to Counsel

Case	Description
Clarkson	Waiver of the right to counsel must be clear and unequivocal; the person who chooses to waive his or her rights must do so with an understanding (1) that the rights were created to protect his or her civil liberties, and (2) of what the effect of waiving those rights may be. An intoxicated person's waiver of his or her rights under s. 10 of the Charter must at least pass some form of "awareness of the consequences" test. Unless the evidence obtained after the right has been waived is urgently required, the court may interpret hasty action as exploitation by the police and exclude the statement. [1986] 1 SCR 383.

Rights Not Invoked

Case	Description
Olivier	Simply asking questions does not invoke Charter rights. A police officer in a bar in Winnipeg asked the accused whether he had any drugs in his possession. It was the officer's duty to investigate and the accused was not detained; therefore, the officer had no duty to inform the accused of his right to counsel. Questioning people is the very basis of police investigations. [1991] MJ No. 299, 74 Man. R (2d) 30 (Man. QB).

ADMISSIBILITY OF STATEMENTS
Persons in Authority

Case   **Description**

Hodgson   A person in authority is someone the accused believes on reason-
              able grounds to be acting on behalf of the state and to therefore
              have influence over the proceedings. This has both a subjective and
              objective component. The accused must perceive the person as
              being a person in authority and that perception must be
              reasonable.

      [1998] 2 SCR 449.

Rothman   When determining whether an individual is a person in authority,
              the court will look at the accused's subjective belief. In *Rothman*, an
              undercover officer was not considered to be a person in authority
              because at the time the statement was made the accused did not
              believe that the officer had any coercive state power over him.
              Thus, the statement was freely made.

      [1981] 1 SCR 640.

Voluntariness

Ewert   Officers who volunteer psychiatric help to a suspect in return for a
              statement *may* be guilty of inducing the statement, depending on
              the circumstances.

      (1991), 68 CCC (3d) 207 (BCCA).

Horvath   The courts are not limited to the definitions of a voluntary state-
              ment established by the *Boudreau* and *Ibrahim* cases—namely, that
              the statement be "free of fear of prejudice or hope of advantage."
              The fundamental question is whether the statement is made
              voluntarily, through the exercise of free choice.

      (1997), 117 CCC (3d) 110 (SCC).

Oickle   Statements made by accused persons to persons in authority will
              be admissible only if they are made voluntarily. The underlying
              rationale is concern for wrongful convictions. Briefly, when deter-
              mining voluntariness, a court will consider four factors: (1) induce-
              ments, (2) lack of operating mind, (3) atmosphere of oppression,
              and (4) police trickery. If these factors, on their own or in combina-
              tion, create a situation that results in the statement not being the
              product of the accused's free choice, then the statement will not be
              considered voluntary and will therefore not be admissible.

      [2000] 2 SCR 3.

Case	Description
R v. N.	The accused was subject to a five-hour polygraph test, a lengthy interrogation, and numerous police tricks. The court held that the police strategies intimidated and confused the accused, thereby inducing him to make a statement, and raising a reasonable doubt as to voluntariness. The accused's confession was excluded under the *Oickle* framework. [2005] OJ No. 357, 63 WCB (2d) 399 (Ont. SC).
Spencer	Not every inducement on its own made by a person in authority to an accused will render a confession inadmissible. A *quid pro quo* is an important consideration—however, the voluntariness analysis will consider the inducement in the light of all circumstances. 2007 SCC 11, [2007] 1 SCR 500.

Preference for Recorded Statements

Moore-Macfarlane	When an individual is in custody, video equipment is available, and the police deliberately set out to interrogate the individual without making a video recording, any confession obtained may be considered suspect. Video-recorded statements are preferable because they provide the court with more information regarding the context in which the confession was made. [2001] OJ No. 4646, 2001 CanLII 6363 (ONCA).

EVIDENCE
Exclusion of Evidence (Charter, s. 24(2))

24(1) Anyone whose rights or freedoms, as guaranteed by this Charter, have been infringed or denied may apply to a court of competent jurisdiction to obtain such remedy as the court considers appropriate and just in the circumstances.

(2) Where, in proceedings under subsection (1), a court concludes that evidence was obtained in a manner that infringed or denied any rights or freedoms guaranteed by this Charter, the evidence shall be excluded if it is established that, having regard to all the circumstances, the admission of it in the proceedings would bring the administration of justice into disrepute.

Case	Description
Grant	Section 24(2) of the Charter allows a judge to exclude evidence where in all the circumstances the evidence obtained in breach of the Charter would bring the administration of justice into disrepute. When faced with an application under s. 24(2), the court will balance the effect of having admitted the evidence on society's confidence in the justice system having regard to (1) the seriousness of the Charter-infringing state conduct, (2) the impact of the breach on the Charter-protected interests of the accused, and (3) society's interest in the adjudication of the case on its merits.

2009 SCC 32, [2009] 2 SCR 353.

Relevant Evidence

Chahley	The accused was charged with murder. Declarations made by the victim a few days prior to his death to a third party regarding the identity of the assailant were admissible circumstantial evidence. The statement was considered logically probative and met necessity and reliability requirements.

[1992] BCJ No. 1121.

Seaboyer	The trial judge always has residual discretion to exclude evidence where the prejudicial effect of the evidence outweighs its probative value. In other words, the trial judge can exclude relevant evidence in situations where its admission would be unduly prejudicial to the accused.

[1991] 2 SCR 577.

COMPETENCE/COMPELLABILITY

Salituro	Irreconcilably separated spouses may be competent to testify against each other even though the charge does not fall within the common-law exceptions or the exceptions mentioned in s. 4(4) of the *Canada Evidence Act*.

[1991] 3 SCR 654, 68 CCC (3d) 289.

STATEMENTS OF CO-ACCUSEDS

B. (K.G.)	A previous inconsistent statement by a witness other than an accused was admitted at trial as substantive evidence of the truth of its contents on an exceptional, "principled" basis. The governing principles were the reliability of the evidence and its necessity. The decision depended on the existence of certain procedures used to support reliability, such as videotaping of the evidence.

[1993] 1 SCR 740, 79 CCC (3d) 257.

DISCLOSURE

Case	Description
Gingras	The Crown must disclose all relevant information in its possession concerning the crime. There is no onus on the Crown to seek out police evidence that has nothing to do with matter in issue in the case. The "Crown," for disclosure purposes, does not encompass other state authorities.
	[1992] AJ No. 107, 120 AR 300 (Alta. CA).
Ryan	The trial judge has considerable discretion as to the manner in which public disclosure of evidence is made. He or she can determine whether a ban should be placed on publication and whether certain parts of the trial must be held *in camera*.
	(1991), 69 CCC (3d) (NSCA).
Stinchcombe	The right to make full answer and defence is one of the principles of fundamental justice, and it imposes a duty on the Crown to disclose all relevant material to the defence, whether or not the material is exculpatory or inculpatory, and whether or not the Crown intends to introduce the materal at trial. Initial disclosure should occur before the accused is called on to elect or plead, and there is a continuing obligation to disclose as additional material is received. The Crown, however, has some discretion to withhold or delay disclosure in some circumstances—for example, to protect the identity of an informant—but this discretion is reviewable by the trial judge.
	[1991] 3 SCR 326, 68 CCC (3d) 225.

Review Scenario

The following scenario and the accompanying questions are provided as a tool for reviewing the material in this book. The scenario can be used as an in-class or take-home test or assignment and for class discussion.

SCENARIO

It is 2:00 a.m. on January 3, 2011. You are on patrol in a marked police car. You receive a report from the dispatcher regarding a robbery that has just occurred about 10 blocks from your location. The dispatcher advises that a convenience store has been robbed by two males wearing ski masks. The dispatcher further advises that the individuals held the clerk at gunpoint and demanded all the money in the cash register. They took about 30 cartons of cigarettes and fled in a 2005 red Ford Mustang.

Moments after you receive the information, a 2005 red Ford Mustang runs a stop sign at the intersection you are approaching and continues on at high speed. You notice two males in the front seat and give chase with your police car's emergency equipment activated. The suspect vehicle sideswipes a pole during the chase. After you chase the vehicle for about 10 blocks, the driver finally pulls over. You and your partner call for backup, and when it arrives moments later you approach the vehicle.

On approaching the vehicle, you notice a number of cartons of cigarettes in the back seat as well as two ski masks on the floor. The suspects are ordered out of the vehicle and the driver is asked for his licence and vehicle registration. The driver produces a valid driver's licence bearing the name Bob Brown. He asks, "Why are you pulling me over? I ain't done nothing wrong." You ask about the cigarettes in the back seat and the driver states, "I got nothing to say." When the driver is questioned about the identity of his passenger, he replies, "This is my kid brother, John, and he ain't done nothing either."

You arrest both individuals on a charge of possession of property obtained by crime and take them into custody. You notify them of the reason for their arrest and inform them of their rights under ss. 10(a) and (b) of the Charter. On inspecting the identification documents carried by the suspects, you find that Bob is 24 years old and his brother John is 16. Bob insists on speaking immediately to his lawyer, and indicates that he has a cellphone with him that he could use to do so. John says that he wants his mother to come to the station with him and that he does not need a lawyer. Both suspects are taken to the police station and placed in separate interview rooms.

QUESTIONS

1. What legal precautions must be taken with each suspect?

2. Would you allow Bob to call his lawyer from his cellphone? Why or why not? Use case law to justify your answer.

3. How would you treat John's request for his mother's attendance at the police station? Are you required to notify his mother? Explain.

4. If John insists that he does not need a lawyer, how will you ensure compliance with the *Youth Criminal Justice Act*?

5. Should the brothers be interviewed together? Why?

6. At the station, Bob speaks to his lawyer in private over the telephone. When he is finished, he tells you his lawyer wishes to speak with you. The lawyer informs you that his client has the right to silence and that he has told his client not to speak with you. He then says that you are not to speak to his client under any circumstances and if you do so your actions will negatively impact the case once it gets to court. What would you do in this situation? Are you prohibited by statute or case law from asking Bob further questions? Explain your answer.

7. Assume that after John and Bob were arrested and the vehicle was searched, a small black handgun matching the description of the weapon given by the store clerk was recovered from under the back seat of the car. What use, if any, would you make of this piece of evidence in your questioning of the suspects? Explain.

8. Assuming that John gives a full statement admitting to the robbery, can his statement be shown to Bob to prompt him to make a statement? Explain your answer.

9. What are the disadvantages of two officers jointly interrogating each of the suspects? What are the advantages?

10. Bob asks for his brother to be in the room while he (Bob) is being interviewed. He advises that he will feel better about talking to the police if his brother is there. How would you handle this situation, and why?

11. Bob says, "If I own up to this thing and give you a statement admitting what I've done, you have to let my little brother off." How would you handle this situation? Explain.

12. While interviewing Bob, you untruthfully advise him that John was interviewed in his mother's presence and gave a full confession implicating Bob in the robbery. In response, Bob provides a full confession. How will the fact that you lied to Bob affect the admissibility of his confession? Explain your answer.

Glossary of Terms

absolute-judgment strategy   strategy whereby a witness decides whether a subject is the offender seen at the crime scene without reference to other subjects

accused   a suspect who has been formally charged with a crime

admissibility   the likelihood of a piece of evidence being allowed by the judge to be presented in court

admissible   a term normally used to describe evidence that is relevant to a determination of the issues in a judicial proceeding and which is allowed to be considered by a trier of fact in making a decision regarding such issues

admission   statement that concedes at least one fact that, if true, is relevant to proving the suspect's guilt

agent   an individual who acts on the direction of police to go out and become involved in an activity under investigation by the police for the purpose of gathering information about that activity and providing it to police

agent provocateur   a person who, acting on the direction of the police, induces another person to do something that they would not ordinarily do or provides them with an opportunity to commit a crime they would not ordinarily have committed

alibi   an excuse, which typically takes the form of a claim that a person was somewhere else when the crime was committed

arrest   the actual seizure or touching of an individual by an officer with the intent of taking physical control of a person for the purpose of detention; or an announcement by an officer of his or her intent to arrest a person accompanied by an attempt to take physical control of that person

base rate   the incidence of a particular behaviour or characteristic in a population

behaviour analysis   an approach to detecting deception that focuses on observing and analyzing different aspects of a person's behaviour in an effort to determine whether the person is being truthful or deceptive

behavioural analysis interview (BAI)   second step of the Reid method, which uses behaviour provoking questions and behavioural observations to detect deception during a suspect interview; used to help an investigator make a decision regarding the suspect's guilt

belief perseverance   people's natural reluctance to give up their initial conclusions about something even when the foundation for their initial conclusion has been completely undermined

Canadian Charter of Rights and Freedoms   the constitutional document that sets out the rights and freedoms enjoyed by all people of Canada

closed question   question that invites a one word or short answer from the subject; for example, "What colour was the car?" or "Did you get a good look at his face?"

coerced–compliant false confession   the most common type of false confession identified in *R v. Oickle* (2000), it is given knowingly by an individual in response to threats or promises

coerced–persuaded false confession   false confession that shares the same characteristics as the non-coerced–persuaded false confession, but in which threats and promises have also been used

cognitive bias   the tendency of humans to make consistent and predictable errors in the way they perceive, recall, interpret, and act on information

cognitive economy   a theory of memory function that describes the shortcuts taken by the brain in an effort to store and retrieve an enormous number of individual memories

cognitive interview (CI)   refers to a group of four techniques (report everything; change perspective; change order; context reinstatement) developed as a result of psychological research conducted on police interviewing practices; designed to facilitate a witness's use of their memory during an interview; *see* enhanced cognitive interview

cold mugshot search   witness's search through a collection of police file photographs for the possible offender or offenders

compellability   being without legal excuse to avoid testifying

competence   being legally permitted to testify (based on the absence of factors such as age under 14 years or mental handicap)

composite sketch   likeness of an offender constructed by combining individual facial features described by a witness

confession   an admission to all of the elements of an offence, including the mental element

confession rule   a long-established doctrine of common law that holds that no statement made by an accused person to a person in authority is admissible against them unless the Crown can show beyond a reasonable doubt that the statement was given voluntarily

confidential informant   an informant who has provided information to the police and has been given a guarantee of anonymity by a police officer; once a person has confidential informant status, their identity cannot be revealed to anyone by the Crown, the court, or the police without the confidential informant first waiving their legal privilege

confirmation bias   the tendency to seek or interpret evidence in ways that support existing beliefs, expectations, or hypotheses

context reinstatement   the establishment of background facts or conditions precedent that help put a statement into its proper context

conversation management (CM)   a technique used in the PEACE model to interview uncooperative subjects; developed to facilitate a working relationship with any interviewee

criminal information   official form on which an individual, typically a police officer, sets out under oath a specific criminal allegation(s) against a person

criteria-based content analysis (CBCA)   a major component of SVA, consisting of 19 different criteria grouped under 4 different headings, that holds that truthful statements will have more of the criteria identified by CBCA than will false statements; *see* SVA

denial   statement in which a person denies any knowledge of or involvement in the matter under investigation

detention   the suspension of a person's liberty by a significant physical or psychological restraint

disclosure   process in which the Crown attorney is required to reveal to the defence all of the evidence (including physical or electronic copies of all documents, statements, and any other evidence) gathered in an investigation that could be potentially relevant to the defence of the accused, including information that the Crown does not intend to use at trial

distracters   lineup members other than the suspect

double-blind procedure   an experiment or study in which neither the test subjects nor the test administrators have been advised of the experiment's hypothesis

duty of care   legal duty of a police officer to those they investigate to conduct an investigation to a reasonable standard; where such a standard is not met, an officer may be found civilly liable for negligence

encoding specificity   a theory of memory function based on the hypothesis that a major factor in how much will be remembered is the degree to which the conditions that exist during memory retrieval match the conditions that existed during one's experience of the to-be-recalled event

enhanced cognitive interview (ECI)   an interview that uses the four original CI techniques, but attempts to maximize their effectiveness by placing them in an appropriate structure and providing interviewers with instructions on how best to use them to minimize the tendency of police interviewers to engage in counterproductive behaviours such as interrupting or using short-answer questions; *see* cognitive interview

estimator variables   factors, such as a witness's eyesight, that affect the accuracy of an eyewitness identification, but over which the police and the Crown have no control

evidence   anything (for example, testimony, document, object) presented in a legal proceeding, such as a trial, for the purpose of establishing the truth or falsity of a fact in issue

exculpatory   that which clears or tends to clear a person of guilt

expert evidence   opinion evidence presented in a legal proceeding by a qualified expert witness drawn from their particular area of expertise

expert witness   witness who by virtue of education, training, or experience has specialized knowledge or understanding beyond that of the average person, whose opinion may be relied on to assist a trier of fact in reaching a conclusion

false positive   refers to a situation in which an observer mistakenly believes that a condition is present when, in fact, it is not

free recall   a witness's uninterrupted narrative of an incident

gaze aversion   in the deception detection literature, refers to the avoidance of eye contact, which is perhaps the most frequently cited non-verbal behaviour commonly thought to be indicative of deception

hearsay evidence   evidence based not on a witness's own knowledge but on a statement that the witness has heard from another source

heuristics   "rules of thumb," or a commonsense guide used in problem solving or investigation; sometimes referred to as an "educated guess" or learning by "trial and error"

hindsight bias   sometimes referred to as the "knew-it-all-along effect," the tendency of people to believe, after an event has happened, that it was inevitable or that its occurrence was more probable than was originally thought

hybrid offence   also known as "dual procedure" offence; a class of offences that can be prosecuted as either minor (summary) or major (indictable) offences, hybrid offences are considered to be indictable offences until the Crown "elects" how to proceed; examples include impaired driving and theft under $5,000

hypnosis   a technique by which a hypnotist purports to put a subject into a trance-like state in which the subject's responses and actions are under the hypnotist's control

hypothesis   a tentative idea or explanation about how something happened or about how something works that an investigator uses to help guide his or her inquiries; also called a "working theory" or "theory"

Identi-Kit technique   identification technique in which drawings of facial features are combined by a witness to generate a composite image of a suspect

inculpatory   that which establishes or tends to establish a person's guilt

inducement   promise, favour, threat, or representation made to an accused that can be perceived as an effort to coerce the accused into making a confession

informant   someone who provides a statement or information to the police regarding an investigation, or someone who supplies the police with facilities to observe and gather information

institutional pressure   factors that make it more likely that an investigator will develop tunnel vision—for example, pressure on the investigator from their superiors, the victims, and the community to solve a case, as well as limited resources

interrogation   an accusatory process, the primary purpose of which is to elicit a confession from a suspect who is believed to be responsible for the offence under investigation

interview   a structured conversation between a witness, victim, or suspect and an investigator, in which the investigator asks a series of questions in order to elicit information from the witness, victim, or suspect about something that they observed, experienced, did, or have knowledge about

investigation   the methodical process of exploring or examining through inquiry and observation

KGB caution   prepared statement read to an interviewee by the police prior to an interview, informing the interviewee that the interview will be electronically recorded and that the interviewee will be swearing an oath to tell the truth and will face potential criminal consequences if they lie to or deliberately mislead police during the interview

leakage hypothesis   a theory that suggests that deception can be detected by observing the ways in which a person's physiological responses are inconsistent with his or her spoken words

material evidence   evidence that is relevant to proving or disproving the elements of the offence with which an accused is charged

material witness   a witness who has observed "material" facts, or facts that are relevant to proving the elements of the offence with which an accused is charged

maximization   an interrogation strategy that seeks to maximize the seriousness of an offence, exaggerate the strength of the evidence against a suspect, and exaggerate the possible consequences of a conviction

minimization   interrogation strategy that seeks to minimize the seriousness of an offence and the perceived consequences of confessing

misleading post-event information   a theory of memory function that suggests that memories are easily distorted by information acquired after the original memory is formed

negligence   legal finding of liability in a civil court where an officer has been found to have acted without due care and concern in conducting an investigation and has failed to meet a reasonable standard of care, as a result of which he or she can be sued

neurolinguistic programming (NLP)   a theory that holds, among other things, that eye movements can indicate deception

non-coerced–persuaded false confession   false confession given as a result of certain police interrogation tactics that have confused a person or caused them to doubt their own memory, and which has temporarily persuaded them of their own guilt

open-ended question   question that invites a detailed answer from the subject, often phrased as a statement rather than a question—for example, "Tell me more about ..."; open-ended questions can also be phrased as conventional questions, such as, "You said x, what did you mean by that?"

opinion evidence   evidence that goes beyond a statement of fact to present an opinion or conclusion

Othello error   the false assumption that a person who acts nervously is necessarily attempting to cover up guilt

PEACE model   a best practice approach to interviewing victims, witnesses, and suspects developed by police, academics, and lawyers in the United Kingdom during the 1990s that focuses on eliciting the maximum amount of information from a subject and, in the case of a suspect, using that information to challenge inconsistencies between the suspect's account of events and the totality of the evidence

person in authority   typically refers to persons who are formally engaged in the arrest, detention, examination, or prosecution of the accused—for example, police officers, prison guards, and Crown attorneys

Photo-Fit technique   identification technique in which photographs of facial features are combined by a witness to generate a composite image of a suspect

polygraph   an electronic device used to measure the body's physiological responses to questioning

polygrapher   an expert in the administration and analysis of polygraph examinations

primary caution   warning given by an investigator to a suspect informing him or her that an officer is conducting an investigation into a criminal allegation; that they are a suspect in that investigation; that they do not have to speak to the police, but if they choose to do so the police will make a record of it that may be used against them in court if they are charged with a criminal offence

propitious heterogeneity   dissimilarities within a group of subjects, each of whom matches a particular physical description

reality monitoring   a scientific technique that attempts to detect false statements

Reid technique   an approach to questioning criminal suspects that consists of three principal elements: a non-accusatory fact-finding interview; a behavioural analysis interview designed to detect deception; and an accusatory, persuasive interrogation designed to obtain a confession

reiteration effect   the tendency for people's confidence in the truth of an assertion to increase if the assertion is repeated, independent of whether the assertion is true or false and/or evidence that suggests that the assertion is false

relative-judgment strategy   strategy whereby a witness decides whether a subject, as compared with other subjects, looks more or less like the offender seen at the crime scene

relevant   tending to prove or disprove a proposition

repressed memories   previously inaccessible memories that are reported to have later been recovered, usually as a result of some sort of therapy or triggering event

right to counsel   the right of a person to consult with a lawyer upon arrest or detention, as guaranteed by s. 10(b) of the Charter

right to silence   the right of an individual not to be compelled to be a witness against himself and to freely choose whether or not to speak to agents of the state, such as police officers

SCAN   an acronym for scientific content analysis and a statement analysis technique premised on the assumption that a statement about something that was actually experienced will differ in quality and content from a statement based on something that was not actually experienced and that one can differentiate between the two by analyzing a person's statement with reference to specific criteria

secondary caution   warning given by an investigator to a suspect where the investigator is not the first police officer to have contact with the suspect, advising the suspect that if he or she has had any previous contact with the police regarding the matter under investigation he or she should not be influenced by anything said or done during that contact, and that he or she remains free to decide whether to speak to the investigator

showup   identification procedure whereby a suspect is brought to a location where a witness has also been brought for the purpose of identifying the suspect

standard of reasonable care   duty of an officer to exercise reasonable care in the investigation of a suspect, the standard for which is defined by how a reasonable officer would act in like circumstances

statement   a witness's, suspect's, or victim's account of an event, usually "taken" from a witness or a suspect in the course of a formal recorded interview, although it can be taken anywhere at anytime and may be written out; electronic recording of statements is the preferred method of preserving a statement for disclosure and court purposes

statement analysis   a blanket term for various techniques that attempt to analyze the truthfulness of recorded statements by applying formal criteria

statement validity analysis (SVA)   a technique for analyzing children's statements alleging sexual abuse that is premised on the belief that a child's account of real-life experiences will differ from his or her account of fictional experiences, and that such differences can be systematically analyzed

stress–compliant false confession   a false confession given knowingly in order to escape from what the person perceives to be an intolerably intense, punishing interrogation, and/or a situation in which someone has been convinced that it is futile to protest his or her innocence

subpoena   a formal request, enforceable by the court, for a person's attendance in court to give testimony

suspect   a person of interest (under arrest or not) suspected by the police on the basis of evidence of having committed a crime

system variables   factors, such as conditions in the lineup room, that affect the accuracy of an eyewitness identification and over which the police and the Crown have some control

testimony   the oral evidence of a witness in court

theme   a technique used in the Reid method to provide a "moral excuse" to the suspect for their commission of the offence or to minimize the moral implications of their conduct

trier of fact   the person or persons charged with making determinations of fact in a trial—namely, the jury in a jury trial or the judge in a trial by judge alone; in contrast to legal rulings that are made exclusively by a judge

tunnel vision   the single-minded and overly narrow focus on a particular investigative or prosecutorial theory, so as to unreasonably colour the evaluation of information received and one's conduct in response to that information

Type 1 error   *see* false positive

varied retrieval   one way an interviewer can assist a witness to use their memory effectively—for example, the subject may be asked to try and recall the details of the event in a different order or from a different perspective; this can help to stimulate a subject's memory and trigger recollections of an event that they might not otherwise have been able to recall

voir dire   a "trial within a trial" to determine the admissibility of evidence, such as a confession given to a police officer or person in authority

voluntary false confession   false confession given voluntarily for a variety of reasons, including mental illness or a desire for attention, and not as a result of the use of police interrogation techniques

waiver   a decision, communicated clearly by words or actions, to decline the exercise of a particular right

walkthrough procedure   identification procedure whereby a witness is taken to a public location (such as a bar) in an attempt to identify a suspect

will say   a formal witness statement prepared for disclosure to the opposing party

witness   a person who has information about a crime or suspected crime and who voluntarily gives that information to the police with no expectation of confidentiality or compensation

witness compatible question   a question designed to take advantage of a witness's personal strengths or knowledge, and their mental images of an event as described to an interviewer; a component of the ECI designed to help maximize the amount of information an interviewer is able to elicit from a witness

References

A.P., R v. (2008) ONCJ 431 (CanLII).

Aamondt, M., & Custer, H. (2006). Who can best catch a liar? A meta-analysis of individual differences in detecting deception. *The Forensic Examiner,* Spring, *15*(1), 6-11.

Adams, S. (1996, October). Statement analysis: What do suspects' words really reveal? *FBI Law Enforcement Bulletin.*

Adams, S., & Jarvis, J. (2006). Indicators of veracity and deception: An analysis of written statements made to police. *International Journal of Speech, Language and the Law, 13*(1), 1-22.

Ahmed, R v. (2002). 2002 CanLII 695 (ONCA).

Amos, R v. (2009). 2009 CanLII 63592 (ONSC).

Ask, K. (2006). *Criminal investigation: Motivation, emotion and cognition in the processing of evidence.* Doctoral Dissertation, Department of Psychology, Goteborg University. http://gupea.ub.gu.se/handle/2077/676.

Ask, K., & Granhag, P. (2005). Motivational sources of confirmation bias in criminal investigations: The need for cognitive closure. *Journal of Investigative Psychology and Offender Profiling, 2*(1), 43-63.

Atkinson, R.C., & Shiffrin, R.M. (1968). Human memory: A proposed system and its control processes. In K.W. Spence (Ed.), *The Psychology of learning and motivation: Advances in Research and Theory* (pp. 89-195). New York: Academic Press.

B. (K.G.), R v. (1993). [1993] 1 SCR 740, 79 CCC (3d) 257.

Bachenko, J., Fitzpatrick, E., & Schonwetter, M. (2008). Verification and implementation of language-based deception indicators in civil and criminal narratives. *Proceedings of the 22nd International Conference on Computational Linguistics,* Coling, UK, pp. 41-48. http://www.coling2008 .org.uk.

Baddeley, A., Eysenck, M., & Anderson, M. (2008). *Memory.* London: Psychology Press.

Bandler, R., & Grinder, J. (1979). *Frogs into princes.* Moab, UT: Real People Press.

Barges, R v. (2005). 2005 CanLII 47766 (ONSC).

Barnes, R v. (2010). 2010 ONSC 546 (CanLII).

Bartle, R v. (1994). [1994] 3 SCR 173, 92 CCC (3d) 289, 33 CR (4th) 1.

Basarke, S., Stanley, D., & Turtle, J. (2011). You have the right to remain silent, so why are you talking? Poster accepted for presentation at the American Psychology-Law Society conference, March 4, Miami, FL.

Beckstead v. Ottawa (City). (1997). 1997 OJ No. 5169 (CA).

Béland, R v. (1987). [1987] 2 SCR 398.

Bernstein, D., & Loftus, E. (2009). How to tell if a particular memory is true or false. *Perspectives on Psychological Science, 4,* 370-374.

Black, R v. (1989). [1989] 2 SCR 138, 50 CCC (3d) 1.

Blair, J., & Kooi, B. (2004). The gap between training and research in the detection of deception. *International Journal of Police Science and Management, 6*(2), 77-83.

Blair, J., & McCamey, W. (2002). Detection of deception: An analysis of the behavioural analysis interview technique. *Illinois Law Enforcement Executive Forum, 2,* 165-170.

Boland, L. (2002). Applying economic methodology: Recognizing knowledge in economic models. *Energeia: International Journal of Philosophy and Methodology of Economics, 1,* 22-31.

Bond Jr., C.F., & Uysal, A. (2007). On lie detection "wizards." *Law and Human Behavior, 31,* 109-115.

Borchard, E.M. (1932). *Convicting the innocent: Errors of criminal justice.* New Haven, CT: Yale University Press.

Borden, R v. (1994). [1994] 3 SCR 145, 92 CCC (3d) 404, 33 CR (4th) 147.

Borrell, B. (2008). What is truth serum? *Scientific American.* http://www.scientificamerican.com/article.cfm?id=what-is-truth-serum.

Borum, R. (2006). Approaching the truth: Behavioral science lessons on educing information from human sources. In National Defense Intelligence College, Center for Strategic Intelligence Research, *Educing information, interrogation: Science and art* (pp. 17-43). Washington, DC: Intelligence Science Board, Phase One Report.

Bowers, K.S., & Farvolden, P. (1996). Revisiting a century-old Freudian-slip: From suggestion disavowed to the truth repressed. *Psychological Bulletin, 119,* 355-380.

Brinsmead, R v. (2006). 2006 NBPC 4 (CanLII).

Brown, R v. (1999). 1999 CanLII 14915 (ONSC).

Broyles, R v. (1991). [1991] 3 SCR 595.

Bruce, V., Ness, H., Hancock, P.J.B., Newman, C., & Rarity, J. (2002). Four heads are better than one: Combining face composites yields improvements in face likeness. *Journal of Applied Psychology, 87,* 894-902.

Bruce, V., & Young, A. (1998). *In the eye of the beholder: The science of face perception.* New York: Oxford University Press.

Bryant, A.W., Lederman, S.N., & Fuerst, M.K. (2009). *The law of evidence in Canada* (3rd ed.) Toronto, ON: LexisNexis Canada.

Brydges, R v. (1990). [1990] 1 SCR 190, 53 CCC (3d) 330.

Buckley, D., & Jayne, B. (2005). *Electronic recording of interrogations.* Eagle River, WI: Hahn Printing.

Buckley, J. (2006). The Reid technique of interviewing and interrogation. In T. Williamson (Ed.), *Investigative interviewing: Rights, research and regulation* (chapter 10, pp. 190-206), Cullompton, UK: Willan Publishing.

Burlingham, R v. (1995). [1995] 2 SCR 206, 97 CCC (3d) 385, 38 CR (4th) 265.

Canada Evidence Act. (1985). RSC 1985, c. C-5, as amended.

Canadian Charter of Rights and Freedoms. Part I of the *Constitution Act, 1982,* RSC 1985, app. II, no. 44.

CBC News. (2003, January 28). *Widely used police interrogation technique can result in false confession: Disclosure.* http://www.cbc.ca/canada/story/2003/01/27/interrogation030127.html.

Central Intelligence Agency (CIA). (2009, March). United States Government, *A tradecraft primer: Structured analytic techniques for improving intelligence analysis.* https://www.cia.gov/library/center-for-the-study-of-intelligence/csi-publications/books-and-monographs/Tradecraft%20Primer-apr09.pdf.

Chahley, R v. (1992). [1992] BCJ No. 1121.

Christianson, S.-A. (1992). Emotional stress and eyewitness memory: A critical review. *Psychological Bulletin, 112,* 284-309.

Clarkson, R v. (1986). [1986] 1 SCR 383.

Collins, R v. (2008). 2008 CanLII 36899 (NLPC).

Conan Doyle, A. (1904; reprinted 1990). The Adventure of Black Peter. In *The Illustrated Sherlock Holmes.* London: Peerage Books.

Coote, R v. (2009). 2009 CanLII 18219 (ONSC).

Cory, P. (2001). *The inquiry regarding Thomas Sophonow.* The Honourable Peter de C. Cory, Commissioner. http://www.gov.mb.ca/justice/publications/sophonow/index.html ("Sophonow Inquiry").

Cotter, R v. (1991). [1991] BCJ No. 42, 62 CCC (3d) 423.

Couture, R v. (2007). 2007 SCC 28, [2007] 2 SCR 517.

Criminal Code. (1985). RSC 1985, c. C-46, as amended.

Crowder, R.G., & Surprenant, A.M. (2000). Sensory memory. In A.E. Kazdin (Ed.), *Encyclopedia of psychology* (pp. 227-229). New York: Oxford University Press and American Psychological Association.

Cruz, R v. (2008). 2008 ABPC 155 (CanLII).

Cuff, R v. (1989). [1989] NJ No. 94, 75 Nfld. & PEIR 1 (Nfld. CA).

Dando, C., Milne, R. (2009). Cognitive interviewing. In R. Kocsis (Ed.), *Applied criminal psychology: A guide to forensic behavioral sciences* (chap. 7, pp. 147-167). Springfield, IL: Charles C. Thomas.

Dando, C., Wilcock, R., & Milne, R. (2009). The modified cognitive interview procedure for frontline police investigators. *Applied Cognitive Psychology, 23,* 138-147.

Darwin, C. (1872). *The expression of the emotions in man and animals.* London: J. Murray.

Department of Justice Canada website. http://www.justice.gc.ca.

DePaulo, B.M. (1992). Nonverbal behavior and self-presentation. *Psychological Bulletin, 111,* 203-243.

DePaulo, B.M., Kashy, D.A., Kirkendol, S.E., Wyer, M.M., & Epstein, J.A. (1996). Lying in everyday life. *Journal of Personality and Social Psychology, 70,* 979-995.

DePaulo, B.M., & Kirkendol, S.E. (1989). The motivational impairment effect in the communication of deception. In J.C. Yuille (Ed.), *Credibility Assessment* (pp. 51-70). Dordrecht, the Netherlands: Kluwer.

DePaulo, B.M., Lindsay, J., Malone, B., Muhlenbruck, L., Charlton, K., & Cooper, H. (2003). Cues to deception. *Psychological Bulletin, 127*(1), 74-118.

DePaulo, B.M., & Pfeifer, R.L. (1986). On-the-job experience and skill at detecting deception. *Journal of Applied Social Psychology, 16,* 249-267.

Devine, R v. (2008). 2008 SCC 36, [2008] 2 SCR 283.

Doran, B., Long, M., & Alison, L. (2009, June). Working against the clock: An analysis of decisions in rape investigations under time pressure. London: *British Computer Society.* Proceedings of NDM9, the 9th International Conference on Naturalistic Decision Making. http://www.bcs.org/upload/pdf/ewic_ndm09_s2paper7.pdf.

Doyle, J. (2005). *True witness.* New York: Palgrave Macmillan.

Driscoll, L. (1994). A validity assessment of written statements from suspects in criminal investigations using the SCAN technique. *Police Studies, 17*(4), 77-88.

Drizin, S., & Leo, R. (2004). The problem of false confessions in the post-DNA world. *North Carolina Law Review, 82,* 891-1007.

Eakin, R v. (2000). [2000] 132 OAC 164, 74 CRR (2d) 307, [2000] OJ No. 1670.

Eastwood, J., & Snook, B. (2010). Comprehending Canadian police cautions: Are the rights to silence and counsel understandable? *Behavioral Sciences and the Law, 28,* 507-524.

Eastwood, J., Snook, B., & Chaulk, S.J. (2010). Measuring reading complexity and listening comprehension of Canadian police cautions. *Criminal Justice and Behavior, 37*(4), 453-471.

Eck, J. (2009). Investigators, information and interpretation: A summary of criminal investigation research. In D.K. Rossmo (Ed.), *Criminal investigative failures* (pp. ix-xii). Boca Raton, FL: CRC Press.

Ekman, P. (1970). Universal facial expressions of emotion. *California Mental Health Research Digest, 8,* 151-158.

Ekman, P. (2009; originally published 1985). *Telling lies: Clues to deceit in the marketplace, politics, and marriage.* New York: W.W. Norton.

Ekman, P., & Friesen, W.V. (1974). Detecting deception from body or face. *Journal of Personality and Social Psychology, 29,* 288-298.

Ekman, P., & Friesen, W.V. (1975). *Unmasking the face: A guide to recognizing emotions from facial clues.* Englewood Cliffs, NJ: Prentice Hall.

Ekman, P., Friesen, W.V., & Hager, J.C. (2002). *The facial action coding system* (2nd ed.). London: Weidenfeld & Nicolson.

Ekman, P., & O'Sullivan, M. (1991). Who can catch a liar? *American Psychologist, 46,* 913-920.

Elliot, R v. (2003). 2003 CanLII 24447 (ONCA).

Elshaw, R v. (1991). [1991] 3 SCR 24.

Ewert, R v. (1991). (1991), 68 CCC (3d) 207 (BCCA).

Fagan, A., & Badgley, P. (2002, October 25). Sniper arrests show limits on profiling: Pundits look to history, not evidence. *The Washington Times.*

Fancher, R.E. (1995). *Pioneers of psychology* (3rd ed). New York: W.W. Norton.

Farwell L.A., & Smith S.S. (2001). Using brain MERMER testing to detect knowledge despite efforts to conceal. *Journal of Forensic Science, 46,* 135-143.

Feynman, R. (1999). *The pleasure of finding things out.* Cambridge, MA: Perseus Publishing.

Findley, K., & Scott, M. (2006). The multiple dimensions of tunnel vision in criminal cases. *Wisconsin Law Review, 2,* 291-397.

Fischhoff, B. (1975). Hindsight ≠ foresight: The effect of outcome knowledge on judgment under uncertainty. *Journal of Experimental Psychology: Human Perception and Performance, 1,* 288-299.

Fisher, R.P., & Castano, N. (2007). The cognitive interview. In B. Cutler (Ed.), *Encyclopedia of psychology and law* (pp. 95-100). Thousand Oaks, CA: Sage.

Fisher, R.P., & Geiselman, R.E. (1992). Memory-enhancing techniques for investigative interviewing: The cognitive interview. Springfield, IL: Charles C. Thomas.

Fisher, R.P., Geiselman, R.E., & Raymond, D.S. (1987). Critical analysis of police interview techniques. *Journal of Police Science and Administration, 15,* 177-185.

Fisher, R.P., Geiselman, R.E., Raymond, D.S., Jurkevich, L., & Warhaftig, M.L. (1987). Enhancing enhanced eyewitness memory: Refining the cognitive interview. *Journal of Police Science and Administration, 15,* 291-297.

Fisher, R.P., & Perez, V. (2007). Memory enhancing techniques for interviewing crime suspects. In S.A. Christianson (Ed.), *Offenders' memories of violent crimes* (pp. 329-354). Chichester, UK: Wiley.

Fisher, R.P., & Schreiber, N. (2007). Interviewing protocols to improve eyewitness memory. In M. Toglia, R. Lindsay, D. Ross, & J. Reed (Eds.), *The handbook of eyewitness psychology: Volume 1. Memory for events* (pp. 53-80). Mahwah, NJ: Lawrence Erlbaum Associates.

FPT Heads of Prosecutions Committee Working Group. (2004). *Report on the prevention of miscarriages of justice.* Department of Justice, Canada. http://www.justice.gc.ca/eng/dept-min/pub/pmj-pej/p0.html.

Frank, J., & Frank, B. (1957). *Not guilty.* London: Gallancz.

Frank, M., Yarbrough, J., & Ekman, P. (2006). Investigative interviewing and the detection of deception. In T. Williamson (Ed.), *Investigative interviewing: Rights, research, regulation* (chap. 12, pp. 229-255). Cullompton, UK: Willan Publishing.

Freud, S. (1900/1965). *The interpretation of dreams.* Trans. by J. Strachey. Reprinted New York: Avon Books.

Frowd, C., Bruce, V. Smith, A., & Hancock, P. (2008). Improving the quality of facial composites using a holistic cognitive interview. *Journal of Experimental Psychology: Applied, 14,* 276-287.

Frowd, C.D., Carson, D., Ness, H., McQuiston-Surret, D., Richardson, J., Baldwin, H., & Hancock, P. (2005). Contemporary composite techniques: The impact of a forensically-relevant target delay. *Legal and Criminological Psychology, 10,* 63-81.

Geiselman, R.E., Fisher, R.P., MacKinnon, D.P., & Holland, H.L. (1985). Eyewitness memory enhancement in the police interview: Cognitive retrieval mnemonics versus hypnosis. *Journal of Applied Psychology, 70,* 401-412.

Gilovich, T., & Douglas, C. (1986). Biased evaluations of randomly determined gambling outcomes. *Journal of Experimental Social Psychology, 22,* 228-241.

Gingras, R v. (1992). [1992] AJ No. 107, 120 AR 300 (Alta. CA).

Goldstein, A.G., Chance, J.E., & Schneller, G.R. (1989). Frequency of eyewitness identification in criminal cases: A survey of the prosecutors. *Bulletin of the Psychonomic Society, 27,* 71-74.

Gonzales, R., Ellsworth, P.C., & Pembroke, M. (1993). Response bias in lineups and showups. *Journal of Personality and Social Psychology, 64*, 525-537.

Goudge, S. (2008). *Inquiry into pediatric forensic pathology in Ontario.* The Honourable Stephen T. Goudge, Commissioner. Toronto: Ontario Ministry of the Attorney General, Queen's Printer for Ontario. http://www .attorneygeneral.jus.gov.on.ca/inquiries/goudge/index.html.

Grandinetti, R v. (2005). 2005 SCC 5, [2005] 1 SCR 27.

Granhag, P., & Stromwall, L. (Eds.). (2004). *The detection of deception in forensic contexts.* New York: Cambridge University Press.

Grant, R v. (2009). 2009 SCC 32, [2009] 2 SCR 353.

Gudjonsson, G. (1992). *The psychology of interrogations, confessions and testimony.* Chichester, UK: Wiley.

Gudjonsson, G. (2007). Investigative interviewing. In T. Newburn, T. Williamson, & A. Wright (Eds.), *Handbook of criminal investigation* (pp. 466-492). Cullompton, UK: Willan Publishing.

Guterman, J. (2002, March). The lost (or never learned) art of debriefing. *Harvard Management Update, 7*(3). http://hbswk.hbs.edu/archive/2940.html.

Haggbloom, S., Warnick, R., Warnick, J., Jones, V., Yarbrough, G., Russell, T., Borecky, C., McGahhey, R., Powell, J., Beavers, J., & Monte, E. (2002). The 100 most eminent psychologists of the 20th century. *Review of General Psychology, 6*, 139-152.

Hazlett, G. (2006). Research on detection of deception: What we know versus what we think we know. In *Educing information, interrogation: Science and art* (pp. 45-61). Washington, DC: National Defense Intelligence College, Center for Strategic Intelligence Research, Intelligence Science Board, Phase One Report.

Hebert, R v. (1990). [1990] 2 SCR 151, 57 CCC (3d) 1, 77 CR (3d) 145.

Henry, R v. (2010). 2010 BCCA 462.

Heuer, R. (1999). *Psychology of intelligence analysis.* Washington, DC: Centre for the Study of Intelligence. https://www.cia.gov/library/center-for-the-study-of-intelligence/csi-publications/books-and-monographs/psychology-of-intelligence-analysis/PsychofIntelNew.pdf.

Hickman, A. (1989, December). *Royal commission on the Donald Marshall Jr. prosecution: Digest of findings and recommendations,* Chief Justice T. Alexander Hickman, Chairman. http://gov.ns.ca/just/marshall_inquiry/default.asp.

Hill v. Hamilton Wentworth Police (2007). 2007 SCC 41, [2007] 3 SCR 129.

Hodgson, R v. (1998). [1998] 2 SCR 449.

Hollis, R v. (1992). [1992] BCJ No. 2066, 76 CCC (3d) 421 (BCCA).

Home Office. (2008, July). The Research, Development and Statistics Directorate, *Crime in England and Wales 2007/8: A summary of the main findings.* http://rds.homeoffice.gov.uk/rds/pdfs08/hosb0708.pdf.

Horvath, R v. (1997). (1997), 117 CCC (3d) 110 (SCC).

Horvath, F., & Jayne, B. (1994). Differentiation of truthful and deceptive criminal suspects in behavioural analysis interviews. *Journal of Forensic Sciences, 39,* 793-807.

Hutchinson, B. (2010, October 28). BC man who spent 27 years in prison as a serial rapist acquitted on all counts. *The Vancouver Sun.* http://www.vancouversun.com/news/spent+years+prison+serial+rapist+acquitted+counts/3734673/story.html.

Ibrahim v. The King. (1914). [1914] AC 599 (PC).

Inbau, F.E. (1942). *Lie detection and criminal interrogation.* Baltimore, MD: Williams and Wilkins.

Inbau, F.E., Reid, J., & Buckley, J. (1986). *Criminal interrogation and confessions* (3rd ed.). Baltimore, MD: Williams and Wilkins.

Inbau, F.E., Reid, J., Buckley, J., & Jayne, B. (2001). *Criminal interrogation and confessions* (4th ed.). Gaithersburg, MD: Aspen Publishers.

Inbau, F.E., Reid, J., Buckley, J., & Jayne, B. (2004). *Criminal interrogation and confessions* (4th ed.). Boston: Jones & Bartlett Publishers.

Inbau, F.E., Reid, J., Buckley, J., & Jayne, B. (2005). *Essentials of the Reid technique: Criminal interrogations and confessions.* Boston: Jones & Bartlett Publishers.

Innocence Project (2010). Retrieved August 14, 2010 from http://www.innocenceproject.org/understand/False-Confessions.php.

Johnson, M.K., & Raye, C.L. (1981). Reality monitoring. *Psychological Review, 88,* 67-85.

Kassin, S.M. (2005). On the psychology of confessions: Does innocence put innocents at risk? *American Psychologist, 60,* 215-228.

Kassin, S.M. (2008). False confessions: Causes, consequences and implications for reform. *Current Directions in Psychological Science, 17*(4), 249-255.

Kassin, S.M., & Fong, C. (1999). "I'm innocent!": Effects of training on judgments of truth and deception in the interrogation room. *Law and Human Behavior, 23*(5), 499-516.

Kassin, S.M., & McNall, K. (1991). Police interrogations and confessions: Communicating promises and threats by pragmatic implication. *Law and Human Behavior, 15,* 233-251.

Kassin, S.M., & Neumann, K. (1997). On the power of confession evidence: An experimental test of the fundamental difference hypothesis. *Law and Human Behavior, 21*(5), 469-484.

Kaufman, F. (1998). *Report of the Kaufman commission on proceedings involving Guy Paul Morin*. The Honourable Fred Kaufman, Commissioner. http://www.attorneygeneral.jus.gov.on.ca/english/about/pubs/morin/.

Kebbel, M, Muller, D., & Martin, K. (2010). Understanding and managing bias. In G. Bammer (Ed.), *Dealing with uncertainties in policing serious crime* (pp. 87-97). Canberra, Aust. The Australian National University, ANU E Press. http://epress.anu.edu.au/dealing/pdf/whole_book.pdf.

Khan, R v. (2010). 2010 ONSC 3818 (CanLII).

King, L., & Snook, B. (2009). Peering inside a Canadian interrogation room: An examination of the Reid model of interrogation, influence tactics, and coercive strategies. *Criminal Justice and Behaviour, 36*(7), 674-694.

King, W., & Dunn, T. (2010). Detecting deception in field settings: A review of the criminal justice and psychological literatures. *Policing: An International Journal of Police Strategies and Management, 33*(2), 305-320.

Kliman, R v. (1996). 1996 CanLII 8364 (BCCA).

Knox, R v. (2006). 2006 CanLII 16479 (ONCA).

Koehnken, G. (2004). Statement validity analysis and the "detection of the truth." In P.A. Granhag & L.A. Stromwall (Eds.), *The detection of deception in forensic contexts* (pp. 41-63). New York: Cambridge University Press.

L.F., R v. (2006). 2006 CanLII 4903 (ONSC).

L.T.H., R v. (2008). 2008 SCC 49, [2008] 2 SCR 739.

Lamer, A. (2006). *The Lamer commission of inquiry pertaining to the cases of Ronald Dalton, Gregory Parson, Randy Druken*. The Right Honourable Antonio Lamer. St. John's, NL: Office of the Queen's Printer. http://www.justice.gov.nl.ca/just/publications/lamerpart1.pdf.

Leipert, R v. (1997). [1997] 1 SCR 281.

Leo, R. (2008). *Police interrogation and American justice*. Cambridge, MA: Harvard University Press.

Leo, R., & Drizin, S. (2010). The three errors: Pathways to false confession and wrongful conviction. In G.D. Lassiter & C.A. Meissner (Eds.), *Interrogations and false confessions* (pp. 9-30). Washington, DC: American Psychological Association.

Leo, R., Drizin, S., Neufeld, P., Hall, B., & Vatner, A. (2006). Bringing reliability back in: False confessions and legal safeguards in the twenty-first century. *Wisconsin Law Review, 26*(2), 479-538.

Leo, R., & Ofshe, R. (1998). The consequences of false confessions: Deprivations of liberty and miscarriages of justice in the age of psychological interrogation. *Journal of Criminal Law and Criminology, 88*, 429-496.

Lepard, D., & Campbell, E. (2009). How police departments can reduce the risk of wrongful convictions. In D.K. Rossmo, *Criminal investigative failures* (pp. 269-293). Boca Raton, FL: CRC Press.

Lesage, P. (2007, January). *Report of the commission of inquiry into certain aspects of the trial and conviction of James Driskell.* The Honourable Patrick J. LeSage, QC, Commissioner, Manitoba Justice.

Lesce, T. (1990). Deception detection by scientific content analysis. *Law and Order, 38*(8), 3-4.

Liew, R v. (1999). [1999] 3 SCR 227.

Lindsay, D.S., & Read, J.D. (1995). "Memory work" and recovered memories of childhood sexual abuse: Scientific evidence and public, professional, and personal issues. *Psychology, Public Policy, and Law, 1,* 846-908.

Lindsay, R.C.L., Wallbridge, H., & Drennan, D. (1987). Do the clothes make the man? An exploration of the effect of lineup attire on eyewitness identification accuracy. *Canadian Journal of Behavioural Science, 19,* 463-478.

Lindsay, R.C.L., Martin, R., & Weber L. (1994). Default values in eyewitness descriptions: A problem for the match-to-description lineup foil selection strategy. *Law and Human Behavior, 18,* 527-541.

Lindsay, R.C.L., & Wells, G.L. (1985). Improving eyewitness identifications from lineups: Simultaneous versus sequential lineup presentations. *Journal of Applied Psychology, 70,* 556-564.

Loftus, E.F. (1992). When a lie becomes memory's truth: Memory distortion after exposure to misinformation. *Current Directions in Psychological Science, 1,* 121-123.

Loftus, E.F. (1997, September). Creating false memories. *Scientific American,* 71-75.

Loftus, E.F. (2003, November). Make-believe memories. *American Psychologist,* 867-873.

Loftus, E.F., Doyle, J., & Dysart, J. (2008). *Eyewitness testimony: Civil and criminal* (4th ed.). Charlottesville, VA: Lexis Law Publishing.

Loftus, E.F., Miller, D.G., & Burns, H.J. (1978). Semantic integration of verbal information into a visual memory. *Journal of Experimental Psychology: Human Learning and Memory, 4,* 19-31.

Lord, C., Ross, L., & Lepper, M. (1979). Biased assimilation and attitude polarization: The effects of prior theories on subsequently considered evidence. *Journal of Personality and Social Psychology, 37,* 2098-2109.

Lykken, D.T. (1981). A tremor in the blood: Uses and abuses of the lie detector. New York: McGraw-Hill.

M.J.S., R v. (2000). [2000] AJ No. 391 (Prov. Ct.).

MacCallum, E. (2006). *The commission of inquiry into the wrongful conviction of David Milgaard.* The Honourable Mr. Justice Edward P. MacCallum, Commissioner. http://www.justice.gov.sk.ca/milgaard/DMfinal.shtml.

MacFarlane, B. (2006). Convicting the innocent: A triple failure of the justice system. *Manitoba Law Journal, 31*(403), 1-78.

MacFarlane, B. (2008). *Wrongful convictions: The effect of tunnel vision and predisposing circumstances in the criminal justice system.* Prepared for the inquiry into pediatric forensic pathology in Ontario. The Honourable Stephen Goudge. http://canadiancriminallaw.com/articles/articles%20pdf/Wrongful-Convictions.pdf.

Major Crime Investigative Techniques Course (2009). *See* Ross (2010).

Makin, K. (2004, February 7). Former prosecutor in Morin case appointed to the bench. *The Globe and Mail.*

Malpass, R.S., & Devine, P.G. (1981). Eyewitness identification: Lineup instructions and the absence of the offender. *Journal of Applied Psychology, 66,* 482-489.

Malpass, R.S., & Devine, P.G. (1983). Measuring the fairness of eyewitness identification lineups. In S.M.A. Lloyd-Bostock & B.R. Clifford (Eds.), *Evaluating witness evidence* (pp. 81-102). London: Wiley.

Mann, R v. (2004). 2004 SCC 52, [2004] 3 SCR 59.

Mann, S., Vrij, A., & Bull, R. (2004). Detecting true lies: Police officer's ability to detect suspects' lies. *Journal of Applied Psychology, 89*(1), 137-149.

Manninen, R v. (1987). [1987] 1 SCR 1233, 34 CCC (3d) 385.

Marsh, E. (2007). Retelling is not the same as recalling: Implications for memory. *Current Directions in Psychological Science, 16,* 16-20.

Marshall v. The Queen (2005). 2005 QCCA 852 (CanLII).

McClelland, J.L, Rumelhart, D.E., & Hinton, G.E. (1986). The appeal of parallel distributed processing. In D.E. Rumelhart, J.L. McClelland, & the PDP research group (Eds.), *Parallel distributed processing: Explorations in the microstructure of cognition.* Cambridge, MA: Bradford.

McCloskey, M., Wible, C.G., & Cohen, N.J. (1988). Is there a special flashbulb-memory mechanism? *Journal of Experimental Psychology: General, 117,* 171-181.

McCrimmon, R v. (2010). 2010 SCC 36.

McEwen, T. (2009, July). *Evaluation of the Phoenix homicide clearance project: Vol. 1. Final report.* Prepared for the National Institute of Justice, Office of Justice Programs, US Department of Justice. http://www.ilj.org/publications/docs/EvalReport_Volume_I.pdf.

McNeil, R v. (2009). 2009 SCC 3, [2009] 1 SCR 66.

Mecklenburg, S.H., Bailey, P., & Larson, M. (2008). The Illinois field study: A significant contribution to understanding real world eyewitness identification issues. *Law and Human Behavior, 32,* 22-27.

Memon, A., Fraser, J., Colwell, K., Odinot, G., & Mastroberardino, S. (2010). Distinguishing truthful from invented accounts using reality monitoring criteria. *Legal and Criminological Psychology, 15*(2), 177-194.

Miller, S. (The Steve Miller Band). (1976, April). Take the money and run. From *Fly like an eagle.* Los Angeles, CA: Capitol Records.

Milne, R., & Bull, R. (1999). *Investigative interviewing: Psychology and practice.* New York: Wiley.

Minde, R v. (2003). 2003 ABQB 797 (CanLII).

Mohan, R v. (1994). [1994] 2 SCR 9.

Monteleone, G.T., Phan, K.L., Nusbaum, H.C., Fitzgerald, D., Irick, J.-S., Fienberg, S.E., & Cacioppo, J.T. (2009). Detection of deception using fMRI: Better than chance, but well below perfection. *Social Neuroscience, 4,* 528-538.

Moore, T.E., & Gagnier, K. (2008). "You can talk if you want to": Is the police caution on the "right to silence" understandable? *Criminal Reports, 51,* 233-249.

Moore-McFarlane, R v. (2001). [2001] OJ No. 4646, 2001 CanLII 6363 (ONCA).

Moran, R v. (1987). (1987), 36 CCC (3d) 225 (ONCA).

Morris v. The Queen. (1983). [1983] 2 SCR 190.

Mullins-Johnson, R v. (2007). 2007 ONCA 720 (CanLII).

Munsterberg, H. (1908). *On the witness stand: Essays on psychology and crime.* Greentop, MO: Greentop Academic Press.

N., R v. (2005). [2005] OJ No. 357, 63 WCB (2d) 399 (Ont. SC).

Nahari, G., Vrij, A., & Fisher, R.P. (2011, January 21). Does the truth come out in the writing? SCAN as a lie detection tool. *Law and Human Behavior,* DOI: 10.1007/s10979-011-9264-6.

National Research Council (2003). *The polygraph and lie detection.* Washington, DC: National Academies Press.

Neuburger, R v. (1995). 1995 CanLII 201 (BCCA).

Newman, A., & Thompson, J. (2001). Rise and fall of forensic hypnosis in criminal investigation, *Journal of the American Academy of Psychiatry and the Law, 29,* 75-84.

O. Reg. 3/99, Adequacy and Effectiveness of Police Services. http://www.canlii .org/en/on/laws/regu/o-reg-3-99/latest/o-reg-3-99.html.

O. Reg. 354/04, Major Case Management. http://www.canlii.org/en/on/laws/ regu/o-reg-354-04/latest/o-reg-354-04.html.

Olivier, R v. (1991). [1991] MJ No. 299, 74 Man. R (2d) 30 (Man. QB).

Osmar, R v. (2007). [2007] OJ No. 244, 2007 ONCA 50.

O'Sullivan, M., & Ekman, P. (2004). The wizards of deception detection. In P. Granhag & L. Stromwall (Eds.), *The detection of deception in forensic contexts,* (pp. 269-286). Cambridge, UK: Cambridge University Press.

O'Sullivan, M., Frank, M.G., Hurley, C.M., & Tiwana, J. (2009). Police lie detection accuracy: The effect of lie scenario. *Law and Human Behavior, 33,* 530-538.

Oickle, R v. (2000). 2000 SCC 38, [2000] 2 SCR 3.

Ontario Ministry of Community Safety and Correctional Services (2004, October). *Ontario major case management manual.* http://www .attorneygeneral.jus.gov.on.ca/inquiries/cornwall/en/hearings/exhibits/ OPC/pdf/56_MCM_Manual.pdf.

Orne, M.T., Soskis, D.A., Dinges, D.F., & Orne, E.C. (1984). Hypnotically induced testimony. In G.L. Wells & E.F. Loftus (Eds.), *Eyewitness testimony: Psychological perspectives* (pp. 171-213). Cambridge, UK: Cambridge University Press.

Petronio, S., Flores, L.A., & Hecht, M.L. (1997). Locating the voice of logic: Disclosure discourse of sexual abuse. *Western Journal of Communication, 61,* 101-113.

Popper, K. (1959). *The logic of scientific discovery.* London: Hutchinson.

Porter, S., & ten Brinke, L. (2008). Reading between the lies: Identifying concealed and falsified emotions in universal facial expressions. *Psychological Science, 19,* 508-514.

Porter, S., & ten Brinke, L. (2010). The truth about lies: What works in detecting high stakes deception? *Legal and Criminological Psychology, 15*(1), 57-75.

Porter, S., Woodworth, M., & Birt, A. (2000). Truth, lies and videotape: An investigation of the ability of federal parole officers to detect deception. *Law and Human Behaviour, 24*(6), 643-658.

Porter, S. & Yuille, J. (1996). The language of deceit: An investigation of the verbal clues to deception in the interrogation context. *Law and Human Behavior, 20,* 443-458.

Post, R v. (2005). 2005 BCSC 1493.

Prosper, R v. (1994). [1994] 3 SCR 236, 92 CCC (3d) 353, 33 CR (4th) 85.

R.E.M., R v. (2004). 2004 BCSC 1596.

Rahman, R v. (2008). 2008 BCSC 647.

Raskin, D.C. (1988). Does science support polygraph testing? In A. Gale (Ed.), *The polygraph test: Lies, truth, and science* (pp. 96-110). London: Sage.

Raskin, D.C., & Yuille, J. (1989). Problems in evaluating interviews of children in sexual abuse cases. In S. Ceci, D. Ross, & M. Toglia (Eds.), *Perspectives on children's testimony*. New York: Springer-Verlag.

Rassin, E. (2010). Blindness to alternative scenarios in evidence evaluation. *Journal of Investigative Psychology and Offender Profiling, 7*(2), 153-163.

Reid, J. (1947). A revised questioning technique in lie detection tests. *Journal of Criminal Law and Criminology, 37*, 542-547.

Richfield, R v. (2003). (2003), 178 CCC (3d) 23, 14 CR (6th) 77 (ONCA).

Rogers, R., Harrison, K.S., Hazelwood, L.L., & Sewell, K.W. (2007). Knowing and intelligent: A study of Miranda warnings in mentally disordered defendants. *Law and Human Behavior, 31*, 401-418.

Rogers, R., Hazelwood, L.L., Sewell, K.W., Harrison, K.S., & Shuman, D.W. (2008). The language of Miranda warnings in American jurisdictions: A replication and vocabulary analysis. *Law and Human Behavior, 32*(2), 124-136.

Roks, R v. (2007). 2007 CanLII 13368 (ONSC).

Ross, R v. (1989). [1989] 1 SCR 3.

Ross, C. (2010). Beyond the crime scene: Building accountable investigations. *RCMP Gazette, 72*(2), 11. http://www.rcmp-grc.gc.ca/gazette/vol72n2/crime3-eng.htm.

Rossmo, D.K. (Ed.). (2009). *Criminal investigative failures*. Boca Raton, FL: CRC Press.

Rothman v. The Queen (1981). [1981] 1 SCR 640.

Ruby, C.L., & Brigham, J.C. (1998). Can criteria-based content analysis distinguish between true and false statements of African-American speakers? *Law and Human Behavior, 22*, 369-388.

Russano, M., Meissner, C., Narchet, F., & Kassin, S. (2005). Investigating true and false confessions within a novel experimental paradigm. *Psychological Science, 16*(6), 481- 486.

Russo, J., & Meloy, M. (2008). Hypothesis generation and testing in Wason's 2-4-6 task. Working Paper, Cornell University. http://forum.johnson.cornell.edu/faculty/russo/Rule%20Discovery%2022%20May%2008.pdf.

Ryan, R v. (1991). (1991), 69 CCC (3d) (NSCA).

Salituro, R v. (1991). [1991] 3 SCR 654, 68 CCC (3d) 289.

Sandham, R v. (2008). 2008 CanLII 84098 (ONSC).

Sapir, A. (1987). *Scientific content analysis (SCAN)*. Phoenix, AZ: Laboratory for Scientific Interrogation, Inc.

Schacter, D., Dawes, R., Jacoby, L., Kahneman, D., Lempert, R., Roediger, H., & Rosenthal, R. (2008, February). Policy forum: Studying eyewitness investigations in the field. *Law and Human Behavior, 31,* 22-27.

Schank, R.C., & Abelson, R.P. (1975). *Scripts, plans, and knowledge.* Proceedings of the Fourth International Joint Conference on Artificial Intelligence. Tbilisi, USSR.

Scheck, B., Neufeld, P., & Dwyer, J. (2000). *Actual innocence: Five days to execution and other dispatches from the wrongly convicted.* New York: Doubleday.

Schollum M. (2005). *Investigative interviewing: The literature.* Wellington, NZ: Police National Headquarters. http://www.police.govt.nz/resources/2005/ investigative-interviewing/index.html.

Schultz, R v. (1990). [1991] BCJ No. 2757, 67 CCC (3d) 360 (BCCA).

Scott, R v. (1990). [1990] 3 SCR 979.

Seaboyer, R v. (1991). [1991] 2 SCR 577.

Seguin, R. (2006, December 22). Mentally handicapped Quebec man receives millions for injustice. *The Globe and Mail.* http://www.theglobeandmail. com/news/national/mentally-handicapped-quebec-man-receives-millions-for-injustice/article862837/.

Shearer, R. (1999, May-June). Statement analysis: SCAN or scam? *The Skeptical Inquirer, 23,* 40-43.

Shepherd, E. (2007). *Investigative interviewing: The conversation management approach.* Oxford: Oxford University Press.

Shepherd, J.W., Ellis, H.D., McMurran, M., & Davies, G.M. (1978). Effect of character attribution on Photofit construction of a face. *European Journal of Social Psychology, 8,* 263-268.

Sherret-Robinson, R v. (2009). 2009 ONCA 886 (CanLII).

Sherriff, S. (2003). *Convicting the guilty: A strategy manual of law and technique for dedicated investigators and prosecutors combating major crime* (10th ed.). Toronto: Steve Sherriff.

Shewood, R v. (1991). [1991] BCJ No. 4041, 29 MVR (2d) 21 (BCCA).

Shuy, R. (1998). *The language of confession interrogation and deception.* Thousand Oaks, CA: Sage.

Sinclair, R v. (2010). 2010 SCC 35.

Singh, R v. (2007). 2007 SCC 48, [2007] 3 SCR 405.

Skinnider, E. (2005). *The art of confessions: A comparative look at the law of confessions—Canada, England, the United States and Australia.* Vancouver, BC: International Centre for Criminal Justice Reform and Criminal Justice Policy. http://www.icclr.law.ubc.ca/Publications/Reports/ES%20PAPER%20 CONFESSIONS%20REVISED.pdf.

Smith, N. (2001). *Reading between the lines: An evaluation of the scientific content analysis technique (SCAN)*. London: Police research series paper 135, London, UK: Home Office, Research, Development and Statistics Directorate.

Smith, R v. (1989). [1989] 2 SCR 368, 50 CCC (3d) 308, 71 CR (3d) 129.

Smith, R v. (1991). [1991] 1 SCR 714, 63 CCC (3d) 313, 4 CR (4th) 125.

Smith, S., Stinson, V., & Patry, M. (2010, August 12). Confession evidence in Canada: Psychological issues and legal landscapes. *Psychology, Crime & Law, 16*, 1-17.

Snook, B., & Cullen, R.M. (2009). Bounded rationality and criminal investigations: Has tunnel vision been wrongfully convicted? In D.K. Rossmo (Ed.), *Criminal investigative failures* (pp. 71-98). Boca Raton, FL: CRC Press.

Snook, B., Eastwood, J., Stinson, M., Tedeschini, J., & House, J. (2010, April). Reforming investigative interviewing in Canada. *Canadian Journal of Criminology and Criminal Justice, 52*(2), 215-229.

Snook, B., & Keating, K. (2011). A field study of adult witness interviewing practices in a Canadian police organization. In *Legal and criminological psychology, 16*(1), 160-172. Pre-print version accessed online from http://www.mun.ca/psychology/brl/publications/Snook_Keating_2010_LCP.pdf.

Spackman, R v. (2009). 2009 CanLII 37920 (ONSC).

Spanos, N.P., Quigley, C.A., Gwynn, M.I., Glatt, R.L., & Perlini, A.H. (1991). Hypnotic interrogation, pretrial preparation, and witness testimony during direct and cross-examination. *Law and Human Behavior, 15*, 639-653.

Spencer, R v. (2007). 2007 SCC 11, [2007] 1 SCR 500.

Sperling, G. (1960). The information available in brief visual representations. *Psychological Monographs, 74* (Whole No. 48).

Spinney, L. (2010, September 2). Is criminal profiling flawed and disorderly? *New Scientist*, (2775), 42-45.

Sporer, S. (2004). Reality monitoring and the detection of deception. In P.A. Granhag & L.A. Stromwall (Eds.), *The detection of deception in forensic contexts* (pp. 64-102). Cambridge: Cambridge University Press.

Sporer, S., Malpass, R., & Koehnken, G. (1996). *Psychological issues in eyewitness identification*. Hillsdale, NJ: Lawrence Erlbaum Associates.

Sporer, S., & Schwandt, B. (2007). Moderators of nonverbal indicators of deception: A meta-analytic synthesis. *Psychology, Public Policy and Law, 13*(1), 1-34.

Statistics Canada (2007). Canadian Centre of Justice Studies, *Police resources in Canada, 2007*, Catalogue no.85-225-XIE. http://dsp-psd.pwgsc.gc.ca/collection_2007/statcan/85-225-X/85-225-XIE2007000.pdf.

Steblay, N.K. (2007). *Double-blind sequential police lineup procedures: Toward an integrated laboratory and field practice perspective*. Final report: Grant #2004-IJ-CX-0044, National Institute of Justice, US Department of Justice.

Steblay, N.K. (2008). Studying eyewitness investigations in the field: A look forward. *Law and Human Behavior, 32,* 11-15.

Stein, L.M., & Memon, A. (2006). Testing the efficacy of the cognitive interview in a developing country. *Applied Cognitive Psychology, 20,* 597-605.

Stelfox, P. (2007). Professionalizing criminal investigation. In T. Newburn, T. Williamson, & A. Wright (Eds.), *Handbook of criminal investigation* (pp. 628-651). Cullompton, UK: Willan Publishing.

Steller, M. & Koehnken, G. (1989). Criteria-based statement analysis. In D. Raskin (Ed.), *Psychological methods in criminal investigation and evidence.* New York: Springer.

Stinchcombe, R v. (1991). [1991] 3 SCR 326, 68 CCC (3d) 225.

Strachan, R v. (1988). [1988] 2 SCR 980, 46 CCC (3d) 479, 67 CR (3d) 87.

Stromwall, L., & Granhag, P. (2002). How to detect deception? Arresting the beliefs of police officers, prosecutors and judges. *Psychology, Crime & Law, 9*(1), 19-36.

St-Yves, M. (2006). The psychology of rapport: Five basic rules. In T. Williamson (Ed.), *Investigative Interviewing: Rights, Research, Regulation* (chap. 5, pp. 87-106). Cullompton, UK: Willan Publishing.

Sophonow, Thomas, inquiry regarding. (2001). *See* Cory.

Tremblay, R v. (1987). (1987), 37 CCC (3d) 565 (SCC).

Trochym, R v. (2007). 2007 SCC 6, [2007] 1 SCR 239.

Truscott (Re) (2007, August 28). 2007 ONCA 575, Docket C42726.

Tulving, E., & Thompson, D.M. (1973). Encoding specificity and retrieval processes in episodic memory. *Psychological Review, 80,* 352-373.

Turtle, J.W., Lindsay, R.C.L., & Isaacs, B. (1998, March). Selecting photos for police lineups: Cloning, photocopying, or roulette? Poster presented at the biennial meeting of the American Psychology-Law Society, Redondo Beach, CA.

Turtle, J.W., & Want, S. (2008). Logic and research versus intuition and past practice as guides to gathering and evaluating eyewitness evidence. *Criminal Justice and Behavior, 35,* 1241-1256.

Turtle, J.W., & Yuille, J.C. (1994). Lost but not forgotten details: Repeated eyewitness recall leads to reminiscence but not hypermnesia. *Journal of Applied Psychology, 79,* 260-271.

Tversky, A., & Kahneman, D. (1974). Judgement under uncertainty: Heuristics and biases. *Science, 185,* 1124-1131.

Unger, R v. (2005). 2005 MBQB 238 CanLII.

Unger (2009, October 23). Kyle Unger acquitted of 1990 killing. http://www.cbc.ca/ canada/manitoba/story/2009/10/23/mb-unger-acquitted-manitoba.html.

United States Department of Justice. (1996). *Convicted by juries, exonerated by science: Case studies in the use of DNA evidence to establish innocence after trial.* Washington, DC: author. NCJ161258.

United States Department of Justice (2006). Federal Bureau of Investigation, Criminal Justice Information Services Division, *Crime in the United States.* http://www2.fbi.gov/ucr/cius2006/offenses/clearances/index.html.

United States Department of Justice (1999). *Eyewitness evidence: A guide for law enforcement.* Washington, DC: author.

Uphoff, R. (2006). Convicting the innocent: Aberration or systemic problem? *Wisconsin Law Review, 26*(2), 739-842.

Vrij, A. (1998). Physiological parameters and credibility: The polygraph. In A. Memon, A. Vrij, & R. Bull (Eds.), *Psychology and law: Truthfulness, accuracy, and credibility* (pp. 77-101). Berkshire, UK: McGraw-Hill.

Vrij, A. (2004). Guidelines to catch a liar. In P. Granhag & L. Stromwall (Eds.), *The detection of deception in forensic contexts* (pp. 287-314). Cambridge, UK: Cambridge University Press.

Vrij, A. (2008). *Detecting lies and deceit: Pitfalls and opportunities* (2nd ed.). Chichester, UK: Wiley.

Vrij, A., Fisher, R., Mann, S., & Leal, S. (2010). Lie detection: Pitfalls and opportunities. In G.D. Lassitter & C.A. Meissner (Eds.), *Police interrogations and false confessions: Current research, practice, and policy recommendations* (pp. 97-110). Washington, DC: American Psychological Association.

Vrij, A. & Lochun, S.K. (1997). Neuro-linguistic programming and the police: Worthwhile or not? *Journal of Police and Criminal Psychology, 12*(1), 25-31.

Vrij, A., Mann, S., Kristin, S., & Fisher, R. (2007). Cues to deception and ability to detect lies as a function of police interview styles. *Law and Human Behaviour, 31,* 499-518.

Wagstaff, G. (2008). Hypnosis and the law: Examining the stereotypes. *Criminal Justice and Behavior, 35,* 1277-1294.

Walsh, D., & Bull, R. (2010). What really is effective in interviews with suspects? A study comparing interviewing skills against interviewing outcomes. *Legal and Criminological Psychology, 15*(2), 305-321.

Walters, S. (1996). *Principles of kinesic interview and interrogation.* Boca Raton, FL: CRC Press.

Wason, P.C. (1960). On the failure to eliminate hypotheses in a conceptual task, *Quarterly Journal of Experimental Psychology, 12,* 129-140.

Watts, D. (2007). *Watts manual of criminal evidence*. Toronto: Thomson Carswell.

Wellford, C., & Cronin, J. (2000, April). Clearing up homicide clearance rates. *National Institute of Justice Journal*. http://www.ncjrs.gov/pdffiles1/jr000243b.pdf.

Wells, G.L. (1978). Applied eyewitness testimony research: Estimator variables and system variables. *Journal of Personality and Social Psychology, 36,* 1546-1557.

Wells, G.L. (1993). What do we know about eyewitness identification? *American Psychologist, 48,* 553-571.

Wells, G.L. (2006). Eyewitness identification: Systemic reforms. *Wisconsin Law Review, 2,* 615-643.

Wells, G.L. (2008). Field experiments on eyewitness identification: Towards a better understanding of pitfalls and prospects. *Law and Human Behavior, 32,* 6-10.

Wells, G.L., & Bradfield, A.L. (1998). Good, you identified the suspect: Feedback to eyewitnesses distorts their reports of the witnessing experience. *Journal of Applied Psychology, 83,* 360-376.

Wells, G.L., Leippe, M.R., & Ostrom, T.M. (1979). Guidelines for empirically assessing the fairness of a lineup. *Law and Human Behavior, 3,* 285-293.

Wells, G.L., & Loftus, E.F. (2002). Eyewitness memory for people and events. In E.A. Goldstein (Ed.), *Comprehensive handbook of psychology: Vol. 11. Forensic psychology*. New York: Wiley.

Wells, G.L., & Luus, C.A.E. (1990). Police lineups as experiments: Social methodology as a framework for properly conducted lineups. *Personality and Social Psychology Bulletin, 16,* 106-117.

Wells, G.L., Memon, A., & Penrod, S. (2007). Eyewitness evidence: Improving its probative value. *Psychological Science in the Public Interest, 7,* 45-74.

Wells, G.L., Rydell, S.M., & Seelau, E.P. (1993). The selection of distracters for eyewitness lineups. *Journal of Applied Psychology, 78,* 835-844.

Wells, G.L., Small, M., Penrod, S., Malpass, R.S., Fulero, S., & Brimacombe, C.A.E. (1998). Eyewitness identification procedures: Recommendations for lineups and photospreads. *Law and Human Behavior, 22,* 603-647.

Wells, G.L., & Turtle, J.W. (1986). Eyewitness identification: The importance of lineup models. *Psychological Bulletin, 99,* 320-329.

Wells, G.L., & Turtle, J.W. (1988). What is the best way to encode faces? In M.M. Gruneberg, P.E. Morris, & R.N. Sykes (Eds.), *Practical aspects of memory: Current research and issues* (pp. 163-168). New York: Wiley.

Wigmore, J.H. (1909). Professor Munsterberg and the psychology of testimony. *Illinois Law Review, 3,* 399-445.

Wright, A., & Holliday, R. (2007). Enhancing the recall of young, young-old, and old-old adults with the cognitive interview and a modified version of the cognitive interview. *Applied Cognitive Psychology, 21,* 19-43.

Youth Criminal Justice Act (2002). SC 2002, c. 1.

Zulawski, D., & Wicklander, D. (1993). *Practical aspects of interview and interrogation.* Boca Raton, FL: CRC Press.

Index

witness
  contamination, 6, 42
  defined, 3
  educational, 40
  identification
    crime scene, arrival at, 4
    search, extension, 5-6
  interviewing techniques, 17-46
  management
    admissibility of testimony, 11
    attendance in court, 9
    compellability, 9, 10
    competence, 9, 10
    distinguishing between informants and agents, 7
    first contact, 6-7
witness compatible question, 41

witness identifications
  accuracy, factors affecting, 134-135
  cold mugshot search, 148-149
  composites, 150-152
  false identification, 135-137
  lineups
    construction, 137-143
    presentation, 143-148
    recording procedure, 148
  recommended protocol, 152-153
  showup procedure, 150
  walkthrough procedure, 149-150
witness statement
  packaging, 32-34

Youth Criminal Justice Act, 52, 53, 61-62
YouTube, 5